WICKED RIVER

WICKED RIVER

THE MISSISSIPPI
WHEN IT
LAST RAN WILD

Lee Sandlin

PANTHEON BOOKS, NEW YORK

ISBN 978-1-61129-641-9

Printed in the United States of America

FOR JOANNE FOX
SINE QUA NON

For if and when we talk of a river we talk of a deep and dank architecture.

Harold Pinter, *No Man's Land*

I do not remember to have traversed this river in any considerable trip, without having heard of some fatal disaster to a boat, or having seen a dead body of some boatman, recognised by the red flannel shirt, which they generally wear. The multitudes of carcasses of boats, lying at the points, or thrown up high and dry on the wreck-heaps, demonstrate most palpably, how many boats are lost on this wild, and, as the boatmen always denominate it, "wicked river."

Timothy Flint, *Recollections*

I hate the Mississippi, and as I look down upon its wild and filthy waters, boiling and eddying, and reflect how uncertain is travelling in this region . . . I cannot help feeling a disgust at the idea of perishing in such a vile sewer, to be buried in mud, and perhaps to be rooted out again by some pig-nosed alligator.

Frederick Marryat, *A Diary in America*

Contents

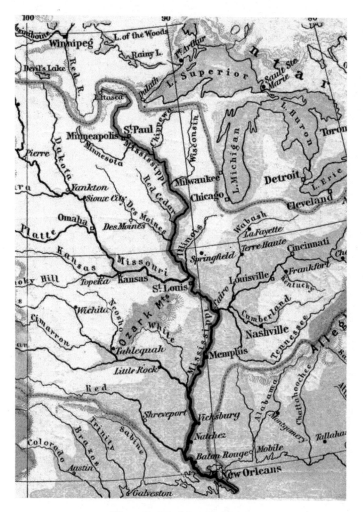

The path of the Mississippi River,
from its source at Lake Itasca to the Gulf of Mexico

Introduction

THERE IS A TRIBUTARY of the Mississippi River running through my neighborhood in Chicago. It's not easy to spot; you have to know just where to look. It's by the bus stop on a cluttered commercial block. Right at the curb is a manhole. The manhole cover is embossed with a decorative pattern of fish, and it carries the message DUMP NO WASTE! DRAINS TO WATERWAYS! Down below is water bound for the Mississippi.

Sometimes when I'm waiting for the bus, I pass the time by imagining the course the water is running. It's invisible at street level, but there is a maze of piping underneath Chicago: water mains and sewer mains and gas mains, electrical conduit and fiber-optic cabling. The water is gurgling through this spaghetti tangle for mile after mile, below the ranges of highrises and the decaying industrial districts and the limitless veldts of bungalows. It doesn't surface until it reaches a pumping station past the southern city limits. There it empties into the Illinois River. The Illinois runs in a meandering course roughly southwest, past the suburban counties around Chicago, out through the exurban fringe, then south through the farm country in the middle of the state, and then west again, until at last, just north of St. Louis, it drains into the Mississippi.

This is a serpentine route, but it's not an unusual one. There are count-less streams just like it. In the nineteenth century, it was estimated that the Mississippi had roughly one hundred thousand natural tributaries—that is, there were a hundred thousand distinct, individually named brooks, creeks, rivulets, and rivers emptying their waters into its gargantuan current. Today there are far more than a hundred thousand, and the majority of them are artificial. They're like the manhole by the bus stop: they're conduits and cisterns and sewage pipes, obscure canals and neglected culverts and out-of-the-way storm drains. The Mississippi is surrounded by a vast network of concealed plumbing that underlies the whole of the American Midwest.

As for the great river at the heart of this maze, it is now for all intents and purposes a man-made artifact. Every inch of its course from its headwaters to its delta is regulated by synthetic means—by locks and dams and artificial lakes, revetments and spillways and control structures, chevrons and wing dams and bendway weirs. The resulting edifice can barely be called a river at all, in any traditional sense. The Mississippi has been dredged, and walled in, and reshaped, and fixed; it has been turned into a gigantic navigation canal, or the world's largest industrial sewer. It hasn't run wild as a river does in nature for more than a hundred years.

Its waters are notoriously foul. In the nineteenth century, the Mississippi was well known for its murkiness and filth, but today it swirls with all the effluvia of the modern age. There's the storm runoff, thick with the glistening sheen of automotive waste. The drainage from the enormous mechanized farms of the heartland, and from millions of suburban lawns, is rich with pesticides and fertilizers like atrazine, alachlor, cyanazine, and metolachlor. A ceaseless drizzle comes from the chemical plants along the riverbanks that manufacture neoprene, polychloroprene, and an assort-

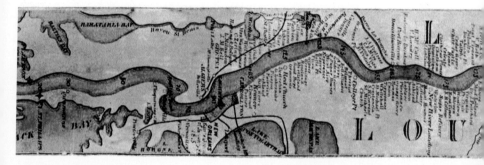

ment of other refrigerants and performance elastomers. And then there are the waste products of steel mills, of sulfuric acid regeneration facilities, and of the refineries that produce gasoline, fuel oil, asphalt, propane, propylene, isobutane, kerosene, and coke. The Mississippi is one of the busiest industrial corridors in the world.

I get a little reminder of the health of this system every time I pass by that bus stop. There's a reason why the one particular manhole stands out among all the clutter of ancient grilles and grates along the block. It reeks. Winter and summer, it emits a peculiar odor, a compound of sewer gas, stale grease, and some kind of pungent chemical reminiscent of sour mint. I can tell how bad it is on any given day by the behavior of the people waiting at the curb. Sometimes they have to hang so far back that the bus blows past the corner without a pause.

Of course it seems all wrong to think of the Mississippi River this way, as an industrial drainage system the length of a continent. It's not how we want to picture Old Man River—the river of the paddle-wheel steamboats, the river that Huck and Jim escaped down when they rode their raft to freedom. That river, we like to imagine, is still running wild the way it always was. The wistful old song "Moon River," popular back in the sixties, caught the feeling perfectly:

> Moon River, wider than a mile,
> I'm crossing you in style some day.

When Andy Williams crooned this, he was obviously not thinking about something as prosaic as driving across the Eads Bridge at St. Louis. He

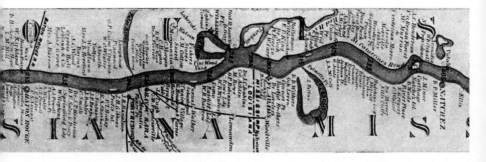

was singing about the mythical river of Mark Twain ("my huckleberry friend," the song calls it, just so we don't miss the point): he was crossing a river bound for the rainbow's end, not one to be found on the interstate map.

This is the image of the river that I grew up with. I knew all about Twain's river long before I ever saw the actual Mississippi. In fact, I knew about Tom Sawyer and Huckleberry Finn before I learned how to read. My mother had an old illustrated edition of Twain, and sometimes when I was a little kid, she would take it down from its high shelf to show me the pictures. The book was filled with glossy plates, each protected by a thin sheet of brittle tissue, which she would delicately peel back to reveal the gorgeously colored image underneath. It never failed to astonish me. I was used to modern picture books, where pop art squiggles were at play in a featureless smear of watercolors, like a cartoon guide to subatomic physics. But here with dream-vivid clarity was Tom Sawyer in church, squirming through the sermon between two pillowy matrons in spectacular floral dresses; there was Huckleberry Finn in overalls, sitting on a barrel on the levee, smoking his corncob pipe, posed against the steepled skyline of Hannibal, Missouri, with a sun-rayed billow of cumulus behind.

My mother didn't try to connect up the images into a story, and I never did get a handle on the story, even when I was old enough to read Twain for myself. To this day, the plot of *The Adventures of Tom Sawyer* is a bit of a blur. I remember the scene where Tom crashes his own funeral, but I couldn't tell you how everybody got the idea he was dead; I know that Tom and Huck find buried treasure at the end, but I had to reread it to figure out where all that gold came from. Much of *The Adventures of Huckleberry Finn* was even sketchier—the truth is, I never could get all the way through it when I was a kid. I had to keep skipping over scenes because

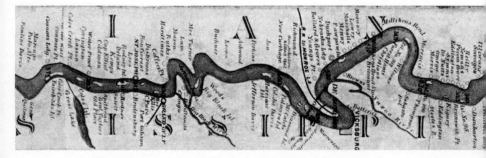

they were too frightening. The chapter where Huck was kidnapped by his monstrous father was so upsetting to me that I couldn't bear to keep the book by my bed; I had to sneak it back onto its shelf in the living room before I could sleep at night.

But none of that mattered: the books still burned themselves into my brain. All the other books I read were ghosts compared with them. Tom tricking the neighbor boys into painting the fence remains as vivid to me as anything from my own childhood. The scene where the steamboat fires its cannon across the water to raise Tom's drowned body from the river is still weirder to me than any fantasy novel. And running deeper even than these was the image of the river itself: the great prairie of water, white veined, impossibly blue, swirling underneath the majestic steamboats like a kind of art deco dance floor. I found it both alluring and unimaginable. There was nothing remotely like it in the Illinois suburb where I grew up. The one river I knew was a dinky, puttering brook that meandered through a nearby forest preserve. It was opaque, it smelled putrid, and its surface was fluorescent green. We were told to stay out of it, because if its water even touched our skin, we'd have to go to the hospital.

Twain's Mississippi was obviously something different, something wholly other. I was haunted by the thought that it was close by, running deep within the landscape, past the last franchise strip and the last strand of freeway. Sometimes I imagined it as a kind of secret subterranean presence flowing around the walls of basement rec rooms. On the maps in my schoolbooks it seemed to cut through the whole of the Midwest like the dark central vein in a leaf: I thought that if I ever managed to reach it, I would be swallowed up in a kind of hidden inland sea, endlessly unfolding from within, dotted everywhere by the glorious islands of the steamboats, edged by the silhouettes of forests against a sunset sky.

That image was so alive to me that it easily survived my real-world encounters with the river. My parents would sometimes take me on trips to visit my great-aunts and great-uncles, who lived on the Illinois side of the Mississippi near St. Louis. The drive led us from the Chicago suburbs down the new interstate—a summer morning's glide through the furrowed green oceans of the farm country, our car and the cars all around us swooping effortlessly along the arrow of highway like an invading army of flying saucers. My gaze was invariably fixed on the horizon, where the grain silos and water towers were creeping past each other like pieces in a titanic board game. I remember a thunderstorm rising up above the horizon line, one of those towering prairie storm fronts that to this day make me think of God long before I think of rain. We were heading straight into it. The highway stretched before us in a brilliant swath of humid yellow sunlight, while ahead was a wall of blackness. We swept into the storm in a furious rush; the car didn't slow at all, even though the windshield wipers were frantically shoving the surging sheaths of rainwater aside as though they were combing the sea. On the far side of the storm front, the world was a sulking monochrome. Off the interstate we headed down a main highway hemmed in by franchise strips, discount furniture stores, and new-car lots; the rain was descending in thin curtains over sodden hills of subdivisions. The road took a bend, and there was the Mississippi.

It was gray. It was hurrying. It was huge. Its surface was mottled and stippled with countless flickering motes of black, like the seethe of snow on a TV screen. It had nothing to do with the river I had imagined. It didn't even seem to be a natural phenomenon. It was an interruption in the landscape, a flood, a mob trampling through a barricade, an endless, purposeless stampede of water. A half a mile off in the deep channel was a

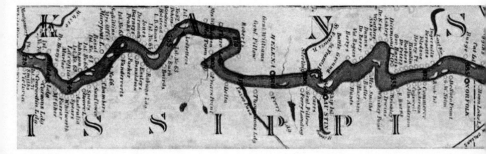

gigantic industrial barge shrouded by rain. On the remoteness of the far bank, more than a mile away, was a line of gaunt dead trees.

There is a pretty much universal idea that Twain has a proprietary relationship to the Mississippi. It belongs to him, the way Victorian London belongs to Dickens or Dublin belongs to Joyce. This is not a new idea—in fact, it dates back to Twain's own time. Some of his original reviewers wrote as though he'd discovered the Mississippi personally and was sending back the first dispatches from an unknown continent. An anonymous critic for *The Hartford Courant* was typical: "With a primeval and Robin-Hood freshness," he wrote after *Huckleberry Finn* was published in 1884, "he has given us a portrait of a people, of a geographical region, of a life that is new in the world."

But this was getting Twain fundamentally backward. The last thing he was trying to do was describe the life of the Mississippi River valley as something "new in the world." His fascination—obsession, really—was with the Mississippi as it had been in the past. He wasn't interested in the contemporary Mississippi and didn't even know that much about it. When he sat down to write *Tom Sawyer* and *Huckleberry Finn,* he hadn't been on the river in decades.

His Mississippi books are works of memory, even of archaeology. They're about the world of the river valley as it had been a generation earlier, before the Civil War. That was the Mississippi he knew firsthand from his childhood: the great age of the Mississippi River culture. It had been a strange and fascinating time. From somewhere in the 1810s until the Civil War, a new society had rapidly sprouted and come to a fantastic height in the river valley: a world of its own, growing on and around the sprawling

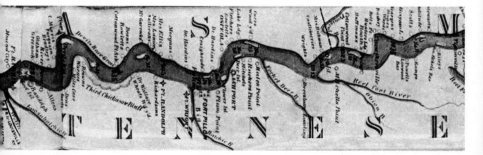

length of the Mississippi, with its own culture and its own language and its own unspoken rules. *Tom Sawyer, Life on the Mississippi,* and *Huckleberry Finn* are lovingly detailed reconstructions of that age. Into them Twain poured all the half-forgotten trivia and pop ephemera he could dredge up from his childhood: the bad pious poetry and the worse folk songs, the primness of river town society matrons and the crazy banter of the river men, the omen reading of the conjurers and the tirades of the drunks on the riverfront levees, the childhood games, the rumors, the ghost stories, the superstitions . . . it was as though the murkiness of the Mississippi had cleared to reveal a drowned town miraculously preserved on the river bottom.

But in taking up this era as his subject, Twain hadn't thought of himself as any kind of intrepid literary pioneer. There had been a long tradition of books about the Mississippi valley already; whole libraries had been devoted to the river long before he started writing about it. In the decades leading up to the Civil War, the foremost authority on the Mississippi had been a journalist and historian named Timothy Flint, whose immense *A History and Geography of the Mississippi Valley* had been regarded as the standard reference work on the river—cited in countless other books and copied uncredited in countless more. But Flint had noted in his memoirs that he'd hesitated even writing about the Mississippi because it had already been done to death:

> There are such showers of journals, and travels, and residences, and geographies, and gazetteers; and every person, who can in any way fasten the members of a sentence together, after having travelled through a country, is so sure to begin to scribble about it, that I have felt a kind of awkward consciousness at the thought of starting in the same beaten track.

This was in 1826—fifty years before Twain published *Tom Sawyer*.

What has happened to all these books? Long gone: banished to the unvisited stacks of university libraries and the unsold inventories of antiquarian book dealers; submerged now somewhere in the bottomless depths of Google Books. In fact, they had already fallen into oblivion by Twain's time. Of the innumerable travelers and essayists and historians of the river who flourished before the Civil War, Twain noted in 1883 that "their books cannot be purchased now."

From a strictly literary point of view, this isn't much of a crime. American literature in those days was in dismal shape, and most of the early books about the river are unreadable today. But if their literary style can somehow be ignored, these books taken together do add up to a vivid collective portrait of the mysterious world of the river culture as it was at its height—and one that makes for a surprising, maybe even alarming, contrast when set next to Twain's.

It must be understood that Twain never pretended to be writing documentary realism. His Mississippi, for all its historical specificity, was still at bottom a nostalgic daydream. The more Twain wrote about the river, in fact, the more it took on a kind of mythic grandeur: it became "the great Mississippi, the majestic, the magnificent Mississippi, rolling its mile-wide tide along, shining in the sun"—a world where every problem fell away down the next turning of the river bend, the perfectly serene, sun-flecked image of the American Eden.

Twain's predecessors hadn't seen it that way. To them the Mississippi had been crowded, filthy, chaotic, and dangerous. Where Twain saw eccentricity and charm, they had seen corruption and unchecked evil. Where he saw freedom, they had seen a jerry-rigged culture swept by strange manias and mysterious plagues, perpetually teetering on the edge of collapse.

Their river valley wasn't Eden; it was, as Twain himself observed in an unguarded moment, nothing more than "a semi-barbarism which set itself up for a lofty civilization."

How could these versions have been so far apart? Simple: the earlier writers were describing the world in front of them; Twain, the world after it had collapsed. Everything we think of as characteristic of Twain's Mississippi—the picturesque river towns, the paddle-wheel steamboats, the whole riotous culture of the river valley—had disappeared by the time he started writing. Even the river itself had fundamentally changed. During the years that Twain published *Tom Sawyer* and *Huckleberry Finn* and *Life on the Mississippi,* the U.S. Army Corps of Engineers had been at work, dredging the channels and building dams and piling up levees—irrevocably destroying the wild Mississippi and putting in its place the artificial substitute we have today. This is why, if we want to explore the old world of the river, we have to begin with those drowned libraries of Mississippi writing and only gradually make our way back to Twain. After all, he wasn't the first laureate of the wild river, the way his original reviewers had supposed; he turned out to be the last.

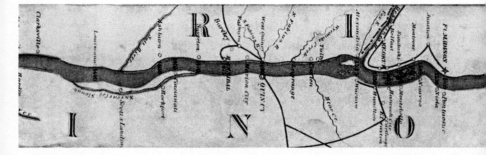

Prologue

ONE OF THE MOST POPULAR art forms in nineteenth-century America was the panorama. A panorama was an oil painting done on a gigantic scale—so gigantic that the first sight of it would make spectators gasp. Today, a painting that fills up an art gallery wall (say, ten feet by thirty feet) would strike people as unusually large; back then, it would have counted as a panoramic miniature. Some panoramas were so big that special halls had to be built to display them.

The subject of the typical panorama ran to the spectacular and violent. One famous panorama (or, to give it its grander name, "cosmoramic view") showed the burning of Moscow in 1812: in the foreground were Napoleon's armies retreating through the snow, and in the background was the skyline of the city in flames. Another panorama showed the cannonades blasting the ships in the harbor of Tripoli during the Barbary Wars. There was a popular panorama of the "magnificent and imposing sight" of Vesuvius in eruption. Another very elaborate panorama displayed a series of biblical scenes, culminating, according to the advertisement, with "the awful destruction of the world."

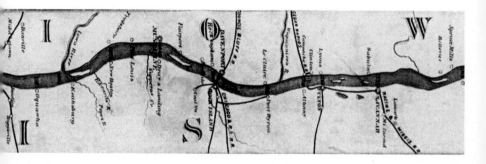

But the most popular—and by far the largest—panoramas were of the Mississippi River.

The choice of subject was a natural one. The Mississippi was famous. It was known everywhere as the wonder of the New World, the American Nile; it had been the subject of worldwide fascination and romance ever since the first European explorers had sent back descriptions of it in the seventeenth century. By the nineteenth century, it had become a major tourist attraction: a steamboat voyage between St. Louis and New Orleans was considered an essential part of an American grand tour.

In those days it was called the Father of Waters. This was said to be the meaning of the original Indian word *Mississippi.* Actually, it was non-sense—a gauzy poeticism born out of white sentimentality about the noble savage. *Mizu-ziipi* was an Ojibwe phrase that meant "very big river." (If any speakers of Ojibwe had felt moved to be poetical about the Mississippi, they would have more likely called it *michu-ziipi,* "endless river.") But even if the phrase was bogus, it did convey something essential about the river—its immensity, the sense that it was a sprawling, dominating presence in the American landscape.

By the middle of the nineteenth century, it had taken on another aspect. The eastern half of the continent was largely colonized by then; the western half was still mostly unexplored. (The prairie and the plains were known as the Great American Desert—a desert more in the sense of deserted than of arid land.) The Mississippi had come to be the natural boundary line between the two. There were no bridges anywhere along its length; a crossing to the far side had something epic about it, a venture from civilization into the unknown. A trip up or down the river, even in imagination, was as exhilarating as a voyage along the edge of the world.

In the early 1850s, when the enthusiasm for panoramas was at its height,

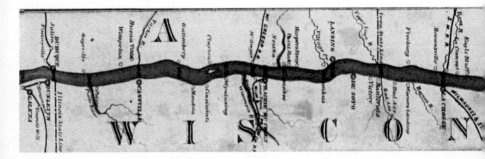

there were five different Mississippi panoramas on tour through America and Europe. Each was advertised as the biggest painting on earth. The most famous of them, John Banvard's *Grand Panorama of the Mississippi River,* was known as the "Three-Mile Painting." The ads said it was the "Largest Picture Ever Executed By Man." Banvard's chief competitor, John Rowson Smith's *Leviathan Panorama of the Mississippi River,* was advertised as "extending over Four Miles of Canvas." It was "One-Third Longer than any other Pictorial Work in Existence." Another, Sam Stockwell's *Mammoth Mississippi Panorama,* was announced as "Three Times the Extent of Any Painting in the World"—which, if that claim had been true (and if the other claims for the panoramas had also been true), would have made it twelve miles long.

Were the claims true? No. The Mississippi panoramas were most likely around twenty feet tall and a couple of hundred yards long, nowhere near miles. But they were still prodigious pieces of work. They were much too large ever to be displayed all at once. Instead they were shown in theaters, by gaslight, like primordial movies. Two cylinders were set on opposite sides of the stage; the panorama was gradually unrolled from one and wound up on the other. There'd be a narrator standing at the side of the stage, keeping things lively by telling stories and cracking jokes and scoring off the hecklers in the audience. There'd also be music—usually a piano or an organ, though at the classier theaters there might be a small orchestra. (The piano score for one of the panoramas survives: "The Mississippi Waltzes, to Accompany Banvard's Three-Mile Painting"; it was on sale in the lobby after each show.) A complete viewing generally took around two hours.

What the audience saw differed from one panorama to the next, but it took the same general form: a succession of scenes as might be witnessed

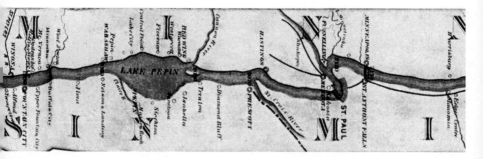

from a steamboat, on a voyage from one of the upper branches of the river down to New Orleans. (Actually the voyage went downriver at one showing and upriver at the next, to save the trouble of rerolling the canvas.) The panoramas rendered the river in the boldest and most gorgeous colors. Vista after vista, spectacle after spectacle, the Father of Waters unfurled itself in serene majesty. One newspaper reviewer described seeing "bluffs, bars, islands, rocks and mounds, points and cliffs without number, and of fantastic varieties of form." The panorama artists crowded the view with eye-catching scenes of natural drama: thunderstorms towering over bluffs, blizzards burying forests, prairie fires stretching from horizon to horizon. There were also scenes of the great calamities and disasters of the day: the desertion of the Mormon city of Nauvoo in central Illinois, for instance (this was a night scene, with the dark rooftops and steeples of the empty city silhouetted eerily in the moonlight). Another favorite was the fire that destroyed the waterfront district of St. Louis in 1849. This was a spectacular scene showing fleeing crowds, desperate companies of firemen, the night sky over the city billowing with black smoke and showering down lurid red sparks; then there followed a scene of the morning after, revealing the charred wrecks of steamboats on the levee and the gutted stumps of buildings behind, with groups of survivors posed here and there in the rubble. This image was always greeted with a shocked hush from the spectators, before the grand flow of the river resumed.

Each vista came with some story attached. A tiny silhouetted figure on a distant bluff, for instance, would prompt the narrator to tell the legend of Winona's Cliff, where an Indian maiden jumped to her death rather than marry a man she didn't love. A view of the skyline of Dubuque, Iowa, would lead to a story about the town's founder, who tricked the local Indian tribes into revealing the location of their secret lead mines. The

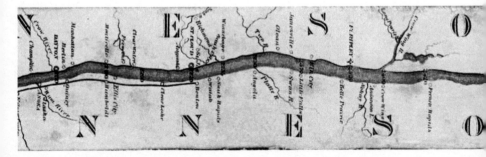

panoramas also naturally touched on the hot-button political issues of the day. The most heated of these questions was the forcible exile of the Native American populations from the eastern half of the continent into the Great Plains. The panoramas seem to have reflected the divided feelings about these expulsions in the country as a whole. Smith's panorama, going by the descriptive pamphlet that was sold at its showings, was robustly scornful of the Native Americans and pictured them as useless primitives who were getting no better than they deserved. The world-famous Indian wigwam, the pamphlet says at one point, was in reality "scarce built with the skill displayed by the beaver in the formation of its home." But Banvard's "Three-Mile Painting" was more elegiac. It showed the Native Americans as proud and statuesque figures of myth; it even took a detour away from the river to survey a new Sioux settlement in the prairie, with scenes of a war dance and children at play and a view of the Sioux's mysterious "village of the dead."

Against these dark images were set upbeat scenes of new growth. The river valley was being colonized at a furious clip, and the panoramas recorded the signs of occupation everywhere: settlements hacked out of the wilderness, vistas of deforested and freshly planted farmland, the plantations occupying the swamps, the new steeple-spiked towns rising on the highest bluffs. The enormous levees being built in the lower valley were favorite topics; one panorama included a dramatic image of a levee breach, with hundreds of slaves running with buckets of sand to fill the widening crevasse.

And above all, there were the world-famous steamboats. They were shown bustling everywhere, from the great harbors of St. Louis and New Orleans to the lonely reaches of the upper river: pausing at levees and docks to unload cargo, stopping off at remote lumberyards to refuel (this

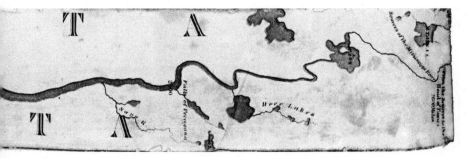

was known as wooding), puffing out proud billows of smoke as they pressed on down bend after bend of the great river—grandly florid emblems of civilization lording it over the wilderness.

The panoramas were like recruitment posters for the new society rising at the edge of the world. Such images seemed to catch up audiences all over America in a tremendous surge of excitement, one they were barely able to explain or describe. Even a famous skeptic of American triumphalism like Henry David Thoreau could feel it. In his essay "Walking," from the early 1850s, he described his fascination with the Mississippi panoramas. He had seen a panorama of the Rhine River in Germany and had been delighted by its scenes of ancient and medieval legend—the Roman bridges, the ruined castles, the walled cities that recalled the setting forth of the Crusaders. He wrote:

> I floated along under the spell of enchantment, as if I had been transported to an heroic age, and breathed an atmosphere of chivalry.
>
> Soon after, I went to see a panorama of the Mississippi, and as I worked my way up the river in the light of to-day and saw the steamboats wooding up, counted the rising cities, gazed on the fresh ruins of Nauvoo, beheld the Indians moving west across the stream, and, as before I had looked up the Moselle, now looked up the Ohio and the Missouri and heard the legends of Dubuque and of Wenona's Cliff,— still thinking more of the future than of the past or present,—I saw that this was a Rhine stream of a different kind; that the foundations of castles were yet to be laid, and the famous bridges were yet to be thrown over the river; and I felt that *this was the heroic age itself,* though we know it not.

PART ONE

THE RIVER RISING

1

Gone on the River

THE UPPER MISSISSIPPI RIVER VALLEY was always a wild and unknown country. Above St. Anthony Falls in Minnesota, the track of the river meandered into vagueness: it wound through pristine forests, and vanished into unexplored valleys, and glinted among mazes of unnamed lakes. The river's ultimate source wasn't established as Lake Itasca in the far north until the 1830s, and the identification wasn't universally accepted for several decades after that—few people were willing to venture up-country to investigate. The pine forests there were trackless and spooky. The valleys were still strewn with monstrous fossils that had lain undisturbed for thousands of years: mammoths and saber-toothed tigers, dire wolves and a species of beaver that was the size of a grizzly bear—relics from the dawn world of the American wilderness, before the first humans arrived.

In the first half of the nineteenth century, the dominant presence in the northern forests was the Chippewa. They lived in wigwam villages, some of four or five hundred people, in glades and clearings scattered throughout the woodlands. These were mostly on the east side of the river. On the west, in the open prairies, were the settlements of the Sioux. The Chippewa and the Sioux were continually skirmishing, and had been for several hundred years. The Sioux believed, not without justice, that when the Chippewa had migrated from the east during the great Iroquois wars, they'd stolen the ancestral Sioux land. There were also white settlers—more and more of them as the nineteenth century went on. Neither the Chippewa nor the Sioux viewed them with much alarm. They generally ignored the rumors of massacres and forced migrations in the lower valley. Both nations had signed treaties with the white authorities, for one thing (the Sioux treaty even recognized their claim to the Chippewa territory), and neither had yet realized that all such treaties with the whites were worthless. Then, too, they wanted to buy from the white traders. They were notorious for taking all the guns and whiskey the traders would sell them, but they were even more eager for cookware. Their enthusiasm for the whites' copper utensils had wiped out traditional pottery through the North Woods almost overnight.

The white settlers mostly lived in new towns along the river. These were muddy and primitive places. A typical one is described in George Byron Merrick's memoir, *Old Times on the Upper Mississippi*. Merrick grew up in Prescott, Wisconsin, which is at the junction of the Mississippi and the St. Croix rivers. In his childhood in the 1840s, the population of Prescott was around two hundred. It was a remote spot; there were no roads, and the closest railroad tracks were hundreds of miles to the south. It was also precariously situated between large settlements of Chippewa and Sioux. Both came into town to trade, and occasionally to fight: the whites all learned how to duck down alleys or crouch behind wagons as soon as they heard war whoops and gunfire.

But Merrick didn't recall ever being troubled by the town's isolation, or its strategic position. The main thing he remembered was the freedom. He and the other boys weren't obsessively monitored the way children routinely are now. In fact, they weren't monitored at all. If they weren't in school, they were on their own—free to go off by themselves and canoe the river, or play with the boys from a nearby Chippewa village, or stage battles around the ruined French fort on the islet just downriver from town. The most romantic of their playgrounds was farther on, below the sandstone bluffs along the west bank of the river: an ancient battlefield, strewn with corroded hatchets and rusted musket nails and arrowheads like fossil fish. The Chippewa boys said it was where their ancestors had won a tremendous victory over the Sioux. Eventually it occurred to Merrick that the Sioux boys probably thought it was where they'd won a victory over the Chippewa.

The lives of the boys were dominated by the Mississippi. Merrick and his friends had a kind of private ritual to symbolize the moment each year when they gave themselves up to the river. On the first hot day of spring, as soon as school was out, they'd run through the town as fast as they could in single file and, one after the next, throw themselves off a bluff into the water. From that moment on, until the first ice sheeted it in the fall, the river was their home.

It was an idyllic and heedless life. "It seems miraculous to me," Merrick wrote, "that all of those boys were not drowned or otherwise summarily disposed of." But nobody ever met with disaster. Merrick himself remembered only a handful of close calls. Mostly they were times when he and the other boys were out canoeing and got caught in violent squalls; their dugout would be swamped by the choppy waters and they had to flounder desperately to the nearest shore. Once, in the open country on the western bank, Merrick was out exploring by himself when he was treed by a wolf pack. He spent a terrified hour clinging to an upper branch as the wolves leaped up to snap at his feet, until the pack inexplicably had a change of mind and ran away.

The nearest he ever came to getting himself killed was a time when he and his brother were out canoeing. They paddled south to a river bend where an immense drift of logs had built up in the shallows. There Merrick's dugout overturned, and as he thrashed around beneath the surface, he got his legs caught in a tangle of cottonwood roots. He barely managed to writhe and jerk and lunge free—and then he had to spend another frantic few seconds scrabbling beneath the drift logs for clear air. At last he burst to the surface. His brother hauled him to safety. Ten minutes later, they were fishing as though nothing had happened.

It certainly never made him love the river less. "We grew into the very life of the river," Merrick wrote, "as we grew in years." Merrick's father owned a warehouse along the levee, and Merrick and his brother commandeered the attic for their bedroom: it gave them a panoramic view of the levee, the docks, and the water. Like sentries, they kept watch on all the arrivals and departures. "At night no steamboat ever landed at the levee," Merrick writes, "without having at least two spectators, carefully noting its distinguishing characteristics."

Most of the traffic was heading downriver. There were wooden barges bearing ore from the mines, and flatboats carrying beaver pelts and sheaves of prairie wheat. If the harvest came in late and the river was already icing over, the flatboats would off-load the wheat and store it in the warehouses until the spring thaw. There were also the big rafts floating down from the logging camps. They were guided by steering oars so large they took dozens of men to maneuver. The crews on the rafts were a notorious lot. Whenever they'd hit town, there would inevitably be a drunken riot. Merrick recalled how the fights would spill into the backstreets and the levee after midnight; all the while, the local marshal waited them out, safely perched atop a high post on the dock, a revolver in his hand, watching the action unfold "with the enlightened eye of an expert and the enjoyment of a connoisseur."

Boats coming up from the lower valley were the most eagerly awaited, because they brought so many essential supplies. The whole town would be on the levee to help unload. There'd be barrels of salt (a prized commodity in the upper valley, so scarce it was often used in place of money), sacks of coffee beans, tuns of cured pork and beef jerky, tubs of rice and axle grease. If the boat arrived at night, torches would be lit up all along the riverfront. People ran everywhere by the flickering light—stacking the barrels, dragging loaded wagons into the warehouses, throwing tarps over the goods that were going to be transshipped farther north. The torches smoked and billowed and flared, shedding a steady drip of pitch and charred wadding into the black water below. And then within the hour the levee would be dark and empty again. Merrick and some of the other local boys would be allowed to stay up until dawn, skylarking among the stacks of cargo, making sure it wasn't stolen by the ubiquitous river thieves.

Now and then, one of the boys on the levee would be on board when a boat pulled out again. He would have stowed away or else talked the captain into letting him hire on as an apprentice—usually for a couple of dollars a month, starvation wages even then. That was what happened with Merrick. When he was a teenager, he left town and was hired as a mud clerk on a boat doing regular runs up and down the valley. Over the next few years, he worked his way up to apprentice engineer, cub pilot, and eventually full pilot. (Later on he went east, where he became a newspaperman and ultimately a publisher.) He thought it was a fine career, but as far as the town was concerned, that was the end of him. They had a phrase they'd use about such a boy: somebody would ask what had happened to this or that kid who used to hang out on the levee, and the answer would be a headshake, or a hand waved contemptuously in the direction of the Mississippi, and a simple dismissal:

Gone on the river.

———

All along its length, on its remotest upper reaches and its most labyrinthine tributaries, people were going on the river. They were sometimes called voyageurs—the word was a survival of the old French culture of the Mississippi, before the Louisiana Purchase. It has a romantic sound, but there was little actual romance associated with being a voyageur. Mostly it meant working the keelboats, barges, and rafts, which was brutal, unremitting, and dangerous labor; or else it meant taking a one-shot trip in a flatboat, loaded down with local goods to sell in the great markets of the river delta. Just about everybody was tempted to try that out at some time or another. It was a simple way of scoring money at a time when most of the river valley was sunk in grinding poverty. One of those who made the trip was Abraham Lincoln: he did his first run on the river in 1831, when he was twenty-two, just out of the family home and striking out on his own. He and some friends, backed by a local businessman, built a flatboat and took it down the Sangamon River to the Illinois, the Illinois to the Mississippi, and the Mississippi all the way down to New Orleans.

What did they carry? It barely mattered. Apples or hemp or whiskey, pigs or turkeys or horses or cattle; maybe there was a local craftsman who made particularly sturdy brooms, or a brewer famous around town for an unusually sweet ale. The delta markets were known to be undiscriminating and insatiable. The voyageurs set out with anything that they could make, grow, barter for, sell on commission, or steal. Ordinarily they set out in the fall, with the pick of the local harvest, or after the thaw in the spring, with whatever miscellaneous load they'd been able to scrounge together over the winter. Sometimes the whole town would gather at the levee for their departure, and the local band would play; sometimes they'd sneak away at dawn, before anybody realized what they'd taken.

The current was a fast jog, nine or ten miles an hour in the deepest channels. It was strong enough to hurry the most heavily laden boat downstream. People didn't have to do much in the way of fancy boating to keep moving. The Mississippi had no waterfalls south of Minnesota, and only one stretch of dangerous white water, along the Iowa-Illinois border (it was successfully dredged by midcentury). The boats were carried forward, hour after hour, day after day, as the valley unfolded around them in endless cascades. There were countless islets and bluffs, feeder creeks and sloughs, marshes and canebrakes receding into the blue depths of the valley; tributaries came rushing in through ravines; clouds skimmed down so low they clipped the pines atop the ridges; drifts of mist floated off the hillsides and melted across the water. Whole days could go by without the voyageurs seeing anyone onshore, and then it might only be a small, silent figure on the near bank, standing for a moment and solemnly raising a hand as they passed.

But the river had its own dangers. Chief among them were the sandbars. The river was deep—more than a hundred feet for much of its length—but the strong drag of the current along its alluvial bottom built up sandbars in countless numbers. The bars cut the effective depth of the channels to a few feet or sometimes a few inches. A boat that went aground on a bar might be stuck there for days or weeks, until help could be found or the river rose. In seasons of low water, these bars made the river essentially impassable. One military expedition, unwisely setting out in late summer, when the river was at its lowest, recorded that between Minnesota and Illinois they went aground on sandbars more than two hundred times.

Then there were the floating trees. There were hordes of them on the river—saplings and fully mature trees and ancient giants more than a hundred feet tall. They'd collect into impassable bottlenecks on hairpin bends and form bobbing, clunking plateaus in the shallows. Sometimes a couple of dozen of them, or a couple of hundred of them, would form into a clump glued together by the mud and debris that were constantly slipping past in the current. These were known as wooden islands, and they would go careening down the river for hundreds of miles at a stretch, until they built up enough momentum to break out of the channels and collide with whatever happened to be in their path along the shore. Everyone got to know the weird creaking, grinding sound that meant a wooden island was approaching. Any boats that couldn't be maneuvered out of the way would be pummeled into flinders by its bristling armor of splintered logs.

But the trees were even more dangerous when they were stationary. Many or perhaps most that fell into the river eventually became stuck in the mud. These were known as snags. Snags were so common that a whole specialized vocabulary was developed to categorize them. A tree that was standing straight up on the river bottom, with its branches just under the waterline, was called a planter. A tree that was stuck sideways into a riverbank or a sandbar so that it stretched out at full length under the water was a sleeper. A tree that waved back and forth in the current with a sawing motion was a sawyer. And a tree that bobbed up and down, rising up out of the water and plunging back again, as though it were performing a river baptism, was a preacher. Any of these snags could stave in or capsize a boat that glided blithely across it, and they were everywhere on the river; by one estimate there was a major snag every five hundred feet.

These perils were almost invisible to the unpracticed eye. Most of them showed up only as odd disturbances on the surface, patterns that had to be decoded from the endless fluctuations of the current. A trailing braid in smooth water was a sure sign of a snag; a quilted ripple was a tangle of submerged logs; a line or fold across the water was an undertow; a persistent swirl of froth was a whirlpool, where a strong tributary flowing quickly into the main current had created a vortex beneath the surface. The voyageurs had to teach themselves all these clues by experience, and the river put a premium on fast learners.

The voyageurs came to call the Mississippi the wicked river. The downriver run was so deceptive and so treacherous that it was said that at least one out of every five boats that set out for the delta wrecked along the way. Every traveler on the river got to know the sight of bodies drifting with the current, or hanging from a floating island, or bobbing among the logs piled up on a river bend—the red shirt that the voyageurs wore, the closest thing the river had to a uniform, could be spotted a mile off, like a distress signal.

The landscape through which the voyageurs passed was still extraordinarily pristine. The most basic traces of human occupation were only sketchily drawn in the valley. There were no main roads or highways; there were barely even any trails. There were no long fences or hedgerows marking out property lines. The countryside hadn't yet been pierced and plotted into an array of carpet scraps, the way it is now; forest and meadow and swamp and prairie still flowed into each other according to their own

logic. The air was uncannily clear. The faintest trace of smoke—a line spi-
raling up from a cabin on a wooded islet, or a smudge over a remote village—could be seen for miles away, as stark as a forest fire.

At night the view was even more glassy and serene. The hills and bluffs
were featureless masses of india ink. There were no lights of towns, sometimes not even when there were towns—streetlights were an innovation
still confined to big cities. People mostly stayed in after dark and went to
bed early. A light on in a house at midnight was a bad sign: it almost
always meant that someone inside was sick. Most nights, the only lights
the voyageurs saw were the moon and the stars—and the stars weren't the
meager scattering of pockmarks we now think of as the constellations, but
the Milky Way in full flood, veil after jeweled veil, reaching down to the
treetops and shimmering on the wrinkled surface of the river. The sharpest
eyes might also pick out, in the remotest depths of the night, a few tiny
flickers of orange: these were enormous bonfires built on the banks of the
river, advertising the wood yards where the steamboats could refuel.

There were no beacons or lighthouses or channel buoys on the river
then; there were no official markers of any kind. Here and there someone
would occasionally paint a warning or an arrow on a prominent rock to
alert voyageurs to danger—but these were often the work of pirates, to
trick boats into going aground. Nor were there any reliable maps. In that
era, mapmaking, even at its best, was a mixture of supposition, obsolete or
garbled information, and pure fantasy; the first rule of travel in the American interior was that only a fool trusted a commercial map.

But the voyageurs didn't care. What did they need a map for? The land
was so wild it was essentially impassable; anyone who didn't go by the river
didn't go at all. In effect, the river served as its own map. A voyageur who
needed to consult it had only to climb the nearest hill. There the route was
unfolded, in all its blue-misted splendor: the great dragon tail of the river
uncoiling through forested valleys and across the tallgrass prairies and into
the vast shrouded swamps, glittering with ten thousand sunflecks, blurred
by drifts of drizzle, blazing with reflected herds of brilliant cumulus, on
and on toward the horizon. As far as the eye could see, the river was the
only road.

To the tourists, the passing landscape was pure monotony; the British travel writer Frances Trollope wrote that the Mississippi was "dismal," "wearisome," "a huge and turbid river with a low and slimy shore," and complained that there was nothing to the scenery but "forest—forest— forest." But a voyageur learned to see every stretch of the river as unique. He needed only one glance at the banks to tell where on the thousands of miles of its course he was. Some didn't even need to raise their eyes to the banks: they could tell their location from the color of the river alone. There were even some connoisseurs who boasted they could do it with their eyes closed, just from how the water tasted.

The river was sky blue near its headwaters, in the white-pine forests of the Far North. The pines came down to the banks, where their roots tangled in a fantastic thorny profusion, and gave the water a clean, pungent tang of pine oil. A little to the south the water became a deep blue-green as the pines gave way to densely overgrown woodlands of oak and elm and maple. The banks grew more lush: in the marshes and along the sloughs and streams were waving fields of cattails and goosefoot and button brush, and below the water's surface in the shallows were mile-long beds of mussels. The marshes were thronged with squabbling crowds of wading birds. The river was busy with catfish and gar and bowfin and buffalo fish and bluegill and walleye; they were so abundant that people claimed there were places you could cross the river by walking on their backs.

By the time the river reached the sandstone bluffs and prairies of Iowa and Illinois, it had become an olive green with hints of brown. Here and there were long wine-red stains trailing along the shallows; the color was from the tannin that had leached from ancient bogs. By that point the forests on either side had thinned out, and the land had opened up. The river ran for hundreds of miles through the tallgrass prairie. The voyageurs would see nothing but the ruffled grass rising and falling in slow swells all the way out to the horizon. In the spring the prairie was a riot of gorgeous wildflowers, endless washes and shoals of white aster and black-eyed Susan and pink phlox and sky-blue spiderwort. In the summer the grasses were ten feet high and were swarmed by game animals like antelope and deer and bison; there were ragged black clouds of passenger pigeons so numerous that a single swarm could take days to pass overhead. In the autumn the grasses turned brittle and were easily set ablaze; after a thunderstorm there'd be a pall of smoke hanging over the horizon marking the spots where the lightning had started fires. Sometimes at night there was a brilliant line of flame edging down a distant hillside, below a titanic churn of smoke underlit by the glare. Now and then the fires swept down to the riverbank, and the voyageurs would be whisked unwillingly along an interminable billowing curtain of smoke and flame. They would be choking and coughing the whole way, and frantically checking the boat to make sure that the burning cinders and tufts of blown grass weren't threatening to stampede their livestock or torch their cargo.

At the southern edge of the prairie was the confluence with the Missouri. The Missouri was a furious torrent bright red with the clays of the Great Plains. Its water was sour and gritty, "too thick for soup but too thin to plow"; its current was so strong that for miles south of the junction it flowed beside the Mississippi in the same bed without mingling, a swift, narrow plume of reddish cream next to a wider swath of greeny murk. Gradually they churned together into an odd pale broth that looked like yellow ash stirred into dark oil. The forests closed in again on either bank. These were some of the densest and lushest woodlands in America. The marshes and canebrakes were tangles of starflower, bloodroot, jack-in-the-pulpit, wild ginger, and mayapple; there were matted beds of maygrass, wild bean, sumac, arrowhead, knotweed, little barley, hickory, and goosefoot. The trees were scrub willow and cottonwood, pin oak and green ash, hackberry and persimmon, black willow and sycamore and honey locust and box elder and pawpaw. They towered up in countless pillars more than a hundred feet tall; the leaf canopy was a remote web of green and black reaching almost to the clouds.

Then the Ohio glided in from the east. It was wide and placid, and its blue water was so rich with topsoil that in some lights it looked black. Its taste was velvety; it was said that if you drank enough of it your sweat would be as sweet as dew. It, too, held aloof from the main current for many miles. But gradually it blended in, and the result was a rich, murky, chocolaty gold. This was the characteristic color that travelers came to associate with the Mississippi. It wasn't very appetizing to drink; the fastidious travelers in the lower valley made a habit of letting the water stand for at least a half an hour to allow the grit and filth a chance to settle out. The hard-core river people didn't bother. They'd just scroop a bucket into the current and guzzle it down straight. They liked to claim the river silt was good for you. They called it "the true Mississippi relish."

Meanwhile, the forests were growing more tropical. Water oaks and water maples were interspersed with catalpas and wild cherries and tupelo gums; there were palmettos unfolding their green spearlike fans and vast stands of gloomy cypresses. Along the water's edge were endless tessellations of Chinese lotus, and the marshlands were radiant with orchids and passionflowers and hibiscuses. Beavers and otters splashed in the sloughs and creeks, the woods were haunted by wolves and panthers, and the air was a deafening riot of millions of songbirds.

The river unfolded into the delta, as the sloughs and bayous and marshes and swamps thickened. It became at times a pale luminous green like lime soda water. Its taste was reminiscent of bitter mildew. On either side the banks were green-shadowed and marshy. Water moccasins and alligators slithered through the mud; the green was spangled with cross vine and trumpet vine, cinnamon fern and Cherokee rose, silver bell and blue lobelia, lily and hyacinth and hydrangea and yellow jasmine. The river glided on past endless receding processions of cypress trees shrouded in Spanish moss; here and there were silent lagoons in perpetual gloom. The river meandered among orange groves and stands of magnolia so pungent the smell made some travelers sick.

Then the great swamp forests began to dwindle. The banks on either side melted away into indeterminate ooze that deepened and widened into borders of reeds and cattails more than a mile wide. The last solid land broke up into a maze of little peninsulas and islets and isthmuses dense with rustles of sea grass and sedge, swarmed by pelicans. The water shone from thousands of brackish ponds and lagoons and lakes. There was no firm line between the river delta and the salt estuaries. But in the end the last islets fell away, and the great freshwater flood of lime, gold, and brown went streaming serenely out into the blue salt of the Gulf.

The river grew more crowded the farther south the voyageurs went. In the upper valley, days could pass without the sight of another boat; below St. Louis there were fresh armadas around every turn. The river traffic was a hectic, crowded, jumbled array of keelboats and flatboats, barges and rafts, pirogues and scows, skiffs and canoes and schooners. "The floating life on the water," one writer called it; he predicted that the people of the Mississippi valley "will ultimately become as famous as the Chinese for having their habitancy in boats."

The basic form of river transport was the broadhorn flatboat. This was essentially nothing more than a rectangular wooden box, with a wide, flat bottom and steep sides. It was typically ten to fifteen feet across, thirty to forty feet long, and three or four feet deep. Its planking was fixed to a lumber frame and held together by wooden pins—iron nails were too expensive. The bottom was sealed with caulk or tar or pitch. There was usually a hut with a peaked roof built amidships. At its stern was an enormous steering oar, sometimes just a big tree limb shorn of its leaves and branches. At either end of the bow were two smaller oars, which were mainly used to shove off from sandbars and steer away from the banks. When these oars were raised, they looked like the horns of a steer—thus its name.

The broadhorn was an ugly, clumsy, primitive boat, almost impossible to maneuver and very easy to wreck. But it had a few crucial advantages: it was cheap, it was easy to build, and it was extremely buoyant. Even when it was loaded down with several tons of cargo, it drew only a couple of feet of water, which meant that it rode high enough to get it over a lot of the sandbars and snags. It was the perfect boat for the first-time voyageur making a one-shot trip to the delta.

The other boat seen most often on the river, at least in the early years of the century, was the keelboat. This was a big, graceful gondola, sometimes fifty or sixty feet long, partially enclosed by an elegantly sloped roof—keelboats were beautiful boats, many of them, with elaborate handcrafted prows. A keelboat typically carried ten or fifteen tons of cargo and was worked by a crew of at least a dozen men. These crews were necessarily more skilled and professional than those of the flatboats; a keelboat wasn't the kind of disposable craft whose loss could be shrugged off by its owners. Its crews tended to be proud of their skills—they often considered themselves to be the only true voyageurs on the Mississippi.

There were many other varieties of boats. Every possible method for moving up and down the current was somewhere being tried, and sometimes brought to a high art form. Canoes of hollowed-out tree trunks, often fifty or seventy-five feet long, were called pirogues; some pirogues were made up of five or six trunks set side by side and nailed together with planking to form a kind of supercatamaran. There were also the traditional birch-bark canoes of the Native Americans, extraordinarily sturdy and angelically light—many people considered them the finest boats ever put on the river. There were great barges bristling with oars and rudders, and there were vast ungainly rafts, cobbled together out of whatever wood was handy and sometimes going downriver in a state of perpetual disintegration. There were shanty boats, houseboats, tugboats, cargo boats, packet boats; there were sleds and skiffs and scows, dugouts, arks, flats, and ferries. And there were irregular and fanciful boats that had no name, built of haphazard materials, of mismatched parts of abandoned boats, of random accretions of flotsam and salvage; some had weird turrets and peaks and railings of ironwork and carved wood like nightmare castles. The writer Timothy Flint described them as "monstrous anomalies, reducible to no specific class of boats, and only illustrating the whimsical archetypes of things that have previously existed in the brain of inventive men, who reject the slavery of being obliged to build in any received form."

All the boats were crammed with cargo. A ceaseless torrent of goods was coming downriver. The big rafts carried pine lumber from the North Woods, furs and hides from the Great Plains, and wheat and corn from the prairies. The barges carried copper and lead ore from Wisconsin and Minnesota, and glistening mountains of coal from the mines along the Ohio. The flatboats and keelboats carried pungent barrels of cider and whiskey; they carried coils of hemp rope and stinking wheels of cheese; they carried avalanches of corn ears, apples, cabbage heads, potatoes; they carried complaining flocks of chickens, turkeys, and geese and herds of skittish horses and cattle and pigs. Some carried the North's most exotic exports, ice and snow, which at their destination were stored in dry wells and deep caves; snow flavored with rose water was always a great treat during a delta summer.

And they were carrying people—immigrants, itinerant laborers, migrant workers following the seasons. People may have been the most common and the least valuable cargo on the river. They were uncounted, uncataloged, unremembered; nobody cared whether they reached their destination or what happened to them once they arrived. The only people who were kept track of were slaves, because they came with a specific dollar value attached. Thousands of slaves were brought down the river each year. Those who transported them were known as soul drivers. Everyone on the river could recognize the soul drivers' boats. They had a peculiar place in the impromptu society of the river. People in the lower valley took the existence of slavery for granted and universally regarded the abolitionist movement with contempt—but there was also a widespread belief that the slave trade itself was a dirty business and that the slavers were the lowest of the low. The boats of the soul drivers glided downriver on their own and were shunned by the other river people wherever they laid up for the night.

Darting among the armadas of the downriver traffic were shifting con-stellations of smaller boats making short hops from port to port. These were the boats of the river merchants. They went from town to village to plantation, anywhere there was a levee or a dock where they could tie up and display their wares. They could be found on any stretch of the river: dealers in kitchenware and cabinetry and furniture, sellers of books and plows, craftsmen of scythes and brooms and spinning wheels. The river had more than one floating smithy with a working forge. There were float-ing greenhouses selling exotic plants. There were floating daguerreotype studios, where people could pose for formal portraits. The river had its own tailors and haberdashers, knife sharpeners and tin workers; there were boats that were fully stocked general stores, with polished countertops and neatly stacked shelves displaying bolts of coarse cloth for sale by the yard, barrels of flat-head nails, and the latest newspapers and gazettes from New Orleans and St. Louis. Then there were the showboats, the traveling troupes of actors and musicians and acrobats. There were the doctors with their medicine shows: steam doctors, magnetic doctors, hydrological doc-tors, milk-sick doctors, homeopaths, vitopaths, mesmerists, baunscheid-tists, and sellers of patent medicines. They traveled with musicians and actors, who'd sing and put on burlesque routines to draw the crowd, and once they'd made their sales, they'd be back on the river again before any-body had a chance to examine the contents of the bottles they'd just bought. And there were the gambling boats and the brothel boats—the latter came to be known as gunboats—that would anchor at a discreet distance from towns and villages, and they'd do their business until the landsmen organized a "vigilance committee" to chase them away.

The most startling sight for many travelers was the houseboats. These were rafts, sometimes eighty or ninety feet long, carrying elaborately constructed and fully furnished houses. The houses were surrounded by pens holding horses and sheep and cattle and hogs; haystacks and farm implements were scattered everywhere as though in a farmyard; children were scampering, men were whittling, and women were at the washtub. Sometimes Grandmother was seen sitting in a rocking chair on the front porch, placidly knitting, as though she belonged to an Americanized version of Noah's ark, riding the flood to a new world.

From just about anywhere on the Mississippi's great branches, the journey down to the delta was a matter of a few days or a few weeks; the return trip could take the better part of a year. An upriver journey, before the rise of the steamboats, was a nearly impossible proposition. There came to be endless varieties of contrivances to force boats against the current. Most often people hoisted sails. If the wind was against them, they'd break out the oars. Some of the simple paddle-wheel boats were powered by hand-cranked treadmills; others had treadmills powered by horses or cattle. Keelboats were moved against the current by a peculiar technique known as poling. It was a strange and mesmerizing spectacle. The keelboat crew, all wearing the bright red shirts of the voyageurs, would line up on deck on the side of the boat nearest to the shore. Each man carried a long wooden pole tipped with an iron shoe. At a signal from the captain, they'd all lower the poles into the water and plant the shoes in the river mud. Then, gripping the poles as firmly as they could, they'd march in a line toward the stern. As each man reached the stern, he'd raise his pole up and hurry to the back of the line, where he'd plant the shoe in the mud again and resume marching. Slowly, lumberingly, the boat would slide forward beneath their feet.

Larger boats required grander techniques. The big barges were moved by warping. This involved running heavy ropes or cables through an anchor that was fixed to the shallows, or else looping them around the biggest tree or boulder onshore, and then out to a tugboat in the channel. The tugboat would move downriver with the current, and the rope would be pulled around the pivot to drag the barge upriver. When no tug was available, the rope would simply be run back from the pivot to the barge itself, and the entire crew would draw it in by hand. Sometimes the crew wouldn't even bother with the rope or the pivot: they'd all just reach out from the barge to grab hold of the bushes on the riverbank, and they'd pull until the boat moved a few feet forward or the bushes were uprooted. This was called bushwhacking.

The most straightforward, brute-force method of upriver movement was also the most exhausting. It was known as cordelling. The crew would go ashore with a heavy rope that had been tied to the bow, and they would simply drag the boat forward. They thrashed through the underbrush, sank to their knees in the mud of the riverbanks, waded chest-deep through reedy sloughs and swamps, untangled the line from bristling stumps, on and on, sunup to sundown. The rule of thumb for a cordelle's progress was this: a boat moving downriver with the current could sometimes make ten miles an hour; a boat going upriver by cordelle was lucky to make ten miles a day.

There were plenty of times when nothing worked. The wind died, and the sails were useless. The current was too strong or the boat was too heavy to be moved with oars. The river bottom in the shallows was so muddy that the iron-shoed poles sank through it like butter. A landslide or a sprawl of fallen timber along the bank made it impossible to go ashore with a line for warping. The shores were swamps a half a mile deep on either side and there was no solid ground for a cordelle. Boats were sometimes stranded for days or weeks, until the wind picked up, the river rose or fell, or a passing steamboat in a rare moment of kindness offered a tow—or until the crew finally abandoned the boat and looked for another way to go on.

It was no wonder that many voyageurs got down to the delta and then couldn't face the thought of bringing their boat upriver again. This was another great advantage to flatboats: they weren't worth anything. They were designed for a one-way trip. Once their goods had been off-loaded and disposed of in the markets of New Orleans, the boats themselves were broken up and sold for scrap. That was how flatboats became known as "the boats that never came back." The writer James Hall found the life cycle of the flatboat to be a melancholy parable:

> She pursues her voyage, like man on his earthly pilgrimage, to that undiscovered country from whose bourne no traveller of her species ever returns; for, being calculated to stem the current, she is useless after she has reached her destination, except as so much lumber.

But even if the voyageurs were freed from the deadweight of their boat, they didn't find their return all that easy. By midcentury, if they were flush, they could buy a cheap passage on one of the steamboats—it was only a few dollars from New Orleans to St. Louis, if they were willing to sleep on deck and work off part of their fare by helping load and unload cargo at the stops along the way. Or they could hire onto one of the big barges returning upriver and spend months cordelling somebody else's boat through the mud of the riverbanks. Many of them found it simpler to walk. Once their business in New Orleans was done, they'd set out on foot—up the forest trails, along the margins of endless swamps, through the trackless tallgrass prairies: month after month, all the way home.

That was the calendar time set by the river. A typical voyageur would set out with a load of cargo bound for New Orleans in the spring, arrive there in a few weeks, and then spend the rest of the spring and into the summer and sometimes the fall getting home. He'd rest up all winter— and then, the following spring, build a new flatboat, pick up a fresh load of cargo, and set out downriver again. Abraham Lincoln after he rode this circuit a couple of times said that it taught him what it felt like to be a piece of driftwood.

The boats ran all day, from dawn till sundown, but only the biggest boats were still on the river after dark. The rafts and barges went barreling on; everybody else looked for some secure place to hole up until morning. A night run in a flatboat or a keelboat was only for the reckless. People might do it if they were desperate, if they had an injured man and thought there might be a town with a doctor somewhere nearby—but they risked being capsized or stove in by an invisible snag, or running fatally aground on a sandbar, or being trapped by a whirlpool, or being swamped or run over by one of the great boats lording over the channels.

Toward dusk each day the boats began to collect into great archipelagoes off the levees of the port towns. It would happen from New Madrid south to the delta: dozens, sometimes hundreds, of boats clustering together, anchoring, tying up at docks, tossing ropes and cables from boat to boat, assembling into loose, floating cities. Soon cook fires in braziers would light up on the decks, dogs on different boats would bark furiously at each other, horses and livestock would shuffle and thump in their pens, and the sounds of fiddle music and stamping and singing and laughing would float up from a hundred places, mingling with the smoke of the cook fires. As the evening deepened and the lanterns were lit, people began moving from boat to boat, clambering over gunwales, hopping across roofs. They were bartering food, looking for jobs on other boats, passing on gossip, making deals for their cargo, and arranging convoys. It was a common practice to "lash" boats into a shoal of ten or twenty and travel downriver together to defend against the river pirates. The parties quickly grew rowdy. Sooner or later drunken fights began breaking out—it wasn't unusual for a voyageur to drink himself into a blind, belligerent stupor every single night of his life. Then, around midnight, there'd be a general exodus toward shore.

Few towns were enthusiastic about welcoming the river people. At St. Louis, there was a night watch with fifty armed men assigned to the dock district, just to make sure that the river people didn't stray too far from the levee. Many towns actually divided themselves in two, giving over one part to the river: that was how Vicksburg, Mississippi, for instance, held itself aloof from its disorderly riverfront companion Vicksburg Landing. Natchez, Mississippi, was divided by topography: the main town stood on a high bluff and was a decorous, gracious place of pillared porticoes, white church steeples, and brick storefronts; while around the base of the bluff was a second town, a crooked, squalid maze of slums and shanties, many of them built from wood salvaged from wrecked or abandoned flatboats. The official names for the two towns were Natchez and Natchez Landing, but more often they were called Natchez-on-the-Hill and Natchez-Under-the-Hill.

On summer evenings, it was the custom for the good people of Natchez-on-the-Hill to stroll to the edge of the bluff and take in the view of their fallen sister town and the boat city below. They'd survey the dirty smoke seething up from the chimneys, and the glare in the back alleys from the saloons and taverns, and beyond, on the river, the constellations of glittering lanterns and flickering cook fires swaying in the darkness. They'd listen with a kind of amused distaste to the disorderly music floating up from open doorways; they'd take in, as though they were spectators at a sporting event, the pops of gunfire and the frequent screams, many of them interrupted. They would congratulate themselves on the way they had carried out their quarantine. Not one of them would have ever admitted to being curious about what was going on down below the hill—much less confess to having, now and then, snuck down the bluff to sample the entertainment on offer there for themselves.

The boat cities hung together at the levees each night until just before dawn. But then, as the last stragglers were drifting in from the riverfront, the assemblies began to stir. The lines and cables between the boats were loosed and coiled up again, the anchors were drawn, breakfasts were frying, and there was a great creaking, thumping, slithering overture of sails raising and oars lowering. At sunrise the signal to depart would come. It was a weird, sonorous boom of a reveille; it came from the huge wooden trumpets known as river horns, sounding out from the flatboats and keelboats and shivering the air for a mile around.

Then the boat cities broke up. In ones and twos, and in the floes of lashed convoys, the boats drifted out into the shining expanse of the river, where they were caught up in the current and went scattering downstream. That was typically the last they'd all see of each other. The immensity of the river, the vagaries of the current, and the crowds of traffic down every bend meant that the next night they'd be sorted into wholly different congregations downriver. It was a rare event for any boats on their way to the delta to encounter each other twice. The river didn't encourage lasting friendships.

2

Old Devil River

IN HYDROLOGICAL TERMS, the Mississippi was something of a freak. It was a titanic volume of ungoverned water flowing across a floodplain of very slight declivity. There were no mountain valleys to funnel it, or deep channels dug in the bedrock to keep it in place. It was traversing a flat and infinitely malleable surface of mud, silt, and clay—and this meant that it was free to move however and whenever its currents shifted.

Its basic form was an endless series of sinuously unfolding horseshoe curves, technically known as meander loops. The exact mechanism by which meander loops are created is still imperfectly understood, but it's believed that the primary force shaping them is the natural tendency of flowing water to fall away from a straight line. The water in a meander loop actually requires far less energy to keep moving, even though it is covering so much more territory, than water traveling through a rigorously ruler-straight canal.

Meander loops tend to form in even equidistant patterns, all other things being equal, but at any given moment their pattern on a particular river usually appears to be wildly irregular. This is because the loops are continually being reshaped by a process of fluid dynamics called helicoidal flow. Helicoidal flow is a secondary type of turbulence that forms around the main current moving in a river channel. Two things happen because of helicoidal flow: the water along the outer curve of a meander loop speeds up and eats into the riverbank, and at the same time the water on the inner curve slows down and deposits the silt that it's already carrying downriver. The result is that the outer bank is worn away while the inner bank is built up, and so the loop becomes inexorably larger and more pronounced within the same area of land. Sooner or later, the growing curves of adjoining loops touch, the current breaks through the banks, and a new connection is formed. On the Mississippi, these connections were known as cutoffs. When the main volume of the current flows through a cutoff, the silt being carried downriver begins to be deposited around it, building up new banks on either side, and the now-landlocked curve of the loop outside the new banks either dries up or else becomes a bayou or an oxbow lake.

On the Mississippi, where the land was flat, the current was vast and strong, and the helicoidal flow was perpetually at work, the meander loops and cutoffs were constantly unfolding into strange new contortions. In the lower valley, where the obstacles were the fewest, the Mississippi bent, doubled back on itself, executed hairpin turns, and twisted around to flow in new directions. A complete map of its meander belt, as the term is, would show that over the centuries the river had writhed around its current route like a nest of anacondas.

At ground level, this shifting tangle was experienced as an unending challenge. Whenever the river people gathered, all they'd ever talk about was how the river was changing. They'd rattle on in a whole specialized technical vocabulary of homegrown hydrology that described the river's peculiar behavior: chutes and points, bends and reaches, false points and sycamore snags. They'd debate about how the river was doing that season, where it had shifted unexpectedly, whether it was rising or falling, what easy stretches were now suddenly dangerous, and which of its most celebrated dangers were wearing away and were now just child's play for a real river man.

The talk was a way of bonding; it enabled total strangers to chatter on together like childhood friends. But it was also an immediate practical necessity. The waywardness of the Mississippi was a constant threat. Every day, somewhere along the river, huge bluffs were collapsing; overgrown banks were falling in on themselves; ancient stands of trees were sliding down into the tide. Sandbars were growing into islets. Islets were accumulating rocks, rotted logs, and mud and sprouting with countless scattered seeds; they were bristling with new trees and underbrush; they were melting away in the current again and turning back into sandbars. On every voyage, the familiar landmarks were disorientingly reshaped or abruptly erased, while new hazards had popped up out of nowhere.

This was another big reason why there were no trustworthy maps of the river. It changed too quickly. Every pilot had to have his own mental map, which was added to, corrected, erased, and redrawn in his head on every run; and no two pilots' maps, if they could have been compared, would have been identical. The river remade itself every day. People who lived on or around the river learned to think of it as untrustworthy, violent, deceptive, and unknowable. While the voyageurs called it the wicked river, the plantation slaves called it Old Devil River, because of its habit of playing bizarre and malicious tricks. A man would go to bed on one side of the river and wake to find that it had changed course overnight and his property was now on the opposite bank. That was not a simple matter, because the river was the boundary line between states: if he went to sleep in a slave state, he might wake in a free state, and he'd find that all his slaves had automatically been emancipated. This was why some people came to call it the abolitionist river—"abolitionist" being a worse insult than "devil."

The most dramatic erasures and remakings of the river course happened in the floods. The floods were annual events. The upper Mississippi would freeze over during the winter; in early spring, the ice would break up and come grinding and tumbling downstream in thunderous cascades; and then in the following weeks, as the meltwater of the North Country came pouring down through thousands of tributaries, the river would rise. Since there was no quick way of getting news downriver, until the advent of the telegraph in midcentury, there were never any warnings about how high the river was running in the upper valley or how bad a flood season the lower valley could expect. The news from upriver arrived at the same speed as the flood itself. People could only wait it out and hope for the best; they'd simply have to watch each day as the waters inexorably crept up over the banks and drowned out their land.

Some of the Indians in the lower valley liked to say that the river was a snake that woke from a doze every seven years and lashed out at anyone foolish enough to live alongside it. As an average for the catastrophic floods—the floods that swept away whole towns and inundated the land for thousands of square miles along either side of the banks—seven years was about right. Sometimes these floods came more often. There were five catastrophic floods on the Mississippi between 1809 and 1816. There were four in the 1820s. There were only two in the 1840s—but the flood of 1844, one of the first for which there is any kind of hard data, is still the greatest volume of water ever recorded descending the river.

The floods were the great given of river life. Everyone who lived on or near the river had to learn to coexist with them somehow. Houses were built on stilts all through the swamps and marshlands; at St. Louis, the warehouses of the dock district had to be set so far back from the river-bank to protect them from the rises that there was a separate hauling fee to get goods carried off the boats into storage. Farmers working the bottom-lands and transient river islets—unbelievably fertile lands, because of the topsoil that the floods dumped on them—would spend their winters building colossal rafts, so that when the river began to rise in the spring, they could herd their cattle and pigs and horses into pens, and load their grain and gear into makeshift barns, and then tie a rope to the tallest tree branch they could find and ride out the next weeks or months till the river dwindled again. They could only hope that their land was still there when the waters retreated. Often their homesteads ended up on the river bottom.

The highest water usually came in June. Everywhere along the river, people waited for the June rise the way they might await the results of a horse race. Some years the river rose only a few feet and swamped the fields adjacent to its banks; other years it rose ten feet or more and drowned the countryside. In 1844 it rose fifty feet and spread out more than ten miles wide and more than thirty feet deep in the central valley all summer long. At its height, the citizens of St. Louis gathered at the levee, as though at a regatta, and watched as Illinoistown on the far bank was wholly engulfed and its pieces carried off by the flood.

On June 5, 1805, at around one in the afternoon, a tornado came out of the hill country south of St. Louis and crossed the Mississippi. It was, accord-ing to one nineteenth-century writer, "the most violent tempest that ever visited Illinois." That area of the Illinois shore was still only thinly popu-lated and there were no reported fatalities, but the tornado brought down countless trees as it crashed through the old-growth forests of southern Illinois. The track of the storm went on for hundreds of miles; some said it went on all the way through to Indiana and even to Ohio—which would have meant it was on the ground for several hours, making it the most powerful tornado on record. For decades afterward, travelers making their way through the wilderness country of southern Illinois were stymied by a natural barrier, a wall of titanic fallen trees a mile wide and hundreds of miles long, rotting and moldering in the forest depths.

This is what routinely stunned visitors and new settlers: the violence and unpredictability of weather in the river valley. It wasn't just the deep freeze of the northern winters, the flooded springs, or the mosquito-swarming summers; it was the daily calamity of the storms. Soldiers in the tallgrass prairies reported being caught in freak thunderstorms, which they called downspouts—presumably what meteorologists now call microbursts—where the rain came down so heavily they had to steeple their hands over their noses to go on breathing.

Even an ordinary spring thunderstorm could be perilous. The journalist Thomas Bangs Thorpe described one. He and a few companions were being led by an Indian guide through the wild country along the wooded bluffs on the east bank of the river when they saw a big storm billowing up over the hills on the far shore. The only shelter they could find was in a crude log cabin on the riverbank that had been abandoned by its previous inhabitants. The storm hit toward sundown, and it grew steadily worse as the evening went on. The rain was pouring in through the chinks in the logs; Thorpe wrote that they "were soon literally afloat." A lightning strike a few hundred yards from the cabin set a huge oak ablaze, and soon the entire stand of trees that surrounded the oak was burning. The fury of the rain turned the fire into a tumult of steam, and the illumination of the lightning falling on the river was so strange that it seemed to Thorpe like something out of the book of Revelation. The river had, he wrote, "a smooth but mysterious looking surface that resembled in the glare of the lightning, a mirror of bronze, and to heighten this almost unearthly effect, the forest trees that lined its most distant shores, rose up like mountains of impenetrable darkness, against clouds burning with fire."

As the storm raged on, Thorpe's companions fell asleep. Thorpe was baffled by their cavalier attitude; he sat sleepless while the sound of their snoring added to his misery. Then sometime toward morning the Indian guide touched him on the arm and gestured for him to listen. Thorpe could hear nothing other than the roaring and drumming of the rain. The Indian suddenly jumped up and headed for the door. That woke one of Thorpe's companions, who immediately grabbed for his rifle and demanded to know what was going on. "River too near," the Indian said. Thorpe's companion listened for a moment, and then shouted, "He's right, so help me. The banks of the Mississippi are caving in."

They made it out just in time. "The Indian was the last to leave the cabin," Thorpe recalled, "and as he stepped from its threshold, the weighty unhewn logs that composed it, crumbled, along with the rich soil, into the swift-running current of the mysterious river."

Even when there were no great events, no land-remaking floods or apocalyptic storms, the sheer scale of the river could be treacherous. Sometimes the issue was the river's titanic lulling sameness, its vast, silent, and unhurried flow day after day: boats often came to grief for no other reason than that their crews simply couldn't stay alert any longer. And when something did go wrong, it would suddenly become blindingly clear just how far one was from any help. A sudden squall or a swell could knock over one of the little braziers the crews kept lit on the deck and within moments the cargo could be set ablaze, or the horses or the cattle could have been panicked into a stampede—and even on the most crowded stretches of the river, the nearest boat was likely to be hundreds of yards away, bobbing along in the current hopelessly out of reach.

The scale of the landscape, too, created its own dangers. Settlements were still thinly spread; if a voyageur had his foot crushed by a loose barrel, he could have gangrene by the time the boat reached the next town with a doctor. Along most of the river the banks were still wholly wild, and going ashore there for any reason was perilous. There were large predators roaming along the riverbanks, bears and panthers and wolf packs; and there were human predators as well, Indian hunting parties and river pirates and armed settlers who didn't like strangers. Lighting a fire was a major risk, for the adversaries it might attract—but in most of the country to go without a fire was even worse: the nights in the North Country could be punishingly cold, and in the South the mosquito swarms were so thick that they could drive people to madness.

The prairies of the central valley were probably the trickiest places to go ashore, because they seemed so simple: just treeless seas of grass spreading out evenly across a gently rolling terrain. They were easily passable in the spring, when the grasses were new, and in the autumn, when the grasses had died and had been burned off by the prairie fires. But in the summer the grasses grew more than ten feet high and offered no landmarks of any kind. Anyone who ventured more than a few feet from shore would become hopelessly disoriented in their rushing, sighing depths, broken only by the crisscrossing tracks left by the grazing deer. People were known to take hours or days to get back to the riverbank after thrashing around helplessly in the interior; inevitably there were stories about the unlucky wanderers who never did get back and whose skeletons weren't found till the grasses dwindled in the fall.

But the greatest danger was the river itself, even when it seemed the most placid. A simple fall overboard could be fatal. The gigantic volume of the current caused complex forms of turbulence in the deep waters that were invisible on the surface, strong vortices and long trailing undertows that could suck down the hardiest swimmer. As one writer noted, "It is said that nothing that ever sunk beneath its muddy surface was known to rise again." But the worst danger for a man overboard was the temperature of the water. Since the river was fed by meltwater tributaries in the Far North, even in high summer it could be bitterly cold. The slow-moving waters in the shallows were warmed by the sun and could at times become almost tepid, but the main current remained hidden in the darkness beneath the immense murky weight of the river and never got much above freezing. Anybody who was drawn down into the river depths for more than a few minutes would most likely succumb to hypothermia.

This was why a man overboard was generally considered a man lost. Even if the rest of the crew noticed in time that he was floundering in the water, there usually wasn't much they could do for him; the boats couldn't be turned around against the force of the current, and most were too unwieldy to be maneuvered quickly into shore—assuming the crew was willing to try. The truth was that most voyageurs took for granted that anybody who went into the water at all was doomed, and they usually wouldn't bother to try throwing out a line. And anyway drowning was probably the most merciful way to go. A man who did manage to make it to shore found himself in a deserted and inhospitable country, perhaps hundreds of miles from the nearest settlement. He was soaking wet and blue from the cold, and with no way of building a fire, he would likely be dead of exposure by morning. The last sight he would get of his boat, it was gliding impassively downriver and vanishing around a bend for good.

3

The Comet's Tail

WHENEVER THE RIVER MEN TIRED of their technical shoptalk, they would fall to reminiscing about the river. The river, for them, wasn't just the most interesting subject in the world; it was the only subject in the world. They would boast of their skill in a crisis. They would tell stories about their exploits on the most remote reaches of the river system—trapping in the wilderness country above the falls of St. Anthony in Minnesota, hunting in the empty lands on the upper Missouri in the shadow of the Rocky Mountains, trading in the mysterious old Spanish territories somewhere out beyond the windings of the Arkansas and the Red. And sooner or later somebody would bring up the river's most celebrated story, its own Iliad—the story of the Crow's Nest and the time of the Great Shakes.

The Crow's Nest was a river islet about 175 miles up from Natchez. It was small, steep, and densely forested; it had a sheltered cove on its downriver bank, and it also had a couple of very deep caves. It was like any other of the countless islets scattered along the river—it stood out only because of its inhabitants. In the late eighteenth and early nineteenth centuries, it was the base for the most feared pirates in the whole river valley.

The river in those days was infamous for its lawlessness. It was infested with thieves, brigands, and pirates. There were also "land pirates" who terrorized travelers on the few existing roads, like the Old Wilderness Road and the Natchez Trace, that ran from the river through the wild country to the east. But even for that time, the Crow's Nest pirates were exceptional. They were renowned for their ruthlessness and wanton cruelty. They snuck aboard docked boats at night, drilled holes in their hulls, and waited until the boats were foundering the next morning before attacking them and killing everybody aboard. They painted false markers on the rocks to indicate channels where there were none, and once the misled boats were wrecked or beached on a sandbar and their passengers killed, they were looted at leisure. They routinely disposed of their victims by gutting them, filling their body cavities with rocks and stones, sewing them up again, and throwing them overboard so they'd sink without a trace.

They stalked the lower river for several decades. At the end of the eighteenth century, the governor of the Louisiana Territory issued a desperate decree banning unlashed boats from the lower river; only convoys of ten or more lashed boats were permitted to proceed past the Crow's Nest toward the delta. The governor had no other recourse. There was little in the way of formal law and order on the frontier then. A few garrisons of federal soldiers were stationed along the river, but they were tasked only with defending the settlers from attacks by small Indian raiding parties— not a large, heavily armed, and well-organized band of pirates. The river people were on their own.

They did their best to stay in business. Their boats were heavily armed to fend off the pirates. One boat making regular runs on the river advertised that it offered "a large crew, skilful in the use of arms, a plentiful supply of muskets and ammunition, an equipment on each boat of six one-pound cannon, and a rifle-proof cabin for the use of the passengers." But in the end the river men had no choice but to take direct action against the Crow's Nest themselves.

The story goes that one night in the late autumn of 1809, a large group of keelboats and barges had been stranded by contrary winds a few miles upriver from the Crow's Nest. The crews lashed boats and created an impromptu floating city in the deserted waters. When they all crossed from boat to boat, hailing acquaintances and passing on gossip, the Crow's Nest was the only thing anybody wanted to talk about. Over the course of that evening, they decided that the time had come to do something about it: they were going to put an end to the Crow's Nest gang once and for all.

By midnight a plan had jelled; in the dead hours afterward it launched. More than a hundred of the toughest raftsmen and voyageurs had agreed to take part. They descended the river silently, in skiffs and canoes, until they saw the shadow of the islet ahead. The pirates had posted no lookouts; after all, there was never any traffic worth looting after sundown. Then the leader of the boatmen stood up in the shallows and waded

ashore. In some versions of the story, he yelled out to the others the traditional fighting cry of the voyageurs: "Hell's afire and the river rising! Up,
boys, and cut their hearts out!"

The boatmen stormed the islet. They took the pirates completely by
surprise. Quickly they fanned out through the interior and seized control
of the caves and of the boats they found docked in the hidden cove. They
didn't turn up much loot—or at least they didn't admit to finding much.
But they did discover a printing press for counterfeit money, which they
ceremoniously wrecked. They also captured a couple of dozen men, two
women, and a teenage boy. They let the women and the boy go. At dawn
they hanged the men.

The news of their astonishing victory rapidly spread up and down the
valley. It was famous in the river folklore for decades afterward: any man
who looked old enough and who could claim to have been on the river for
long enough would modestly admit, after a few drinks, that he had taken
part in the storming of the Crow's Nest. But in the real world, the triumph
proved to be short-lived. The Crow's Nest wasn't put out of business.
Maybe the surprise of the attack hadn't been perfect; the worst of the
pirates might have had some advance warning and escaped. Or maybe it
had gone perfectly, but the gang had simply sprouted up again with new
leaders. Or maybe the raid had never happened at all, and was just a story
the river people told to buck themselves up. In any case, by 1811, the
Crow's Nest was as feared on the river as it had ever been.

The year 1811 was a hard one on the river anyway. The spring flood was
disastrously high; towns were swamped all along the Ohio and Mississippi. By summer there was a bad outbreak of yellow fever, the worst that
anybody had seen in years. In the fall there was another deadly fever, never
identified, that swept the length of the valley. (It was described by the doctor Daniel Drake as a "bilious remitting and intermitting fever . . . clearly
referable to the vegetable putrefaction which was the consequence of that
flood.") And then in the autumn there was the comet.

The comet appeared in the first week of September. Initially it was just
an unusually large new star that burned brightly each evening in the after-
glow of sunset. As the weeks passed, it didn't wink out or dwindle away,
the way strange sights in the sky usually did; every night it was more brilliant, and within a month it was growing a tail. This tail was an alarming,

two-pronged fork like a devil's tail. By December the comet was a dazzling point of light surrounded by a vague milky halo almost as large as the moon, and the forked tail had stretched out into two enormous ghostly plumes that covered half the sky.

Everyone knew what it meant: some strange disaster was imminent. Then there was another sign—or so it was said long afterward. "As the splendid comet of that year continued to shed its twilight over the forests," the British travel writer Charles Joseph Latrobe wrote decades later, "a countless multitude of squirrels, obeying some great and universal impulse, which none can know but the Spirit that gave them being, left their reckless and gamboling life, and their ancient places of retreat in the north, and were seen pressing forward by tens of thousands in a deep and sober phalanx to the South."

Soon after the squirrels left, the comet disappeared. And then the earthquakes began.

The first quake was on December 16. Its epicenter was on the Missouri side of the river south of the junction with the Ohio. According to one eyewitness account, the quake was felt first in the boat city off New Madrid. When the crews were awakened in the middle of the night by the commotion, they had no idea what was happening. They all thought they must be under attack, by the river pirates or by the Indians. But the river was deserted. There had only been the sound—a deep, hollow, rolling thunder—and the brief violent chop of the river. Everyone went back to sleep; they had the vague idea that some large nearby stretch of the riverbank must have collapsed into the current.

A bigger jolt came at dawn. First there was a new sound, a hissing roar that was, according to one witness, "like the escape of steam from a boiler." Then the surface of the river shivered, stirred, and erupted into violent swells. The boats were heaved about in wild convulsions as the men clung on desperately; all around them the banks and sandbars were collapsing and the cottonwood trees along the shore were hurled into the surf—"tossing their arms to and fro," one witness remembered, "as if sensible of their danger." The crews in the boat city maneuvered frantically to keep their boats in the middle of the channel, as far away from the sandbars and the falling debris as possible. The river was becoming bloodred with the clay churned up from its bottom. Its surface was alive with whirlpools and was sheeting over with drifts and swirls of foam. The air was particularly strange; it seemed to be "filled with a thick vapor or gas, to which the light imparted a purple tinge, altogether different in appearance from the autumnal haze of Indian summer, or that of smoke."

Then the river calmed. The aftershocks, according to one account, were "becoming lighter and lighter until they died away in slight vibrations, like the jarring of steam in an immense boiler." The water was a soup of foul effluvia that had been stirred up from the river bottom. Few were willing to risk drinking it—not for days and weeks afterward, no matter how thirsty they were. They would hang on until they had gotten as far away from New Madrid as they possibly could. Some of them waited for two hundred miles.

Nobody believed the crisis was over yet. The aftershocks never quite stopped. There were hundreds of them over the next month. One traveler on the river a few weeks later recorded twenty-seven in the space of twelve hours; a doctor keeping track in Louisville that winter counted almost two thousand. A pendulum hanging in a store window in Cincinnati didn't stop swaying until the spring. River travelers making their way through that country in December and into January reported all kinds of odd sights. It was said that just before the first earthquake hit, two pillars of lightning were seen towering up from the hills to the clouds. (This is a phenomenon known as earthquake light, which has a long history of eyewitnesses but still no documentary evidence or scientific theory to back it up.) Afterward there were lights and glows and flashes every night here and there in the hills along the river. There was also a pervasive horrible smell, like burning sulfur, that drifted all through the quake zone but had no detectable source. People added all this up and came to the only possible conclusion: it was the comet. Maybe it had disappeared from the sky because it had crashed to the earth somewhere around New Madrid. Or somehow the earth had become tangled up in its tail, which was lashing the river like a whip. The Scottish botanist John Bradbury, who was traveling on a keelboat when the first quake hit, recorded the discussions of the crew. One man offered the view that the earth was now stuck between the two tails of the comet and the earthquakes were its attempts to roll out again. "Finding him confident in his hypothesis," Bradbury added, "and myself unable to refute it, I did not dispute the point."

The next great quake came on January 23. With this quake the stretch of the river south of New Madrid gave up all its snags: hundreds of thousands of planters, sawyers, sleepers, and preachers shook loose of the mud and came bobbing to the surface. Centuries' worth of rotted logs accumulated in vast plateaus; they covered the river for miles downstream from the quake zone. Scattered in among them were coffins: the cemeteries along the riverbanks, caught in the general collapse, had disgorged their inhabitants into the water.

Two weeks later, on February 6, was the third great quake. It came to be known as "the big shock." It was so strong that it cracked pavements in Baltimore and rang church bells in Montreal. (It's still the most powerful quake ever recorded in the continental United States.) At the epicenter, near New Madrid, the land was in a frenzy. The earth undulated like a stormy sea; forested hillsides came sliding down into the river in roaring collapses; geysers shot up from ruptured crevasses; waterspouts hissed and rushed and snaked down into the furious depths of the channels. The shock was so large that a titanic backwash of water went flashing northward upriver against the current, swamping boats, flooding levees, and drowning houses on the riverbanks: an impossible apparition terrifying everybody caught up in its furious rush. That strange backwash became the talk of the river for decades afterward. There was no agreement at all about how far it had gone or how long it had lasted—some of the standard histories of the region claimed that the river ran backward for days. (This was in fact a physical impossibility; what's more likely is that the shock waves sent water washing upriver over the surface for several hours while the main strength of the current continued to flow normally underneath.) One prominent geologist, reviewing the whole story later in the century, was so skeptical about the backwash that he concluded not just that it hadn't happened, but that the earthquakes themselves were mythical. But it remained the defining event for anyone who lived in the river valley in those years: they all knew where they had been and what had happened to them the day the Mississippi ran backward.

The big shock was the last of the great New Madrid quakes. Together the quakes left the town of New Madrid flattened and had brought down every building in the countryside for miles around. But because the land in that part of the country had been so thinly settled, there were few reports of serious casualties—it was said that only two deaths among the locals could be directly attributed to the quakes. The river was another matter. The first quake had come when the river traffic was traditionally at its highest, right as the boats were bringing the northern harvest down to the markets of New Orleans. There was never an official count, but the death toll was probably in the hundreds. For weeks afterward bodies were found floating downstream, and there were wrecked and abandoned boats stuck on sandbars or drifting in the current all the way down to the delta.

But the traffic resumed. Cautiously, over the next several weeks after the big shock, the first boats came making their way south. They found the wilderness country around New Madrid in ruins. On either side of the river for miles the hills were split and shattered by slips and subsidences and sinkholes and fissures. There were areas where whole forests had sunk into the ground and been covered over by floodwaters; they were now strange, menacing lakes, bristling with the spikes of drowned trees beneath the waterline. A greater surprise awaited them on the river itself. As they approached New Madrid, the view of the waters ahead was lost in mist and spray, and there was an unfamiliar sound: a deep, continuous, full-throated roar. (Ordinarily the river in the channels was preternaturally silent.) With incredulity, and then with mounting panic, the boatmen frantically maneuvered their craft out of the current and into the shallows. Then they got out onto the riverbank and warily approached the source of the noise on foot. There they found what they had suspected but could not bring themselves to believe: the land below the riverbed had split and tilted, and the course of the lower Mississippi was now broken by immense, river-spanning waterfalls.

The river itself was quick to recover. The great waterfalls—there were two of them, one above New Madrid, and one below, about twenty miles apart—proved to be ephemeral. The relentless drag of the current rapidly wore them down; within several weeks they had eroded to the point where that stretch of the river became navigable again, and by spring no trace of them remained.

Then the river rose: the spring flood that year was a big one, even worse than the flood of 1811, and it cleared away the snags and the wreckage and the bodies. The strange stench and pollution of the river were washed away as well. The great muddy flow resumed its old steady course, and the water was as drinkable as it had ever been.

The landscape around New Madrid came back more slowly. The big open scars and fissures in the hills were gradually smoothed over by the wilderness. The new lakes and rivulets eventually aged into place, until they seemed as venerably weathered as any other feature of the country-side. But the terrain remained broken and jumbled. People were very leery of returning to it. In the years and decades that followed the time of the Great Shakes, wave after wave of new settlers came into the river valley; the population doubled, and doubled, and doubled again—but the area around New Madrid remained deserted. It didn't regain its sparse pre-quake population until the middle of the century. Those that did return, and the few new settlers willing to chance life there, reported that the land never did settle down; there were accounts of weird rumbles and tremors and quiverings until at least the 1840s.

The legal and economic aftershocks went on for just as long. The federal government made its first major foray into disaster relief after New Madrid; it passed an act granting compensation to property owners for their losses. The result was a fury of speculation and an instant, rapidly expanding, and inextricable tangle of lawsuits. Many of these suits dragged on for decades. The Supreme Court was hearing appeals on New Madrid cases in the 1840s; the last one wasn't settled until the middle of the Civil War. By then a "New Madrid claim" had become a byword throughout the river valley for legal chicanery and fraud.

But the most immediately significant event of the aftermath went unnoticed by everybody except the river people. When the boats came gliding again downriver into the lower valley, the voyageurs all braced themselves for their inevitable encounter with the Crow's Nest pirates. But nothing happened. They saw no pirates. As they approached the Crow's Nest itself, still expecting the worst, they discovered why: there was no Crow's Nest any longer. There was only a dissolving sandbar where the island had been.

Almost a century later, a monograph about the quakes published by the United States Geological Survey offered a description of the fate of the Crow's Nest, as summarized from the eyewitness testimony of one Captain Sarpy. This Sarpy claimed that his boat had been lured to the Crow's Nest on the evening of December 15, just before the first quake. He quickly realized that it was a trap, and before the pirates spotted him, he dropped back into the river out of sight and set in to wait until morning. The earthquake came, and when the haze cleared in the dawn light, he found that the island was gone. The pirates, their hideout, their hidden stashes of loot—the river had taken them all.

4

Like Bubbles on a Sea

TIMOTHY FLINT CAME TO THE RIVER as a missionary. That was in 1815, during the first big wave of migration to the Mississippi valley. The towns of the Mississippi were believed to be sorely in need of ministers: they already had a reputation for wild licentiousness, for gambling, for prostitution, for casual violence, and for prodigious, near-suicidal drinking. The churches and missionary societies of the East Coast were commissioning every warm body they could find. But Flint was in fact a reasonably good prospect. He had trained as a minister straight out of the highest and most conservative Puritan tradition—he was born in Massachusetts in 1780, was graduated from Harvard in 1800, and had already spent more than a decade serving at local churches in New England. His religious training had put the stress on sobriety, purity, and unquestioning obedience to church doctrine. He added to that his own personality—stiff-necked, querulous, and perpetually aggrieved. A college friend observed of him that there were two striking aspects to his character: he was useless at social intercourse and he was entirely ignorant of human nature. This all made him (it was surely felt by the Missionary Society of Connecticut) perfect for his job.

When Flint set up at his first church in St. Charles, Missouri, it didn't take long for him to make a pest of himself. With a wide and clear field of sinfulness before him, he decided that there was one particular vice he needed to target: Sabbath breaking. He was driven to a denunciatory rage when he observed the people of St. Charles working, dancing, partygoing, or laughing out loud in public on a Sunday. This didn't endear him to his flock. He further alienated them by involving himself in a highly unpopu-lar land deal: he bought and fenced in a large patch of forest where people had been accustomed to collecting their firewood in the winter, and he tried to have anyone who went on foraging there prosecuted for trespassing. Even his fellow ministers in town took sides against him for that. It got even worse for him when he tried to resell the land and found no takers. His letters back to the missionary society were filled with laments about how the deal had cleaned him out and how little support he was getting from the town.

But then he was never one to keep silent about his problems. His letters east weren't primarily about his money troubles and his conflicts with his neighbors—in fact, those topics come as something of a welcome break in the main flow of his complaints, which centered on his health. He had evidently never been very vigorous, and the climate of the river valley seems to have turned him into a perpetual invalid. He contracted countless diseases—measles, influenza, smallpox, and an assortment of fevers and infections named and unnamed. All this, he repeatedly pointed out, explained why he was able to spend so little time actually attending to the business of his church. He could not work, he said at one point, because he had "a bilious complaint accompanied by spasm." "I suffered fever and ague sixty days," he wrote another time. On another: "I had seventy fits of the ague."

Eventually he was forced to give up on the church in St. Charles. He and his family spent the next decade wandering up and down the Mississippi. His luck didn't change for a long while. He wasn't a fast learner and the basics of life on the river still eluded him. In 1820 he had an all-too-typical experience. He and his wife, Abigail, and their children were traveling from southern Arkansas to Missouri when they made what would now be called a classic newbie mistake—they tried to go upriver against the current during a season of unusually low water.

The trip was a nightmare. They thought it would take a few days; it prolonged itself into weeks. They petered out in exhaustion while they were still in the wilderness country above Memphis, with several hundred miles left to cross. By then they were in bad shape physically. Abigail was pregnant and nearing term, and she was sick with a fever. Soon they all were coming down with the fever and were too weak to move. Their food was running out. They had counted on buying supplies from the boats passing in the opposite direction, but they'd had the bad luck to find themselves in a lull in the downriver traffic: eight days passed without their seeing another boat. At last a flatboat appeared around the bend ahead of them, and Flint hailed it. The crew, seeing how desperate he was, sold him a barrel of salt pork and a barrel of flour for thirty dollars each—extortionist prices he was still furious about when he wrote his memoirs a decade later.

The family spent the following night in a secluded cove. Even though it was November, it was miserably hot and the cove was shrouded by mosquitoes. The next day was no better. By first light it was already sweltering, and by midmorning the signs were everywhere that a big storm was coming. It was then that Abigail went into labor.

The river was still running low and it was impossible to move forward to look for better shelter. The shallows on the eastern shore were a maze of sandbars; the western shore was a huge cypress swamp. The river was deserted. There was no choice but to ride out the storm and hope for the best. Flint lashed the boat to the trees along the eastern bank, and he had his children wrap themselves in blankets and lie down on a wide sandbar to wait. He did what he could to make Abigail comfortable. She was very weak with the fever, and she'd been "salivated"—meaning that she'd been given a large dose of calomel as an expectorant. Calomel is mercurous chloride; so whatever else Abigail had been enduring before, she was now suffering the effects of mercury poisoning.

The storm broke over them toward noon. It was a rage of hail and lightning, followed by torrential rain. Flint's only comfort was Abigail: she regarded, he said, the prospect of her imminent death with "perfect tranquility." She was so tranquil, in fact, that she regarded the fate of their children, who were just then huddled in their blankets out on the sandbar, with total indifference. For Flint, a deeply pious and conventional man, this was proof of her sanctity.

As for Flint himself, he was nowhere near as placid. He was terrified to the point of madness; he felt like King Lear on the heath. The storm kept getting more intense hour by hour. Around midafternoon, a sudden, intense gust of wind tore the roof off their boat, and the rain came pouring in. Flint didn't dare move his wife; he resolved that he would risk carrying her into the forest to look for shelter only if the boat started to tear loose from its moorings and float downriver.

The storm began to spend itself by late afternoon; the clouds broke up and there was a magnificent sunset. The children all came back aboard the boat—they were waterlogged but still alive. Abigail gave birth at eleven that night. The baby girl, Flint could tell at once, was too weak to survive.

The boat remained stuck on the sandbar. After two days, the baby died. Flint emptied out a small trunk to use as a coffin and buried it in the rushes along the bank. The next day, the river began to rise, and the winds returned with it. Flint and his family hoisted their sails and they went on north without further incident. Flint remembered the location exactly: it was "on a high bank opposite to the second Chickasaw bluff."

Flint would spend the rest of his life, off and on, traveling the river, and he would pass by that spot many times. Invariably he did so with his thoughts on how he was "carrying . . . my miserable and exhausted frame, with little hope of its renovation, and in the hourly expectation of depositing my own bones on the banks of the Mississippi."

The death of his child didn't come as a great shock to Flint. It wouldn't have been a shock to any parent: the rule of thumb in the river valley was that one in four children died before their first birthday; one in two didn't make it to their twenty-first. The situation might have been different if Flint's family had been able to reach a nearby town and find a doctor—but probably not, given the nature of medical care on the frontier in those days. After all, it was a doctor who had given Abigail the mercurous chloride, and another doctor would have most likely succeeded only in killing her along with the baby.

But then, too, Flint had a certain natural callousness. He was curiously unmoved by the suffering and death of other people—even people in his family. It was characteristic of him that in his account of the river journey, he didn't spare a single thought for what his other children had gone through that night, left to fend for themselves on the sandbar while the storm raged. But in this he was actually a fairly typical inhabitant of the valley: people did not as a rule display a lot of empathy for other people's problems. The river discouraged it—life on the river was so dangerous, so unpredictable, and so casually violent that it couldn't help but leave its inhabitants coarsened. Flint doesn't seem to have been that interested in other people to start with, and the river never taught him to feel otherwise. So as a minister, his main concern was simple outward obedience to church doctrine; as a father, he viewed the death of his child primarily as an occasion to reflect on his own mortality. This all made the river his natural home.

Over the next several years, Flint took charge of churches in Arkansas, Tennessee, Louisiana, and Florida. He stayed nowhere long, forced out in each place by poverty or sickness or the opposition of the citizenry. In one town he alienated his neighbors by doing amateur chemistry experiments in his parlor; they thought he was either a necromancer or a counterfeiter, and they couldn't decide which was worse.

He proselytized everywhere he went. When he met up with Cajuns and Creoles, he addressed them in French. His biographer John Ervin Kirkpatrick noted: "He did not then speak French well enough to preach in it but that he could and did use it to reprove and warn." The years continually sharpened his inborn knack for the exasperating moral judgment. He once visited a naval garrison in Baton Rouge, where he came across a simple white monument on the esplanade dedicated to the memory of the naval officers who'd died on the river. It was inscribed with a quotation from Alexander Pope's *Essay on Man*:

> Like bubbles on a sea of matter borne,
> They rise, they break, and to that sea return.

Flint didn't recognize the source, misquoted it in his book, and in any case was infuriated by the sentiment. He had no hesitation about outraging his hosts by saying so. Writing about the incident several years later, he didn't bother to hide his contempt:

> It is a matter of regret, that in a country professedly christian, any inscription should ever find a place on a funeral monument, that bears no allusion to our hope of immortality.

Inevitably his meanderings took him in and out of New Orleans. This was a rich prospect for any missionary: it already had a reputation for being the wickedest city in America. The city was notorious for its brothels, its slave markets, its stores selling occult charms and amulets, its voodoo ceremonies held openly in public squares—all of which would seem calculated to torment a prim soul like Flint. And in fact he did find countless things to complain about. The city, he wrote, was "disgusting." The saloons and brothels had "such an aspect of beastliness and degradation, as to render them utterly *unbearable*." He also didn't like the weather; it was "debilitating and exhausting." He thought the fruit produced by the local orchards was "less flavoured, and more insipid" than the fruit of New England. He found the presence of so many Catholics "a painful sensation"—"not . . . a single Protestant house of worship," he complained about Louisiana. "We need not cross the ocean to Hindostan to find whole regions destitute of even the forms of christian worship." (Catholicism did not in his eyes count as Christianity.)

On the other hand, the more of his complaints that one reads, the more one gets the curious feeling that he liked the place. He was uncharacteristically forgiving of its situation—he wrote that "New Orleans is of course exposed to greater varieties of human misery, vice, disease, and want, than any other American town," but in the end he believed it was probably no more sinful than New York or Boston. He was fascinated by the crowds, the babel of languages, the daily storm of color on the streets. He got in the habit of visiting the great cathedral—a new experience for him, as he'd never been inside a Catholic church before—and he was awed by its great taper-lit interior, perpetually shrouded in silent gloom. "This deep and unalterable repose," he wrote, "in the midst of noise and life, furnishes a happy illustration of the state of a religious mind, amidst the distractions of the world." He was also enchanted by the ornateness and peculiarity of the city's famous cemeteries, so cluttered with fantastic crypts and mausoleums. He particularly liked visiting them at night, after the other visitors had cleared out. Their silent delirium reminded him of "how uncertain is the dream of life."

He eventually took over a church and a school north of New Orleans, in the small town of Alexandria, Louisiana, on the Red River. It proved to be the happiest time of his life. He loved the town; it was a placid and well-groomed place, gorgeously green with catalpa and China trees. In the summer he and his family moved into a cabin in the pinewoods; there was a glade on the riverbank where several of the other families in town had cabins and lodges, and they all passed the hot days in an idyll of games and picnics. The river was swarming with fish; Flint estimated that he caught two thousand trout, "beautifully mottled with white and gold." In the serene, leaf-glowing evenings he and his friends "had public chowder-parties, where sixty people sat down under grape-vine arbours."

But it wouldn't have been like Flint to be at ease in such contentment. "A kind of sad presentiment used to hang over my mind," he recalled, "to embitter even this pleasant summer, an impression, that as it was so delightful, it would be the last pleasant one allotted to me on the earth." In the fall he fell sick again. He convinced himself that it was the end. His family hoped that he might recover his health if he were away from the putrid atmosphere of the delta, so they sent him to visit relatives back east. When he got to Massachusetts, he told people that he "had come home to die."

Idly, with no particular motive other than to occupy his time before his funeral, he began writing his memoirs. He worked quickly, even hectically, with only a loose plan. The book is cast as a series of letters to a friend—a common device in those days (Jonathan Swift remarked in *A Tale of a Tub* that he thought it was used by an actual majority of contemporary books). This enabled Flint to be casual, amusing, and digressive—qualities that tended to be missing from his actual letters. He put in whatever occurred to him: natural history, political history, sociology, anecdote, folklore, poetry. He indulged in his private obsessions—he was, as his biographer called him, "morbidly fascinated" with the Great Shakes, which had occurred four years before his arrival in the valley, and he passed on every scrap of news and folklore he'd heard about the quakes. He constantly wandered from his point; he launched into stories and forgot to finish them; he fumbled and weaved and meandered as wildly as the river did. The result was a fascinating double study: as much a vivid (if inadvertent) portrait of a peculiar, bigoted, obnoxious, and curiously endearing man as it was of the chaotic life on the river itself.

He was lucky in his theme: by the 1820s, the increasing tide of migration to the Mississippi valley was catching the interest of people all over America and Europe. Travelers, particularly European travelers, were beginning to think of the Mississippi as an essential tourist destination; travel writers describing their experiences in America were more and more likely to include an epic account of a Mississippi steamboat voyage. But Flint had grown to know the Mississippi far more intimately than any tourist could. As he wrote: "I cannot certainly be classed with those writers of travels, who . . . are wafted through a country in a steam boat, and assume, on the ground of having thus traversed it, to know all about it." The title of his book was itself a claim to his status as a real river man. He called it *Recollections of the Last Ten Years, Passed in Occasional Residences and Journeyings in the Valley of the Mississippi.*

The book was published in 1826. It was an immediate success—so much so that it gave Flint a surprising new life. He recovered from his illness—but he found that he no longer wanted to continue his wandering life as a minister. While he was determined to go back west, he didn't want to risk the climate of the lower valley. So instead he took his family to the rapidly growing new town of Cincinnati on the Ohio. He and his brother opened up a bookstore, and he became a professional writer.

For the next several years, he turned out prose at a furious clip. He wrote novels—mostly about virtuous ministers bearing up with great fortitude under a succession of misfortunes and natural disasters. He translated French novels and works of philosophy (his French had been greatly improved by his years in the delta). He ghostwrote the memoirs of a trapper in the Far West. He wrote a biography of Daniel Boone that was praised by later historians for its scrupulous accuracy (most contemporary biographies about Boone were full of shameless romancing). He wrote and compiled his immense ragbag of a compendium, *The History and Geography of the Mississippi Valley.* And he founded and edited a magazine called *The Western Monthly Review.* Each issue ran about fifty pages in minuscule type and contained essays on education, theology, politics, culture, literature, English grammar, and current events—almost all of which were written by Flint himself. His perpetual complaints about his weakness, his exhaustion, and his imminent death came as he labored at his craft like a stevedore.

For better and for worse—mostly worse—he wrote his later books just as he'd written his first one: at a hectic pace, without looking back. "Lack of finish," his biographer noted, "is one of the greatest evils of the page. . . . There are so many obvious faults, in plot, sentences, and even in use of words, that one often regrets that he did not spend more time in the revising of his work." He was also brazen about recycling his own prose: phrases, paragraphs, whole pages from one book will turn up unexpectedly in several others. Much of *Recollections* was absorbed into his *History* almost word for word. But then Flint never claimed to be a literary artist. He thought of himself at best as a kind of archivist, recording the life of the river valley for the use of posterity. "We can easily enjoy in anticipation," he wrote about the back issues of *The Western Monthly Review,* "the eagerness with which the future historian will repair to them, as a synopsis of most of what has been said and written in the Western Country, touching its own natural, moral, and civil history."

But he did very well in the present time. He grew to be a popular and highly regarded author, and he became a local celebrity in Cincinnati. When the celebrated British writer Frances Trollope stopped there for an extended stay during her American travels, Flint was the person she was most eager to look up—and, as it turned out, the only person there she actually liked. In the travel book she published shortly afterward, titled *Domestic Manners of the Americans,* she called him "the most agreeable acquaintance I made in Cincinnati, and indeed one of the most talented men I ever met." She particularly admired Flint's mild manners, beneath which she was delighted to find "first-rate powers of satire, and even of sarcasm." She even felt indulgent toward Flint's ferocious patriotism: "He is the only American I ever listened to, whose unqualified praise of his country did not appear to me somewhat over-strained and ridiculous."

But Flint didn't reciprocate these warm sentiments—at least not after her book was published. He felt a profound exasperation with outsiders venting opinions on his own turf, even when the opinions were ones he might otherwise agree with. (He was personally opposed to slavery, for instance, but he loathed the abolitionists because he thought they had no firsthand knowledge of what they were talking about.) Trollope's harsh judgments on American manners, which in another mood Flint might have endorsed, he found unforgivable. In his magazine he wrote that Trollope's views were "absolutely without value," and he later published a sketch where he courteously described her as "a coarse, flippant, and vulgar man-in-petticoats."

Meanwhile, he had the money and leisure to begin traveling himself.

He retired from his magazine and left Cincinnati in early 1834 to return to the lower Mississippi. He resettled in his beloved town of Alexandria, Louisiana. But almost immediately he left on an extended tour of Canada. He enjoyed it enormously: he adored Montreal; he was awestruck by the natural grandeur of Quebec and the St. Lawrence Seaway; he was impressed by the canals (he called them "prodigious works of art"); he even admired the local steamboats, which he said were finer than those on the Mississippi. He then went on to Europe. This didn't go as well: it wasn't as interesting as the New World. He wrote that Boston, New York, and Philadelphia were "intrinsically handsomer towns" than any of the great European capitals. He was bored by all the museums and monuments. The European landscapes left him just as cold; after the sight of an American mountain range, the Alps and Apennines were "bald, ragged, revolting."

He returned to America and his home in Alexandria. Once again he fell to brooding about the end. "I draw into my shell, abandoned by all others," he wrote in a letter. In a poem he wrote:

Fondly I thought that, years ere this, my breast
Would cease to swell with joy or sorrow.

In May 1840, Flint and his son James were taking a steamboat trip up the Mississippi from Alexandria. Flint was sixty then; he was, needless to say, in poor health, and he'd retired from professional writing a few years earlier. He and James stopped off on May 7 in Natchez-Under-the-Hill. The town was at that point in the middle of one of its periodic attempts to clean up its image: there were still gambling houses, saloons, and brothels, but there were also dry-goods stores and haberdashers and barbershops, and there was a new hotel, called the Steam Boat Hotel, catering to the upscale river traveler.

Flint and his son had lunch in the Steam Boat Hotel's elegant new dining room. It was a hot and humid day, and the tall windows were standing open. The sky was hazy and overcast, and beneath the clatterings and babble of the crowded room Flint could hear the mutterings of an approaching storm. He later described the sound as "a continual rumble of a hundred low thunders all melting together." At around half past one, the sky grew so dark that the hotel staff had to bring out candles. By then the thunder had grown much louder. But nobody was alarmed. It still seemed to them like a typically stormy spring day in the lower valley.

After Flint finished his meal, he wandered restlessly through the lobby into a new barroom. It, too, had an impressive set of windows; these overlooked the main street and the levee. The levee was swarming, as it always was on spring afternoons: hundreds of flatboats, barges, and steamboats were gathered in the waters off the docks, all caught up in their routine frenzy of loading and unloading cargo. Beyond was the grand sweep of the river. Natchez had been built on the outer bank of a hairpin turn, and from where Flint was standing, he could look down the river for miles, as it flowed to the southwest between the Louisiana and Mississippi shores.

The view that afternoon was dominated by a rapidly approaching storm front that had swallowed up most of the sky. As Flint stood at the window, he had an unimpeded sight of "a terrific-looking black cloud, as though a well defined belt of black broad cloth, seeming a mile and a half wide, shooting up the river with fearful velocity." He looked more closely and saw a weird specter: "At the end it poured out dark wreaths, resembling those of the steam-boat pipe." He was looking at a tornado that had touched down on the river's surface to the southwest, about twelve miles downstream, and was moving directly up the center of the channel straight at Natchez.

Another witness to the events of that day, J. H. Freleigh, the captain of the steamboat *Prairie,* recounted his experiences for a St. Louis newspaper. He had heard the storm coming, too—"a continual dull roaring," he said, that was broken at intervals by "sharp heavy claps, attended with the most vivid lightning." But as the storm came up the river, he remembered, "the distant rolling thunder assumed more the sound of moaning." Still, he took only the ordinary precautions: he put his men on alert, he had more lines tied to the dock, and he ordered the pilot to the wheel and the engineer to the boiler room. He himself went up on the roof with one of the hands to string out a hawser to the forecastle. He never saw the funnel cloud the way Flint did. Instead the storm came directly overhead in a titanic roar and a wave of blackness. As the steamboat roof began to break up beneath him, he jumped down the gangway to the boiler deck, and there he held on desperately to keep from being sucked into the vortex. The storm shrieked around him for barely a minute and was gone. In those few moments, the roof had been torn loose and carried away; the deckhand who had been working with him had been levitated to the forecastle and dropped uninjured.

Freleigh climbed up to the forecastle to survey the damage. His boat had been ripped free from all its moorings and had been blown upstream, where it was drifting and pitching in the shallows. The water was still furiously choppy. The forests on the western bank had been leveled; Freleigh said they "were transformed into mere stubble-fields of splinters." Freleigh's boat was "a dismantled and useless wreck, floating a shapeless hulk on the boiling and maddened waters." One of his crew was dead; five or six were severely injured; five were missing and their bodies were never found.

Meanwhile, Flint had been watching at the hotel window as the storm crossed ashore and engulfed Natchez-Under-the-Hill. As the funnel approached the hotel, Flint finally broke away and went running back to the reading room to find his son James. They had no time to get out before they were hit. All the windows and doors simultaneously blew in. In the fury of the storm, everyone was bolting for the front door. "The rush closed the passage, and kicking, fighting, and cursing ensued," Flint wrote. "Part were trampled underfoot, and part, such as James and I, thrown over their heads." They found themselves shouldered into a narrow hallway between the barroom and the reading room. As the building came down around them, Flint remembered, he "expected the next moment to have all my maladies effectually cured." The walls and pillars closed in, the rains poured over them in torrents, and the last light vanished.

Then the storm was gone. The funnel skipped up the bluff, crossed through Natchez-on-the-Hill, and raced on into the wilderness country beyond.

Within a few minutes, people all over Natchez were emerging from their shelters to survey the damage. Natchez-Under-the-Hill had taken a direct hit. The scene there, Captain Freleigh said, was of "horror, devastation, ruin." A reporter for the local newspaper, the *Natchez Daily Free Trader,* found that "on the river the ruin of dwellings, stores, steamboats, flatboats was almost entire from the Vidalia ferry to the Mississippi Cotton Press." Above the bluff, the scene was as bad or worse. In Natchez-on-the-Hill, the *Free Trader* reported, "scarcely a house, escaped damage or utter ruin." The towers of the town's two big churches had been toppled and the roofs caved in; the buildings in the business district had lost their roofs or had collapsed completely; the courthouse was destroyed; the Natchez Theatre was a pile of debris; most of the houses had been brought down. Particularly heartbreaking to the reporter, "the beautiful and splendid villa of Andrew Brown, Esq., at whose place the most gorgeous and splendid fete ever given in this city to the city guests from Vicksburg last year, is totally ruined." Even the office of the newspaper itself was a shambles (the reporter apologized in advance for any shortfalls in coverage over the next few days). "We are all in confusion," the reporter concluded, "and surrounded by the destitute, and houseless, the wounded and the dying. Our beautiful city is shattered as if it had been stormed by all the cannon of Austerlitz. Our delightful China trees are all torn up. We are peeled and desolate." The headline for the story was DREADFUL VISITATION OF PROVIDENCE.

The best estimate from the rescue parties and vigilance committees was that upwards of three hundred people were dead. There couldn't be an exact count because most of the casualties were voyageurs and river people who'd been working their boats off the levee. Nobody had any idea how many boats there had been; most of them had sunk or had been blown to scatterings of flotsam. The *Free Trader* predicted, "There will be mourning all along the banks of the Wabash, the Salt River, and the Ohio."

Almost unnoticeable in the long record of destruction was a report from under the hill. Work gangs of slaves lent by local plantation owners were excavating the ruins of the Steam Boat Hotel. Eleven bodies had been recovered so far, and a few people had been found alive, including the landlord and his wife—and also "Timothy Flint, the historian and geographer, and his son from Natchitoches, La."

Flint was characteristically detailed and copious about his situation: "I found myself alive though much bruised and crushed, and a nail had gone through my hat and grazed my temple, so as to cause some bleeding." About his son, he said only that he lost his hat. About the death and destruction in the town, he said it was "sickening," but no more. As ever, he wasn't one to dwell on other people's sorrows.

His own sufferings continued in the aftermath of the storm. "The weather turned very cold, the night I began to ascend the river," he wrote, "and my long drenching and exposure, with my previous sickness, gave me severe chills." But he continued his journey; then he crossed the prairie to the Great Lakes and rode a steamboat to the East Coast, where he paid a visit to his brother. His chills worsened along the way. He'd had his inevitable presentiment by then; his letter describing the Natchez tornado, written that summer, ends in the same spirit as so many of his others:

> I had not thought when I began, that I could scrawl so much. Take it, not for what it is worth, but for what it has cost me. You will, probably, be one of my last correspondents.

This time he was right; the letter is the final writing of his that survives. He died at the end of that summer, at his brother's home in Salem, Massachusetts. The most suitable epitaph might be a remark of perhaps unintended self-description he made in *Recollections*:

> Man is every where a dissatisfied and complaining animal; and if he had a particle of unchanged humanity in him, would find reasons for complaining and repining in paradise.

PART TWO

"DO YOU LIVE ON THE RIVER?"

5

The Desire of an Ignorant Westerner

THE MIGRATION TO THE RIVER VALLEY was the wonder of the age. New settlers were arriving in a ceaseless torrent. They were coming across the Alleghenies through the Cumberland Gap; they were riding keelboats and flatboats and arks down the Ohio; they were taking steamboat passages across the Great Lakes; they were voyaging by sailing ship down the Atlantic seaboard around the Florida peninsula up through the Gulf to the river delta and New Orleans. Travelers reported that their entire way to the river valley, along the only passable main roads beyond the Alleghenies—the Old Wilderness Road and the Natchez Trace—they were never out of sight of other wagons.

The migration began with the Louisiana Purchase in 1804, and it became a major phenomenon after the War of 1812. "The old America," one traveler wrote in 1816, "seems to be breaking up and flowing westward." The scale of the movement was hard for people to comprehend. At the beginning of the century, there may have been a couple of hundred thousand people scattered along the length of the Mississippi; by the time of the Civil War, there were tens of millions.

Few if any doubts were expressed about this immense transfer of people—some sentimental regret about the necessity of removing the Native Americans, none at all about the obliteration of the wilderness. The taming of the land was a self-evident good. A typical expression of this feeling can be seen in a best seller from the 1830s, *The Indian Captivity of O. M. Spencer.* It describes the terrifying experience from the author's childhood when for several months he was held hostage by an Indian tribe in the wild country of Ohio, and it concludes with the reassuring moral that such things could never happen again, because the river valley had grown so thoroughly civilized in the meantime:

> Nearly forty years have since passed away; our rivers teem with commerce; their banks are covered with farms, with houses, villages, towns, and cities; the wilderness has been converted into fruitful fields; temples to God are erected where once stood the Indian wigwam, and the praises of the Most High resound where formerly the screams of the panther or the yell of the savage only were heard. O, "what hath God wrought!"

The same language can be found in the descriptive pamphlet that accompanied one of the great Mississippi panoramas:

> In America the country itself is ever on the change, and in another half century those who view this portrait of the Mississippi will not be able to recognize one twentieth part of its details. Where the forest now overshadows the earth, and affords shelter to the wild beast, corn fields, orchards, towns and villages will give a new face to the scene, and tell of industry and enterprise, which will stimulate to new and untiring efforts. Places of small population will have swelled their limits, and there will be seen cities where are now beheld hamlets—mansions in the place of huts, and streets where the foot path and deer track are now only visible.

But this description is cast in the future tense—evidently God wasn't working fast enough. And in fact that was the common experience of the settlers. They didn't reach the river valley and find the orderly, stable, developed civilization that O. M. Spencer described; they found an ad hoc and jerry-rigged scaffolding for a civilization yet to be constructed.

By the time the largest waves of settlers arrived, the river valley had already been carved up into states, counties, and municipalities. But these were notional arrangements on maps and bills and legal briefs; they didn't have much practical effect. The mechanism of government was feeble and atten-

uated, and it tended to break down at the simplest obstacles. The courts
and government offices of the frontier were a hopeless morass—what one
writer described as "a gulf of land-claims, settlement-rights, preemption-
rights, Spanish grants, confirmed claims, unconfirmed claims, and New
Madrid claims." The simplest legal action routinely meant an eternity of
bureaucratic frustration. One of the first pioneers, Christiana Holmes Tillson, described a typical encounter with the frontier government. She and
her family were homesteading in western Illinois near the Mississippi, and
her husband went to the state capitol at Edwardsville to register their claim.
He found that the office of the recorder of deeds was so buried in unsorted
paperwork that the clerks couldn't tell him when, or even if, his documents
would ever be filed. But the man in charge of the office, a Mr. Randall,
offered a solution: "Mr. Randall proposed that he should enter the office as
clerk and write until his deeds were recorded." Tillson accepted the deal;
the backlog was eliminated and his deeds were duly recorded. It only took
a year and a half.

The story was unusual in one respect: it had a happy ending. Most people were left to flounder. This was one reason the people of the river valley
so quickly developed a reputation for truculent independence. "The desire
of an ignorant westerner to stand up for his 'rights,' as he called them,"
Christina Tillson observed, "was the predominant feeling of his nature." It
was a necessary form of self-defense, even of survival, in a place where so
many of the elements of a functioning society were absent. There were no
schools, no hospitals, few roads, only the most rudimentary arrangements
for public sanitation, an erratic and unpredictable mail service, a welter of
free-floating paper that passed for currency, and little or nothing in the
way of law enforcement. People were guided by their own sense of their
natural "rights" because in most cases they had absolutely nothing else to
go on.

Even morality and propriety were improvised. The American heartland
would eventually develop a reputation for suffocating primness—and
while this was a real phenomenon, it was something that developed slowly,
over many decades, and only in reaction to the prevailing moral anarchy
of the early years of the frontier. Excessive propriety didn't really become
the dominant mode in the river valley until around the time of the Civil
War. Before then, immorality (by the rest of America's standards) was

taken for granted. Prostitution was so common as practically to be the fundamental structural element of society. In fact, no clear line was drawn between it and marriage. In many of the logging and mining towns, the ratio of men to women was twenty to one; a woman who wanted to establish her respectability, and yet still retain her income, would arrange to marry several of her regular clients simultaneously. After the wedding ceremonies were over, she would spend nights with each of her husbands on a prearranged schedule, or else would live with them all communally. Prostitutes were considered in some army garrisons to be essential military personnel: they lived full-time in the barracks, and were listed on the payroll as seamstresses or laundresses, or sometimes were recorded as officers' wives. The opulent brothels of St. Louis and New Orleans were famous tourist destinations; they advertised openly in newspapers, they held fundraisers with the most celebrated local politicians in attendance, and the local churches only objected to them when they scheduled fancy costume balls on the Sabbath.

The traditional forces of morality were in perpetual disarray. Waves of preachers and missionaries came spreading through the river valley; even the most dismal logging camp could afford to build at least one church. But these clergymen routinely wasted their righteousness on hairsplitting debates over doctrinal purity. Some churches were ready to go to war over the biblical validity of river baptisms. Earthly law was just as erratically enforced. By midcentury, only St. Louis and New Orleans had professional police departments, and they were notoriously feeble, incompetent, and corrupt. About the police in New Orleans before the Civil War, the writer Henry Castellanos observed that "a more worthless and contemptible body of men never assumed the functions of office in any other city." But New Orleans was still better off than most communities. Villages and even large towns rarely had more than one full-time sheriff or marshal. He had the authority to deputize more men in an emergency, but ordinarily he had to enforce the law on his own, by any means necessary—which primarily meant through intimidation and violence. It wasn't uncommon for sheriffs to be career criminals or highwaymen themselves. Their employers often felt they were the only men tough enough for the job.

The routine business of keeping the peace fell to civilians—to groups of volunteer citizens who formed associations known as committees of safety and committees of vigilance, and to quasi professionals called regulators (some regulators were volunteers; others were mercenaries who traveled from town to town). The committees and the regulators had wide latitude regarding their duties and responsibilities. All strangers could count on being questioned closely by members of the local committee about who they were, what their business was, and where and how long they were expecting to stay. In most towns, they would also be expected to turn over to the committee any firearms they were carrying—despite the cliché of the frontier-town shoot-out, communities did not as a rule permit armed strangers to wander their streets (though there were many exceptions, and local citizens were generally free to do as they pleased). The committees in the lower valley also watched over the slaves. On the plantations, slaves were kept in close confinement by their overseers, or at least were in theory, but in towns they were generally left unsupervised during the day, and they routinely mingled on the streets with the free citizens. Many slaves were allowed out in the evenings as well, and would often hold private gatherings known as darky parties. The committees would typically only stop and detain slaves for gross breaches of the peace. Thievery and public drunkenness were probably the most common offenses, followed closely by insolence. (In the plantation country there was a slightly different system of supervision, called the slave patrol, which searched for runaway slaves and was supposed to keep slaves from having any contact between plantations; service on the patrols was compulsory for white male citizens, but it was despised and widely evaded, and the enforcement of the rules was generally lax.)

Along the Mississippi, the main concern of the committees was the river people. The voyageurs had a bad reputation—partly for their rowdiness when they came onshore, but mostly for their casual, incessant, and universal thievery. The river made theft easy. If the crew of a boat saw something they wanted onshore—some plow or horse or cow, some cotton bale or wagonload of corn that had been left unattended, a stack of barrels on a deserted dock, a flock of sheep without a shepherd, whatever they could carry or push on board before they were noticed—they'd simply help themselves, adding it to the cargo bound for the New Orleans market. Even if they were spotted, there was little that the victim could do. There was no way of catching up with a boat once it was back in the current; there were no roads that would let a victim ride furiously to the next port town, no way of alerting the authorities downriver—when there were authorities downriver. The thieves were safe with their loot, just another anonymous boat in the armada, lost forever down the next bend.

This was one reason the boats congregated before the riverfront districts each night: they weren't welcome anywhere else. It might seem, given how sparsely settled so much of the river was, that a boat could lay up almost anywhere and be undisturbed, but the banks away from towns were thought of as fantastically risky places for the river people. Farmers and plantation owners took for granted that anybody coming onto their property from the river was a thief. They hired regulators to patrol the banks, or else they armed their own farmhands—and none of them was shy about shooting trespassers. It could happen almost anywhere the voyageurs tried to beach a boat after sundown, in a secluded creek or a pristine wooded cove: they'd suddenly find themselves greeted by a bristle of shotguns. If they weren't killed there and then, they'd quickly be conveyed to the local branch of the most powerful and most dreaded institution on the river—the courts of Judge Lynch.

The name came from a vigilante court that had been set up in Virginia during the Revolutionary War. The presiding judge had been a local planter named Charles Lynch; the defendants put on trial had been loyalists to the king. In the first few decades of the new Republic, the institution of the lynching court spread throughout the South and into the river valley. The judges were most often prominent local citizens—some of them justices of the peace, some of them at least with a smattering of legal training. The defendants were usually people who had been put on trial already in a government court and been found innocent when everybody knew they had done it, or else had been found guilty but given too light a sentence. Nobody thought of a traditional jury verdict as the last word. In the river valley it was sometimes cynically referred to as an "advisory opinion."

Today we think the word "lynching" automatically means death by hanging. But that didn't become the primary meaning till after the Civil War. Before then, it meant any sentence handed down by a lynching court. This might be a beating, or it might be a branding. Some of the lynched were tarred and feathered and rode naked out of town on a rail— a split wooden rail, and they rode the sharp edge: the punishment could leave the genitals permanently damaged. All of these were known as lynching. A sentence of death by lynching—by hanging, or by firing squad— was reserved for the worst criminals: murderers, horse thieves, slave stealers, and counterfeiters.

The typical defendant at a lynching court was poor. Rich people routinely bought their way out of trouble, or else they hired their own regulators and bodyguards to keep the townspeople at bay. The defendant was most often one of the river people, or a stranger in town, or somebody who was a known troublemaker, or somebody who had been seen acting in a suspicious manner, or somebody who was just generally thought of as odd. While we think now that most of the defendants were people of color, that again wasn't typically true before the Civil War. The courts in the lower valley didn't ordinarily punish slaves. Slaves detained by the regulators and the vigilance committees were turned over to their owners for punishment. This wasn't out of any concern for the slaves' rights—it was because slaves were property, and property rights were regarded as sacred. The lynching court would only intervene and punish the slave when it was suspected that the owner was going to be too lenient.

This system, if it can be called a system, was known for its arbitrary and capricious results. The committees and the regulators often made a great show of legal formality in their arrests, but they weren't bound to obey any law and were answerable only to the authorities of their local town. The lynching courts weren't answerable to anybody. A perpetual fog of doubt shrouded the actions of those involved in the dispensation of lynch law. Nobody knew what officer or judge was acting fairly, who was seeking revenge, who was simply a criminal himself. One town's regulator was likely to be another town's wanted murderer; a chief justice in a county's lynching court could be the most infamous highwayman in the state. There were celebrated cases where in the end it never was sorted out just what side everybody had really been on.

During the early years of the frontier, the most notorious of these cases involved a man named James Ford. Ford owned a ferry service on the Ohio just up from its confluence with the Mississippi. From around 1810 to the 1830s, Ford's Ferry was a local landmark: the crossing of choice for everyone traveling between Kentucky and Illinois. Its prominence wasn't a fluke of geography or custom. Ford worked very hard to establish its reputation. He practiced an early form of saturation advertising, nailing up signs pointing to his ferry along all the roads on either side of the river. He also had posters made proclaiming the safety of his ferryboats and the professionalism of his crews, and he put them in all the inns and taverns on the Kentucky and Illinois shores.

These ads probably weren't lies. Ford did try to make his ferry practical and safe—more so than most ferries, anyway (ferrymen were legendary for their indifference to the lives of their passengers). He was also concerned with easy access to his ferry point. He cajoled and bribed the county government to improve the road on the Kentucky side; ultimately they agreed to clear and repair eight miles of roadway leading up to the riverbank. The road on the Illinois side was even worse. It was very old and in poor shape, and it routinely flooded out every time the river rose. It was known by a dismal name that informed everyone under what conditions it was passable: Low Water Road. But Ford had no luck persuading the Illinois government to fix it. So he paid out of his own pocket for a new twelve-mile stretch of road on the Illinois shore. He had it built on land above the flood crest, and he picked a name that would ensure that everybody knew what it was for, how superior it was to the Low Water Road, and who had provided it: Ford's Ferry High Water Road.

Ford became a prosperous and respectable citizen. With the ferry fees rolling in, he grew rich enough to buy several large local farms. He became an appraiser of properties and an administrator of estates. He was a justice of the peace for many years. He grew to be so highly regarded that items on the agenda in the county courts were passed immediately so long as they were offered with the magic phrase "on motion of James Ford." He was, one of the locals said, a man who excelled in having things come out his way.

In a book written many years later, *Chronicles of a Kentucky Settlement* by William Courtney Watts, Ford is described this way: six feet tall—much taller than the average then—and very powerfully built, "a perfect Hercules" in his youth but by his fifties grown corpulent. He was handsome, with graying brown hair and penetrating steel-gray eyes. He had a florid face, a short and thick nose, a "remarkably long" upper lip, a "full and sensuous" mouth, a deep and sonorous voice. "On the whole," some-one said, "when in repose, he gives one the idea of a good-natured, rather than a surly, bull-dog; but, if aroused, I should say he would be a lion tamer."

His skill at lion taming came out in his other occupations: he ran the county's regulators, and he presided over the local court of Judge Lynch. These were heavy jobs. That region along the Ohio was extraordinarily dangerous. There were many bands of pirates working the river; one of their hideouts, Cave-in-Rock, about ten miles downriver from the ferry, was notorious all over the frontier, the successor in evil to the Crow's Nest. There were also gangs of highwaymen who could be counted on to challenge every lone traveler on the roads all around the junction of the Ohio and the Mississippi. Ford earned a reputation as an implacable foe of these outlaws. He was fiercely protective of the roads on either side of the ferry. Any bandit preying on his ferry passengers who came before his lynching court was certain to be put to death. He often went out patrolling with the regulators himself. Newspaper accounts of robberies along the ferry road routinely concluded, "Jim Ford found the robbers and ran them out of the county."

And yet, for all his determined crusading, the region never got any safer. By the late 1820s, there was one remarkably persistent outlaw band that seemed to be responsible for most of the robberies, deaths, and disappearances on the Illinois side of the river. They became known, doubtless to Ford's intense displeasure, as the Ford's Ferry Gang. They were so successful that people began to say darkly that some other factor had to be involved: surely they must be in league with some apparently upstanding local citizen who was providing them with both information and cover. Suspicion fell particularly on a man named Billy Potts. Potts owned an inn in Illinois just up the road from Ford's Ferry. The rumor was that he was a spotter for the Ford's Ferry Gang, alerting them to which of his guests had money, and which didn't need to be bothered with. It was also said that the big field behind Potts's inn was where the unlucky travelers ended up buried. The field was excavated, over Potts's outraged protests. The bodies were indeed there. Potts was immediately arrested and turned over to the government court for trial.

But nobody believed that this was the end of it. Potts was regarded around the area as a simpleton—or at least not somebody clever enough to have come up with this spotting system on his own. That was when people started wondering about Ford himself.

It made perfect sense. If he really was the ringleader of the Ford's Ferry Gang, it would explain why the gang was never caught. As the presiding judge at the lynching court, he could guarantee that any member of his gang detained by the regulators or the committees could be found innocent and set free. Then, too, as the head of the regulators, he could ensure that all the rival gangs could be killed or driven away, leaving his own gang with a monopoly.

The talk slowly poisoned Ford's reputation. Nobody had any proof—but nobody could quite dismiss the idea out of hand, either. (In *Chronicles of a Kentucky Settlement,* even Ford's daughter isn't entirely certain of his innocence.) Of particular concern were the men he associated with; while he himself was a distinguished and respectable citizen, his regulators, and even his employees at the ferry, tended to be "vicious and bad men," as one writer put it, whom he kept in line through insult and intimidation.

Finally, some of the area's prominent citizens decided to find out for themselves. They hired a new and secret group of regulators to put an end to the Ford's Ferry Gang. They didn't tell Ford about it. The regulators immediately began investigating some of the vicious and bad men in his employ. Their interest fell upon a man named Vincent Simpson. Simpson ran the day-to-day operations of Ford's Ferry. He was also known to be bitterly unhappy with Ford, who had recently humiliated him by winning their nasty lawsuit over the sale of a slave and then crowing over the victory afterward. Simpson was the ideal man to rat Ford out. It wasn't long before a new rumor was spreading around town: Simpson had confessed to the regulators that he was a member of the gang, and he was going to reveal to a grand jury everything he knew, including the identity of the gang's leader.

It's not clear whether Simpson did in fact confess, or for that matter whether he had ever talked to the regulators at all. What is certain is that he never ended up testifying before the grand jury. It so happened that he was involved at that time in another nasty lawsuit with an associate of Ford's, a man named Henry Shouse. Simpson, evidently a hot-blooded man even by the standards of the river valley, decided to have it out with Shouse before the lawsuit was heard. One afternoon he planted himself in Shouse's front yard and began yelling for Shouse to come out. Nobody answered. But as Simpson bellowed and taunted and challenged Shouse to show himself, a shot was fired from the upper window, and Simpson fell dead.

Shouse was immediately arrested. He maintained (and went on maintaining through his trial, and all the way to his execution) that he'd had no secret motive; it had simply been an act of self-defense when he saw Simpson trespassing on his property. But nobody believed him. Obviously he'd done it at Ford's behest, to keep Simpson from testifying before the grand jury. So, after Shouse was in custody, the regulators next went to arrest Ford.

Ford had been away when Simpson had been killed. He'd been visiting one of his farm properties about a day's ride from the ferry. The regulators found him coming home on a remote country road. They told him what had happened; they said they were going to escort him to the county seat, where he would be expected to appear before the grand jury and tell what he knew about the dispute between Shouse and Simpson.

This was toward sundown. There were several hours of riding ahead of them. Ford declared that he would stay the night at a nearby roadside inn and proceed on with the regulators the next morning. The entire party went to the inn. Ford took a room, while the regulators made as if to camp outside. Sometime after sunset, before Ford retired for the night, somebody asked him for a favor. In one version of the story, it was an associate who had been traveling with him back from the farm; in another, it was one of the regulators. In any case, somebody produced a letter he'd recently received and asked Ford to read it aloud—Ford was known to be one of the few literate men in the county. Ford agreed. He was sitting then in the common room of the inn. A candle was set on the dining table in front of him, and he began reading out the letter. The candle was the only light in the room. This was a moonless night; Ford's face, shining in the candlelight, was the brightest object not just in the room, but for miles around. The regulators used it as their target. They gathered outside and opened fire through the window, the doorway, and the chinks in the log walls. Ford was hit seventeen times.

Ford's death marked the end of the investigation into the Ford's Ferry Gang. Nobody was ever charged with Ford's murder, and no further evidence was found about his involvement in the gang. So was Ford in fact guilty? To a modern eye it looks unlikely. At least, if he was, then much of his other behavior is hard to account for. Why, in particular, would he deliberately go out of his way to antagonize Simpson, when Simpson was so well situated to betray him? But this is not an objection that occurred to anyone at the time. People, even prominent and respectable citizens like Ford, routinely acted with near-suicidal recklessness for the sake of absurdly short-term or trivial benefits. Thinking through the consequences of a rash act simply wasn't a favorite activity on the frontier.

Ford's funeral proved to be a dire affair. None of his friends, none of his colleagues, nobody from town showed up. Only his wife and children were in attendance at the gravesite. A group of slaves carried the coffin. Just as they were lowering it into the grave, a savage thunderstorm erupted all around them. The slaves, terrified, let go of the coffin and it fell perpendicularly into the hole, where it immediately sank into the mud and stuck. The gravedigger left it where it was and filled in the grave all around it. People said afterward that Ford was the only man on earth to go to hell headfirst.

6

Bloody Island

FOR NEARLY TWO DECADES, from the early 1830s until his death in 1851, William Johnson kept a diary. He was a barber in Natchez, and was in a position to hear all the local gossip, but the ordinary round of small-town infidelities and scandals left him cold. One subject did fascinate him: the casual violence on the streets.

> Mr Bledsoe and Mr Hewitt had a small fist fight. After a blow or two, Mr Bledsoe went and got his pistols.

> Today Mr James in a small dispute with Mr Stanford struck him with his fist twice. Stanford drew a dirk and Mr James ran into his store and got a hatchet.

> Jim Welch and Oblenis had a fight in the sheriff's office.

Johnson rarely bothered to record what the fights were about. There was no point: they could have been about anything. Any event at all, no matter how benignly it began, could end up in a riot.

> I rode out today to see the balloon ascend, but the man did not attempt to put it up at all, and told them that they would put it up tomorrow. A mob was soon raised and they tore it all to pieces, destroying everything as they went.

It was as though they were all walking around in a perpetual state of rage. They'd lash out at each other about politics, or a gambling debt, or the outcome of a lawsuit; they'd explode over a mistimed joke or a long-simmering feud. They would often get into fights over other people's fights—even the fights of people they'd never met. Johnson records one fight that broke out over the question of whether a celebrated duel in South Carolina had been a sham: "When Mr Charles Stewart stated that those gentlemen that fought actually fought with bullets, Mr Dahlgren said that they must have fought with paper bullets. Mr Stewart then said that if any man would say that they fought with paper bullets that he is a damned liar and a damned scoundrel and a damned coward." The two men began pummeling each other, Stewart with a walking stick and Dahlgren with an umbrella. They then pulled out pistols and began shooting at each other. Dahlgren was wounded in the side and Stewart was hit in the jaw. When Stewart fell to the ground unconscious, one of his friends went after Dahlgren with a bowie knife, and by the time the bystanders finally managed to break it up, Dahlgren's head had been slashed twice, the palm of his hand had been split open, and one of his fingers had been almost entirely severed. "It was," Johnson concludes, "one of the gamest fights that we have ever had in our city."

Johnson doesn't ever appear to have taken part in the fights himself. He preferred to remain a spectator. In fact, his diary is the work of an exceptionally prudent man—as it piles up, day after cautious day, year after quiet year (the most frequent entry is a relieved note, "Nothing new"), it reveals itself to be the autobiography of someone who spent his whole life trying, and ultimately failing, to stay out of the line of fire.

Johnson's situation might seem to be inherently precarious. He was a free man of color living in the heart of the slave country. But that wasn't in itself all that unusual. Tens of thousands of free people of color lived in the lower valley. There were two hundred living in Natchez alone, out of a total population of three thousand. Most of the women were domestic servants; the men were farmers, or small-time craftsmen—typically coopers or smiths—or in Johnson's trade, barbering. Johnson stood out only because he was so successful. He owned several pieces of land and he also owned many slaves. (This was also not unusual—any prosperous man of color would as a matter of course be a slave owner.) He did so well that he was able to buy the shabby clapboard building where he had his barbershop, tear it down, and replace it with a sturdy three-story building with a brick façade. It cost three thousand dollars, a fortune in those days, but he paid for it out of his own pocket. He opened a second shop around the corner from the first, in the lobby of an upscale hotel, and eventually a third shop in Natchez-Under-the-Hill. This shop was the result of yet another civic campaign to clean up Natchez-Under-the-Hill by encouraging respectable businesses to move in. Johnson was one of the first businessmen the campaign approached.

Johnson was such a successful man because he was smart, civil, discreet, and unrelentingly cautious. His diary wasn't a vehicle for self-expression or self-examination, but a way of keeping everything in his life precisely on track. The lurid violence he reported in the outside world was a kind of dark counterpoint to his abiding interest: the careful outlay of petty cash. The diary records the unending parade of odd objects he had to purchase for his barbershops—razors and razor straps, roller towels and hand towels, shaving brushes, toothbrushes, hairbrushes, hat brushes. He bought bottles of lemon water, orange water, lavender water, and rose water; his shops stocked expensive Macassar oil and cheap bear's oil, imported cologne and exotic pomades and Crème de Perse and Winship's Camphor Soap. He also recorded all manner of one-off purchases that sound almost like impulse buys: a barrel of sweet potatoes for $3.00; a keg of nails for shingles for $8.00; $8.50 for a satin vest and a pair of pants. He was always hungry for bargains—even when it's hard to imagine what use he could have made of them. One time he recorded splitting with a neighbor the cost of a cask of bacon. The neighbor paid $13.00 and Johnson paid $16.25. Since bacon sold in bulk for around 3.25 cents a pound, that means the cask held almost nine hundred pounds.

The larger issues of his life ultimately came down to the same kind of accounting. When he rebuilt his barbershop, he decided to lay out extra money to add a bathhouse. It was an unusually risky move for him, because bathing had never been popular on the frontier—even the most respectable men avoided immersing themselves in water, which was thought to be unhealthy, and instead doused themselves with perfume and cologne (which is why Johnson did such a brisk business in both). But in the 1830s hot baths were becoming something of a fad, prompted by a popular form of alternative medicine known as Thompsonism. Its practitioners claimed to cure all kinds of diseases by means of saunas and sweatboxes—Thompsonians were known as steam doctors. Johnson himself had no opinion on whether steam medicine actually worked; he just made a bet on its popularity, and it paid off. The bathhouse took in a small but steady stream of customers, giving Johnson a pleasant and consistent income even in hard times.

That was the one self-revelation the diary discloses: Johnson was secretly a bit of a gambler. He didn't much like playing cards, and he was indifferent to roulette and other games of chance. But he did dearly love racing—horse racing in particular. He was a regular for decades at the local tracks, and he believed he knew horses well. But then he'd bet on any kind of racing. One time he bet a friend about which of two toy boats would get across a pond first.

He was as prudent in his vices, though, as he was in his virtues. He never risked any substantial amount of money gambling, and his diary never records any disappointment or guilt when he lost—which is fortunate, because he lost consistently. Johnson didn't see that, or wouldn't admit to seeing that; it was the one area of his life where he deliberately avoided totaling up his outlays. Like any longtime gambler, he preferred to think of himself as a sharp operator. In the diary he sometimes calls himself, with a kind of secret, self-amused pride, "the old shark."

He was also a family man with a large and thriving household. His diary records the ceaseless dailiness of his doings with his wife, his children, his apprentices, his servants, and his slaves. He was a loving husband, a strict father, and a stricter employer. He was highly disapproving of his apprentices for consorting socially with his slaves; he frequently notes the occasions when one or another of the apprentices snuck off to attend a darky party, where the slaves and the free people of color would mingle. By his own telling, he wasn't a particularly kind or indulgent slave owner. He dispassionately writes up the times when he had to flog one of his slaves for disobedience or drunkenness or theft. But he could also be secretly fond of the most difficult of them: the closest he comes to naked emotion in his diary is when he regretfully sells off a favorite slave on account of his perpetual troublemaking.

He didn't aspire to be accepted by white society. He was always careful to be courteous with well-to-do whites—particularly those to whom he lent money. He had a brisk sideline in making small private loans at interest, and he cultivated a reputation as a trustworthy lender who'd never try to gouge a customer or violate his confidence. But none of this was to gain their friendship. It was a practical necessity: he needed to be able to call on the best people to pay back a favor by discreetly applying pressure to other debtors who'd fallen behind. Other than that, he never socialized with his customers. He certainly never recorded any feeling of envy, any resentment that he was permanently excluded from their world. His attitude can be best seen in the odd mocking pseudonyms he sometimes used in his diary for his prestigious customers: "Mr. Thermometer," "Colonel Troublesome," "Little Low Man."

He had his own circle. Mostly he associated with the other free men of color in Natchez who were as successful and respectable as he was. One of these was a farmer and landowner named Baylor Winn. Johnson and Winn never became close friends, but for many years they were civil enough. In 1848 they had a bet going on the outcome of the presidential election; Johnson untypically won. Johnson did note in his diary some unpleasant gossip about Winn, how he was known around town to have had bitter fights with his children over what they considered to be his tyrannical ways. But Johnson himself doesn't seem to have been much troubled by any of that. He took for granted that a man's family affairs were his own business. It certainly never prevented him from passing an hour or two with Winn in leisurely conversation whenever they met— a form of socializing known in Natchez as "stopping to light a cigar." (Cigars were notorious for being difficult to light; getting one to draw was always a time-consuming process.)

Johnson even took Winn's advice about property. In the late 1840s, at Winn's urging, Johnson bought land in the marshy terrain south of town along the river—an area known unimaginatively as the Swamp. He then hired crews to clear it and cultivate it as farmland. After a few seasons, he began hearing from these men about a problem. Winn happened to own the adjoining property, which he was also having cleared, and his crews were taking the lumber downriver to the market in New Orleans. According to Johnson's men, Winn's crews were trespassing onto Johnson's land to cut lumber there as well.

Johnson's first response was typical of him: he went to Winn and offered to settle the issue with a handshake. But Winn refused to discuss it. After that their dealings grew increasingly tense. Johnson offered to pay to have a survey done of their properties in the Swamp to establish the exact boundary line. Winn became enraged and said that if any surveyors—or, for that matter, Johnson himself—came onto his land, he'd shoot to kill. Johnson refused to take the threat seriously and had the survey done. The results proved him in the right. He showed them to Winn, but Winn would not budge. Johnson then sued him. He knew that with the results of the survey in hand, he was certain to win—but just before the case was heard, he made another offer to settle, on terms far less advantageous to him than what he was likely to get in court. Winn accepted, and the case was dropped.

Johnson returned to his ordinary routine; his diary entries for the next couple of weeks show nothing but the usual daily drift:

The river rising tolerably fast. Mr James Curry's son was drowned yesterday evening at the landing. He fell off a log. Business rather dull

I was up at auction today and bought a barrel or ½ pipe of gin at 30 cts per gallon

Business only so so.

I rode out today with the children and got a lot of blackberries Business extremely dull

Business very dull indeed but nothing like as dull as was yesterday.

On June 16, 1851, two days after this last entry, Johnson visited his property in the Swamp. He took along one of his sons and an apprentice. On the way back, they passed a farm belonging to one of Winn's sons; Johnson decided to stop off to light a cigar. The conversation was perfectly amicable. Johnson's son and his apprentice later remembered seeing Winn there, but as far as they could recall, he and Johnson didn't speak.

Johnson's party rode back toward Natchez. As they neared the outskirts of the Swamp, they were surprised to see that Winn was following them. They slowed down to wait for him; instead he left the road and began paralleling them through the heavy underbrush. They still weren't alarmed. They went on down the road for a few hundred more yards. Then Winn began shooting. Johnson's apprentice was hit in the shoulder; Johnson himself was wounded in the stomach. Winn rode off.

Johnson was brought back into Natchez. He was still conscious, and as he weakened, he described the attack to his family and to the sheriff. He died later that night.

Winn was immediately arrested. He would give no explanation for his actions. People who knew him, though, did report that he had been complaining constantly about Johnson; even with the settlement of the lawsuit, he supposedly said that he didn't think the troubles between them would ever come to an end. But at his trial he said nothing about any of this. Instead he stymied the prosecution with a surprise legal maneuver. According to Mississippi law, people with Negro blood weren't allowed to be called as witnesses except against defendants who also had Negro blood. Winn claimed that, even though he was a man of color, he had no Negro blood: he was part white and part Seminole Indian. If this claim was upheld, the case could not proceed. The only witnesses to what had happened were Johnson's son and his apprentice; without them, there would be nobody to testify. The jury deliberated the claim for a day and a half. In the end they were deadlocked. The judge declared a mistrial.

Johnson's murder had been met with an upwelling of genuine shock and anger among the white people of the town. Johnson was "an excellent and most inoffensive man," wrote a reporter in the *Natchez Courier,* "holding a respected position on account of his character, intelligence, and deportment." It might be thought, then, that such a manifest injustice as the mistrial would lead to action by the local court of Judge Lynch. But the whites were prepared to go only so far in avenging a man of color; in this case they let the legal system take its course. Winn was duly retried. He raised the same defense: he could show that he had voted in at least one election and had once served on a jury at the trial of a white defendant. The result was another hung jury.

At the next trial the venue was changed. Johnson's family paid for an investigation in Winn's home state of Florida, where they found that there he had been legally classified as a mulatto—which meant that Johnson's son and his apprentice could indeed testify against him. But the judge in the new venue would not allow this evidence to come in. The witnesses were barred from testifying. The trial then proceeded to a verdict. Winn was found not guilty of murder. After two years in jail, he was a free man.

In the diary, the highest term of praise Johnson had for any man, black or white, was that he was a "gentleman." He never defined what he meant, but then he didn't need to. Everybody in the river valley knew what a gentleman was, even if they couldn't have explained how he got that way. It was breeding, it was dress, it was manners—but more than any of that, it was honor. A gentleman was concerned about his honor just as an ordinary man was obsessed with his rights. This provided people with a handy rule of thumb. Where an ordinary man might commit manslaughter, a gentleman would fight a duel.

The duel was the defining trademark of the aristocrat in the lower valley and throughout the South. Every gentleman was expected to know the Code Duello, as it was called—an elaborately ritualized etiquette of single combat adopted from the old European aristocracy that laid out what was and wasn't a dueling offense, how challenges were to be offered and accepted, how the duel was supposed to be conducted, and when to shoot to kill. The core of the code was its uncompromising rigor. Gentlemen were expected to fight duels over any affront to their personal honor, no matter how slight or absurd it might seem to an outsider. A misunderstood word, a political dispute that turned personal, an invitation to a dance that went awry—these were all legitimate occasions for a duel.

The code, if followed scrupulously, would have led any gentleman to fight duels on almost a daily basis. In fact, full-blown duels with real bloodshed seem to have been relatively rare. Going by Johnson's diary—and this was the sort of thing he was sure to note down—Natchez saw on average only one formal dueling challenge a year, and almost all of these were settled without violence. When a duel was carried out to the point of actual combat, it became the subject of universal fascination.

One of the most famous duels fought in the river valley took place in St. Louis in 1831. The participants were both prominent Missouri gentlemen. Major Thomas Biddle was a distinguished veteran of the War of 1812, a quartermaster at the local army garrison, and a member of one of St. Louis's most aristocratic families. The Honorable Spencer Pettis was a well-regarded local politician who had been Missouri's secretary of state and was currently Missouri's only representative in the United States Congress. The cause of their dispute was both personal and political. It centered on the Bank of the United States—an institution that seems during the few decades of its existence to have been the occasion for near-constant quarreling all over the country. In this case, Pettis was running for reelection and made the corruption and incompetence of the bank into a major campaign issue. Thomas Biddle's brother Nicholas happened to be the president of the bank. Thomas regarded all attacks on the bank as attacks on Nicholas and therefore as affronts to the family honor. After Pettis attacked the bank in a speech, Thomas Biddle published a rebuttal in one of St. Louis's newspapers, in the course of which he referred to Pettis as "a dish of skimmed milk." Pettis replied with a letter impugning Thomas Biddle's manhood. Biddle then escalated by breaking into Pettis's room at the St. Louis Hotel early one morning while Pettis was still asleep and beating him with a rawhide whip. (Pettis later claimed to have been too groggy to defend himself, because he'd been tormented all night by a swarm of mosquitoes in his room.) Pettis then challenged Biddle to a duel.

The whole city was caught up in the drama. Both parties agreed to postpone the duel for a few weeks, until after the congressional election. This gave time for the suspense to build. On the appointed morning, thousands of people gathered at the levee to watch Pettis and Biddle and their seconds depart for the dueling ground. The crowds lined the streets; they shouldered each other aside in the downtown windows; they perched on the rooftops. There were cheers when the boat bearing the duelists pushed off into the river.

The boat's destination was a wooded islet in the Mississippi just off St. Louis. This was where Missouri gentlemen habitually fought their duels. The islet offered privacy—duels, after all, were supposed to be discreet affairs handled among gentlemen, not vulgar public spectacles. It also offered, or was at least believed to offer, a certain amount of legal cover: although dueling was rarely prosecuted, it was illegal according to both Missouri and Illinois law, and since the islet was in the river between the two states, it might technically be considered outside the jurisdiction of either. So many duels had been fought there that it had come to be known as Bloody Island.

When Pettis and Biddle reached Bloody Island, they took their places in a clear glade screened from the shore by a stand of trees. This was the traditional dueling ground. In fact, everything up until then had been traditional—they had both been punctiliously following the Code Duello. The issuing and acceptance of the challenge had been orthodox. The terms of their encounter had also been set out and agreed to in formally correct terms: an exchange of pistol fire at a specified distance. (The modern image of a duel, where both parties begin back to back, walk away from each other, and turn and fire, seems to have largely been a Hollywood invention.) On the dueling ground, they correctly proceeded to the formal gesture of reconciliation. It was offered and refused. They were now ready to begin.

This was the point at which the duel revealed its unusual nature—the little detail that guaranteed it would become famous. In the course of accepting the challenge, Biddle had insisted that they fight not at ten or twenty paces, as was generally accepted as appropriate, but at five paces. He claimed that it was necessary because of his poor eyesight. That was probably a lie; he was a frequent and expert duelist and nobody had ever noticed anything wrong with his eyes. It's more likely that he was trying to set a preposterous condition on the duel so as to panic Pettis into chickening out. But if it was a bluff, it didn't work. Pettis had accepted the terms. This meant that when the two men raised their pistols to fire, the barrels were close enough to touch.

In the European tradition, there had always been a certain tacit understanding that the duelists didn't actually have to try to kill each other. The point was simply to demonstrate that a gentleman had the courage to die for his honor if he had to. Once that was established, the offending party could apologize and the offended party could accept, without either one looking like a coward. The gentlemen of the river valley scorned all this as craven. If two gentlemen were going to fight a duel at all, they were going to do it for real. So nobody had tried to dissuade Biddle and Pettis from carrying out their absurd duel, even though the terms amounted to mutual suicide. Their seconds had in fact discreetly approached another gentleman, the most famous gentleman in the territory, Senator Thomas Hart Benton (great-uncle of the painter)—the only man who could have forced the two to call it off or at least modify its terms through the sheer authority of his prestige. But Benton wholeheartedly approved. He is reported to have said, "There will be no child's play in the meeting."

So the two men faced each other. There was a count of three, and they fired simultaneously. As Pettis fired, he ducked into a crouch—possibly he was panicking in the end, or else he might have come up with this maneuver as a clever last-ditch gimmick to keep himself from being killed. In any case, it was useless. He was shot in the chest, and the shot passed clear through his body. Meanwhile, his shot struck Biddle in the stomach.

Before they were carried away from the dueling ground, each man forgave the other. That was also traditional—not only did it reassert their honor, but it also served as an additional hedge in case either man survived to be charged with murder. But the precaution turned out to be unnecessary. They barely lingered on for a few days; each died in horrible agony. Their friends all came by to console and praise them. Pettis was particularly concerned that his last-second crouch would be considered cowardly. He was comforted when everyone assured him that his honor was intact. Senator Benton said they were "the bravest of the brave." Newspapers eulogized their willingness to put death before dishonor. Pettis's funeral was later said to have drawn the largest crowd in St. Louis's history.

Dueling wasn't something that happened only between enemies. Anywhere in the valley, it was seen as perfectly appropriate between close friends. This is the way it played out in the life of the famous Mississippi attorney and politician Henry Stuart Foote. One of his lifelong friends was a fellow attorney, the celebrated prosecutor S. S. Prentiss. They were, Foote writes, friendly rivals in court and good companions in their off-hours for decades—except, of course, for those times when they tried to kill each other.

Their duels arose because of their professional competitiveness. Both

men were lawyers of the classic school: that is, they were known as much for
their showmanship as for their jurisprudence. The gallery of the courtroom
in Vicksburg was always packed when they gave their closing arguments.
With good reason: this was, after all, an age where public speakers of all
sorts—preachers, attorneys, politicians, medicine men—were expected to
offer as many rhetorical thrills as a Shakespearean actor. Foote and Prentiss
always delivered.

One time it got out of hand. They found themselves on opposite sides in
a murder trial. During the trial there was a moment where Foote thought
Prentiss had impugned him unnecessarily. In his memoirs, Foote doesn't
spell out exactly what Prentiss said—evidently it was some needling personal witticism made during an exchange of objections. Foote did say that
he felt the insult "had been sufficiently retaliated by me at the time." But
when he thought it over later, the feeling of sufficiency wore off. After the
trial ended, he challenged Prentiss to a duel.

It was a mistake, he admitted in his memoirs: Prentiss was a much better shot than he was. They fought with pistols at dawn in a meadow outside of Vicksburg. Foote shot to kill, but he missed; Prentiss's shot left
Foote badly wounded in the shoulder. Foote as the aggrieved party
declared that his honor was now satisfied. Even before they'd left the dueling ground to find a doctor, they had followed the code and made up their
quarrel. They swore to each other that they were friends again for life.

A few weeks later, their reconciliation came undone. According to
Foote, he had heard that Prentiss's friends were passing around some kind
of nasty gossip about the duel. He doesn't say what the gossip was
exactly—only that they "spoke disparagingly of my conduct on the occasion." Foote was enraged, and wrote Prentiss a stiff note "demanding
whether he had given his sanction to this act of injustice." Prentiss immediately wrote back to say that he hadn't. Probably this should have satisfied
Foote, but he was so rankled by the perceived slight to his reputation that
he published the two letters. Prentiss then publicly claimed to have been
insulted by the whole exchange: "He placed such an interpretation upon
my letter to him as gave him much offense," Foote recalled. "He proposed
reopening the fight, which we did on exceedingly desperate terms."

It sounds like some sort of schoolyard squabble, not the behavior of two of the most respected attorneys in the Mississippi valley. And yet they were now bound by honor to return to their dueling ground. In the second duel, Foote missed again. Prentiss shot him in the hip. The wound was so bad that Foote almost died. He took months to recuperate; he was still on crutches when he came into the courtroom for the first time afterward to contend with Prentiss again.

They met over the case of one of the most notorious thieves and murderers in the river valley. Prentiss was prosecuting; Foote was defending pro bono—he may have volunteered just to spite Prentiss. The defendant was a man named Alonzo Phelps. Phelps was a mysterious and sinister figure: a highwayman who had long been haunting the wilderness along the river north of Vicksburg. This was inaccessible country, a region of steep, lushly overgrown hills and countless winding ravines; even locals got lost in it. Despite frequent manhunts by large groups of regulators, Phelps had remained hidden in its depths for more than a decade. It was said that he never set foot in a human habitation and lived off squirrels and other small animals caught and eaten raw—because a campfire would have given away his position.

Phelps was a rare sort of highwayman: he almost always let his victims go alive. He reserved his murderous rage for the vigilance committees and the regulators. He is supposed to have killed eight regulators who tried to bring him in. He was also notorious for his stream of abusive and threatening letters to members of the local vigilance committees, demanding that they leave him alone. No one knew how the letters were sent—they would simply show up in mailboxes out of thin air. One of Vicksburg's leading committee members got a long succession of these letters, and they grew to be so menacing that he at last hired, on his own dime, an unusually large band of regulators and trackers to find and bring in Phelps, no matter what the cost. It took them weeks of systematic searching, but they finally cornered him in the remotest interior of the wilderness region, and they brought him into Vicksburg in chains.

At his trial the courtroom was packed. Everybody wanted to see the strange apparition who had terrorized them for so long. Seated in the courtroom under armed guard, Phelps proved to be tall, handsome, tanned, and muscular; but he had peculiar, snake-curling bloodred hair and a perpetually ferocious expression. Foote found him a brilliant man, "a ripe and accurate scholar," well versed in classical literature, which he read in the original—"when taken prisoner," Foote wrote, "a few weeks subsequent to the perpetration of his last murder, [he] had, as I personally know, a much-worn pocket-copy of Horace in his possession."

Prentiss presented an ironclad case at the trial. In his summation he spoke at great length, conjuring up Phelps's decade of terror with his grandest sallies of vividness, scorn, and impassioned eloquence. (At one point he called Phelps "the Rob Roy of the Mississippi.") The longer Prentiss went on, the more Phelps's face swelled and empurpled into a mask of rage. Foote recalled:

> Seeming presently to grow desperate, he bent forward a little and whispered in my ear: "Tell me whether I stand any chance of acquittal, and tell me frankly; for if my case is hopeless, I will snatch a gun from the guard nearest me and send Mr. Prentiss to hell before I shall myself go there."

It was a bad moment for Foote. He later wrote, "Never was I more embarrassed in my life." What would happen if he told Phelps the truth—that conviction was an absolute certainty? Phelps would grab for the gun, Prentiss would most likely be killed, and Phelps would then be shot dead by the guards. But was that such a bad outcome? Foote would have had his revenge on Prentiss for the two duels without lifting a finger. And yet, Foote hesitated. "If he should slay him, he would deprive of life one whom I could not help loving and admiring much, despite the unkind relations then existing between us." Then, too, there was the question of whether he could get away with it: "Were Prentiss assassinated by the hands of this fiendish ruffian, immediately, too, after this whispering intercourse with me, who, of all that vast crowd, would hold me guiltless?" The conclusion was inevitable.

> I may have been wrong, but frankness constrains me to confess that I whispered back to Phelps, "you are not in the least danger; we shall have no difficulty whatever in preventing your conviction, and shall

presently introduce a motion for a new trial, or in arrest of judgment, which will save you from all further annoyance."

"I may have been wrong"—meaning, presumably, that he was troubled by the thought that he lied to his client. Or else he meant that he still regretted not telling Phelps to go ahead and damn the consequences.

In any case, Phelps acquiesced and did nothing. He remained placid as the jury found him guilty on all counts and the judge sentenced him to death. He didn't seem to resent that Foote had lied to him, even after (as Foote himself knew perfectly well would happen) the motions for a suspended sentence and a new trial went nowhere. He went to prison without a fuss and spent his time before his execution working furiously on his memoirs.

Just before Phelps was scheduled to be hanged, he wrote to the governor asking for a reprieve. He didn't want a full pardon; he was still only midway through his memoirs and he needed a couple of weeks more to finish them. The request was denied. Phelps made no complaint when he heard the news; he simply returned to his work at an even more frantic speed. Foote visited him at the end of that day and guessed that by dinnertime he'd written thirty more pages.

That same evening, after Foote left, Phelps had two visitors: the jailer and a priest. During their visit, Phelps revealed another way he'd been passing his time. He'd been working out a method for sawing through his manacles.

He abruptly reared up from his bench and threw the chains aside. The priest immediately bolted. Phelps advanced on the jailer and beat him unconscious with a makeshift weapon: a heavy lead inkwell (on loan from Foote) that he'd wrapped in a sock. Then he armed himself with the jailer's knife and pistol. He picked up the jailer's unconscious body, held the knife to his throat, and started dragging him toward the prison gate.

The noise of the fight had caused a commotion in the prison yard. But everyone gave way when they saw Phelps emerge from the cell with his hostage; even the toughest of the other prisoners were intimidated by Phelps. The guards didn't hesitate to throw open the gates. A crowd had gathered outside—some had been waiting for the hanging, and others were running up to find out what the noise was about. They all fell back as Phelps advanced from the yard into the wide evening air.

The prison stood at the edge of a bluff where a steep grassy slope descended toward the Mississippi. Phelps started down the slope while the crowd followed warily at a distance. Then somebody threw a rock at Phelps's back. It glanced off him without slowing him down. More rocks followed; then brickbats, bottles, and shards of wood. Phelps lumbered on silently. About midway down the slope, one of the brickbats finally staggered him. He let his hostage sag limply to the ground and turned around to face the crowd. The sheriff was cautiously coming toward him with pistols drawn. Phelps lowered his hands and told him to fire. The sheriff killed him with one shot.

Afterward Phelps's unfinished memoir was turned over to Foote. It contained confessions to several murders Phelps hadn't yet been suspected of committing, as well as an elaborate defense of his criminal career. It built up to a long and furious denunciation of slavery and a call for all slaves to be emancipated immediately. If this was not done, Phelps wrote, he was debating whether he should take direct action himself. Foote summarized: "He mentions, in his rude and coarse phraseology, his inclination to break forth from the prison in which he was confined, for the purpose of bringing about an insurrection of the slaves. He discusses the expedience of the measure very freely; but finally relinquishes the project, from considerations of humanity."

Phelps's manuscript was never published. In Foote's own memoirs, written after the Civil War, he was vague about what happened to it. At one point he claims he no longer had it because he did send it out for publication, but this may be his memory failing him, because there's no record now of such a book existing. Another passage implies that he destroyed it. This is more likely. Not only was Phelps's memoir unpublishable—publicly advocating abolition was a felony in Mississippi—but if Foote had been found in possession of such an incendiary manuscript, it's likely he himself would have gone to prison.

The Phelps incident did have one positive consequence for Foote. After it was over, he and Prentiss reconciled. They remained close friends for another fifteen years, until Prentiss's death. They never fought another duel—at least not with each other. Prentiss had a long career as a prosecutor. Foote went into politics: he became governor of Mississippi and a U.S. senator. He was one of the authors of the Compromise of 1850, legislating the spread of slavery into the new states of the Union, which was sometimes said to have staved off for a decade the outbreak of the Civil War.

7

The Roar of Niagara

THE MOST CELEBRATED PHRASE to describe the typical river man was "half horse, half alligator." There's no record of who coined the phrase or who was first called it—sooner or later it was used about every prominent man on the river, up to and including Abraham Lincoln. But the figure it was most associated with was a voyageur named Mike Fink. Stories about Mike Fink were told all over the valley. He was famous for what one writer described as "his wild freaks and daredevil sprees." "He war," as one story in frontier dialect put it, "a helliferocious fellow, and made an awful fine shot. . . . There ar'nt a man from Pittsburgh to New Orleans but what's heard of Mike Fink, and there aint a boatman on the river, to this day, but what strives to imitate him."

The Mike Fink stories were a kind of primordial example of literary realism. At least, they weren't set in the absurdist universe where most tall tales unfold; they took place in what was recognizably the real Mississippi River valley, the world of keelboats and flatboats, of frontiersmen and Native Americans, of bluffs and points and chutes and levees. The only fantastic element in them was Fink himself. In the archetypical Fink story, he was floating down the Mississippi in a keelboat when he picked up his rifle for no reason at all and shot at somebody onshore. His target might be an Indian brave on a hilltop, or a slave boy carrying a bucket along a plantation road. In an instant, the victim would have his earlobe sliced off by the bullet, or a spur on his heel blasted away with surgical precision. Fink's boat glided on; before the victim or the bystanders could react, Fink was around the river bend, leaving nothing behind but the sound of his laughter.

That was the appeal of Fink: he was a creature of pure impulse—and yet whatever he did, no matter how bizarrely random it might be, he did perfectly. He achieved without effort what nobody else could do in a lifetime of labor. His air of godlike grace, of what in classical literature was called *arete*, transcended everything about his personality—which was in all other ways appalling. In story after story, he was casually shown to be a psychotic thug. He had no morals, no conscience, no principles, and no remorse. His signature quality was his murderous rage, which in him seems indistinguishable from happy-go-lucky high spirits. There's one story where he cheerfully boils up puppies in a stew and laughs uproariously at the horrified reaction of his dinner guests. In another he puts kindling around his wife's bed, sets it on fire, and watches in delight as she wakes up in terror and has to jump through the flames.

And yet the storytellers perpetually rhapsodized about him. They sang the praises of his great soul, his invincible backwoods wisdom, and his heart as big as the river itself. He was, in the words of one writer, "the tallest, strongest, longest-winded fellow in the section, carried the truest rifle, knew more Ingin ways, was the wildest hand at a frolic, and withal, was the greatest favorite in the country."

Maybe they could praise him like this because they no longer had to live with him. The submerged theme running through all the Mike Fink stories was that he belonged to the heroic days of the river's past. He was often called the Last of the Gintys. "Ginty" was river slang for a tough guy—Fink was the last because the old-style tough guys were falling out of favor on the increasingly tamed and civilized river. He was also called the Last of the Keelboatmen. The keelboats were vanishing from the river as the century went on. Or else he was simply the Last of the Boatmen, because the voyageurs had the feeling that their livelihood was rapidly becoming obsolete.

There is even a Fink story about what was happening to the old river culture. It describes Fink's first sight of a steamboat. As he saw it go cruising serenely up the river during a flood, he thought it must be Noah's ark. The white puffballs furiously billowing from the smokestacks, he decided, were the breath of all the animals inside.

Fink wasn't given to reflection; any thoughts he had about this vision he

kept to himself. But the point of the story would not have been lost on the
river men in the audience. The increasing dominance of the steamboat on
the river meant the end of their way of life. If the steamboat was Noah's
ark, after all, then Fink must have been left behind, part of the world that
was drowning.

Fink himself seems ultimately to have gotten the message. In the end he
gave up the river life and struck out again on his own. The later stories in
the Fink saga describe how he went off on a new adventure in the wilderness country up the Missouri. One night on a riverbank he was playing his
favorite game of marksmanship and, for the first time in his life, missed his
target. He was trying to shoot a tin cup off somebody's head at fifty yards,
and instead the man fell dead. In some versions of the story, Fink missed
because he was drunk—"corned too heavy," as they said on the river. In
others, he deliberately missed because he and his victim were having a
fight over an Indian squaw. But what happened after that was abrupt and
final: a bystander picked up a gun and shot Fink dead.

In some stories, the bystander was a stranger. Sometimes he was the victim's brother. In one version, he was Fink's best friend. That didn't matter;
the point was the same. It ended for Fink brutally and thoughtlessly, the
way things had always happened with Fink, the way life had always gone
on the river.

Was Fink a real person? Doubtless not—but people talked like it. Sometimes they seemed to be bursting out with the need to reveal the truth
about him, as though they'd had to keep glancing over their shoulders
while he was alive for fear he was listening in. There was an anonymous
letter in the *Western General Advertiser,* in 1845, claiming to be by somebody who knew another anonymous somebody—"a friend of mine, one
of the oldest and most respected of the commanders of steamboats in the
Nashville trade"—who actually had known Mike Fink personally. According to the letter writer, this friend had said authoritatively that the real
Mike Fink was "worthless and vile." The letter goes on: "Mike was one of
the very lowest of mankind, and entirely destitute of any of the manly
qualities which often were to be found among the bargemen of his day."

Not the sort of thing usually written about a folklore hero. Perhaps letters like this make it slightly more plausible that Fink did exist.

There was at least one thing about Fink that wasn't purely fantastic. He reflected, in a distorted and abstracted way, an attitude that people in the river valley actually held. They all lived for the spontaneous, heedless surge of wild exuberance, the sudden recourse to violence with no provocation—the violence if not of act then of thought and of language. They routinely did and said extraordinarily foolish things for no reason other than joie de vivre. John James Audubon, in solemn correspondence with the most distinguished scientists in Europe, often enlivened his descriptions of the fauna of the Mississippi with absurd creatures out of his own head that he claimed were as real as the alligators and the passenger pigeons. He had nothing to gain by this kind of shameless romancing; in fact, his reputation could easily have been destroyed, given how self-evidently preposterous some of his inventions were. It was as though he couldn't help himself. After pages of scrupulously accurate observations of the river's wildlife, he was somehow obliged to imagine the gigantic Devil-Jack Diamond-Fish, with scales that were impervious to bullets and that could be used as flints to strike fires.

This kind of submerged taste for the manic became familiar to the people around Abraham Lincoln. In the White House he was well known for his air of forbidding gloom, but he would also frequently interrupt the most serious discussions of military strategy with nonsensical tall tales about two squirrels fighting on a log, or an old woman and a chicken thief. In the middle of a debate over a desperate battle, he would suddenly snort with laughter and say, "This reminds me of when I was a boatman on the Mississippi" or "This reminds me of a fight in a bar-room at Natchez, but I won't tell that story now." Such moments of private levity gained him a reputation among the sophisticates of Washington as an incomprehensible barbarian. Even those who admired him had to admit that they usually had no idea what he could possibly think was so funny.

The voyageurs had a ritual game they'd play called shout-boasting, the point of which was to make up surreally violent claims about themselves and then dare to fight anybody who challenged them. Here is one shout-boaster, on a raft heading down the Mississippi at midnight:

Then he jumped up in the air and cracked his heels together again and shouted out: "Whoo-oop! I'm the old original iron-jawed, brass-mounted, copper-bellied corpse-maker from the wilds of Arkansaw! Look at me! I'm the man they call Sudden Death and General Desolation! Sired by a hurricane, dam'd by an earthquake, half-brother to the cholera, nearly related to the small-pox on the mother's side! Look at me! I take nineteen alligators and a bar'l of whiskey for breakfast when I'm in robust health, and a bushel of rattle-snakes and a dead body when I'm ailing! I split the everlasting rocks with my glance, and I squench the thunder when I speak! Whoo-oop! Stand back and give me room according to my strength! Blood's my natural drink, and the wails of the dying is music to my ear! Cast your eye on me, gentlemen! and lay low and hold your breath, for I'm 'bout to turn myself loose!" All the time he was getting this off, he was shaking his head and looking fierce, and kind of swelling around in a little circle, tucking up his wrist-bands, and now and then straightening up and beating his breast with his fist, saying, "Look at me, gentlemen!"

The scene is from the original manuscript of *The Adventures of Huckleberry Finn.* Twain might be thought to be burnishing to an especially high glow his nostalgia for the old river world, but in fact he wasn't exaggerating what shout-boasting was typically like. Similar dervish dances of language can be found throughout the early literature of the river—particularly in an odd series of joke books that began circulating around 1840, spoofs of the famous *Farmer's Almanac,* featuring the supposed adventures of the frontier hero Davy Crockett.

The real Davy Crockett, who had died a few years earlier at the Alamo, actually had been a wild and charismatic man, a kind of true-life Mike Fink. But in the almanacs he was reimagined as something much grander—as a demigod of the river valley, a mythic superhero who wrestled wild animals for fun, wiped out whole Indian tribes out of pique, and rode his pet alligator up waterfalls. The stories were written in a bizarre parody of frontier slang, where illiteracies like "satisfakshun" and "Kornill" (for "Colonel") and heavy dialect like "I war skeered" were jumbled together with weirdly pompous nonce words: "explunctify," "flustification," "insinnivation," "absquottleated," "tongariferous," "sarcledicular." Crockett was always bellowing things like "My name are Thunder and Lightning!" and claiming that he once fought a bison a thousand years old, "with eyes like two holes burnt in a blanket, or two bullets fired into a stump." A typical story began:

> I was laying asleep on the Mississippi one day, with a piece of river scum for a pillow, and floating downstream in a rail free and easy style . . .

Crockett had a friend named Ben Harding, who could blast enemies away by the stench of his breath, and he also had a woman—a vague shape-shifter who was sometimes his mother, sometimes his sister, and sometimes his wife. She could "jump a seven rail fence backwards, dance a hole through a double oak floor, spin more wool than one of your steam mills, and smoke up a ton of Kentucky weed in a week." On the day of her marriage, she chased a crocodile half a mile. Her sneezing "lifts the roof of the house about one foot, and breaks the crockery." She wore clothes made of the skins of the bears she'd wrestled to death, and a necklace made of the eyes she'd gouged out of the skulls of her rivals. She went by a variety of extravagant names—usually she was called Florinda Fury—but her grandest incarnation is as Sally Ann Thunder Ann Whirlwind.

This was another given of the frontier imagination: in the tall tales, the women were just as exuberantly powerful as the men. The wild men of the valley were "ring-tailed roarers"; the women were "riproarious she-males." "She-male" wasn't meant as an insult. The implication was that their strength and their appetites were the equal of any man's.

The wildest stories of these appetites weren't in the Crockett almanacs. They showed up in print only in fugitive pamphlets and broadsheets, and many of them weren't written down at all until they were collected by the folklorists of a later century. These were the stories of the valley's prostitutes. Some of the folklorists invented a female version of Crockett to hang these stories on. They called her Annie Christmas, and her stories were all about prostitutes so skilled and so voracious they could intimidate Crockett himself. One Annie Christmas story told of a prostitute traveling up and down the river with a bucket of gold; she would bring it with her into the brothels and the gunboats and offer to bet the bucket against the house till that she could take on more men in a night than any woman there. It was said that she never lost.

There was one simple explanation for the wildness of the river culture: everybody was drunk. The great temperance movements of the nineteenth and early twentieth centuries, which ultimately resulted in Prohibition, weren't outbursts of foolish moralism, or not only that: they were legitimate responses to the astonishing volume of alcohol consumed on the frontier. New arrivals were routinely horrified by it. One writer observed that a typical inhabitant put away "a whiskey keg in the morning, and a keg of whiskey at night; stupid and gruff in the morning, by noon could talk politics and abuse the Yankees, and by sundown was brave for a fight." Another recorded the alcohol consumed at one picnic attended by only two people: two bottles of claret, one bottle of champagne, one large bottle of anisette, one small bottle of muscat, and a bottle of honey brandy.

It was taken for granted that people had alcohol at every meal. On the steamboats, travelers were at least a little tipsy from the moment they woke up—their custom was to stop off at the bar and down a glass of wine and bitters on the way to breakfast. There would be no slowdown in the bar service till long after midnight. Steamboat meals were famously lavish; the drink menus just as much so. The British traveler Alexander Marjoribanks recorded some of what was offered: mint juleps; spiked eggnog; rum punch with milk and nutmeg; sherry cobbler made with lemon, strawberries, and sugar; gin sling with rum; a brandy cocktail with bitters and lemon peel; and a drink of brandy, mint, and ice called a brandy smash.

The voyageurs and the other river people didn't have that kind of variety available to them. Their drink of choice was Monongahela rye, which was distilled in Pennsylvania, brought down the Ohio, and distributed all through the river valley. It was rough and it was potent, and the custom was to drink it three times a day. (The menu didn't vary, either—on most flatboats and rafts, it was beef or pork at each meal, fried in a skillet with bread dough and a lot of grease; the voyageurs as a rule disdained fish.) The result was predictable: the crew was drunk all day, every day. Drunken fights on the boats were almost an hourly occurrence. Drunken riots in the river districts at night were routine. The captains on the boats would use any means necessary to restore order. In one celebrated incident in the 1810s, a keelboat captain broke up a fight on deck by beating an oar repeatedly over the head of the most drunken and abusive crewman, until the man fell to the deck unconscious and then slithered overboard and drowned. The case became famous only because the captain was conscientious enough to turn himself in to the authorities at the next port. There a hasty inquest was held, and the verdict was "accidental death."

But there seemed to be something other than mere drunkenness at work in the valley. The wildest passions of the frontier legends—the rages of Fink, the lunatic exuberance of Crockett and his cohorts, the extravagant energies of Annie Christmas—all had a basis in daily life; they all shared in that mysterious upwelling of outsize exuberance that inspired the shout-boasting and Audubon's dabblings in imaginary natural history. Maybe nobody ever rode alligators around the river, but they really did keep alligators as pets. They also made pets of mountain lions, pumas, and bears.

There was one regular occasion where the collective energies of the valley found a natural outlet: the religious gathering known as the camp meeting. Camp meetings were a routine fixture of life in the valley from the beginning of the nineteenth century until sometime in the 1840s. They were wild and disorienting events. One witness, the minister James Finley, wrote that they "exhibited nothing to the spectator . . . but a scene of confusion, such as scarcely could be put into human language." The British traveler William Newnham Blane said: "One of these meetings, at which many thousands are often assembled, and which commonly last for several days, fills the spectator with the utmost alarm and wonder. An Indian war-dance is a bagatelle to it, and I verily believe that it exceeds the wildest orgies of the Bacchanalians or the Corybantes."

Camp meetings were usually held somewhere deep in the wilderness, typically in a large forest glade or clearing. They tended to last for around a week. They were almost always held in high summer, when farmers could afford to take that much time off from their fields. During the meeting, the grounds were transformed into a kind of tent city (which is why they were sometimes also known as tent meetings). There were large tents serving as makeshift hostels, taverns, and hospitals, and open-air kitchens were everywhere. Around the central meeting grounds was a ring of smaller tents where families set up housekeeping and where hawkers and peddlers put their wares on display. People who couldn't get a place to sleep in one of the tents, which were invariably overcrowded, would find what shelter they could in the surrounding forest—this was not seen as a big hardship because the summer nights in the valley were usually sultry, and anyway these events were supposed to be about something other than material comfort. Some of the meetings were remarkably large. There was one at Cane Ridge, Kentucky, in the summer of 1804 that drew more than twenty thousand people—at a time when New Orleans, the biggest city in the river valley, had a population of around ten thousand.

A typical meeting began in a low-key, almost solemn way. A preacher gave a sermon of welcome and led a prayer for peace and community. This was followed by the singing of several hymns. Then there would be more sermons. Gradually, as the hours went by, the atmosphere changed. The preachers became more lively; the audience grew more excited. One attendee recalled that "the order of preaching was for the first speaker to be somewhat logical, and to show forth to the listening audience his great learning and wisdom; for the last speaker was left the sensational. He would 'get happy,' clap his hands, froth at the mouth; the congregation responding, some groaning, some crying loudly, 'Amen,' some calling 'glory, glory, glory to God!' " The sermonizing went on past sunset, and when it ended, everyone broke off with the sense of a day well spent.

The next day, and the day following, the sermons grew increasingly sensational and impassioned, and the excited response of the crowd grew more prolonged. By the second or third day, people were crying out during the sermons, and shouting prayers, and bursting into loud lamentations; they began grabbing at their neighbors and desperately pleading with them to repent; they sobbed uncontrollably and ran in terror through the crowd, shoving aside everybody in their path. Many of the preachers were famous for their hysterical intensity—none more so than the Reverend James McGready, who gave at tent meetings a sermon called "The Character, History, and End of the Fool" (the fool being the one who said in his heart that there was no God). The character and history of the fool were scanted; all of the reverend's fury was devoted to evoking the fool's end:

> He died accursed of God and the black, flaming vultures of hell began to encircle him on every side! His conscience woke from its long sleep, and roared like ten thousand peals of thunder! When the fiends of hell dragged him into the eternal gulf, he roared and screamed and yelled like a devil! When, while Indians, Pagans, and Mohammedans stood amazed and upbraided him, falling like Lucifer, from the meridian blaze of the Gospel and the threshold of heaven, sinking into the liquid, boiling waves of hell, the accursed sinners of Tyre and Sidon and Sodom and Gomorrah sprang to the right and left and made way for him to pass them and fall lower down even to the deepest cavern in the flaming abyss!

The response of the crowd to this sermon, one witness wrote, "was like the roar of Niagara."

As the days passed, the crowds got so big and clamorous that the preacher couldn't be heard across the whole assembly, so multiple preachers began sermonizing simultaneously at different points on the meeting grounds. At one camp meeting James Finley counted seven ministers at one time haranguing everyone in earshot—"some on stumps, others in wagons, and one . . . was standing on a tree which had, in falling, lodged against another." As the preachers ranted without letup, the crowd was driven into a kind of collective ecstasy. In the night, as the torches and bonfires flared around the meeting ground and the darkness of the trackless forests closed in, people behaved as if possessed by something new and unfathomable. As Finley wrote: "A strange supernatural power seemed to pervade the entire mass of mind there collected." Finley felt it happening to him: "My heart beat tumultuously, my knees trembled, my lip quivered, and I felt as though I must fall to the ground." His immediate response was to run away. He found himself racing frantically off from the campground and stumbling alone deep in the forest. There, he wrote, "I strove to rally and man up my courage." He returned to find that the scene was growing even more frenzied; that same power, the irresistible urge to fall to the ground, was overtaking hundreds in the crowd, while all around them other people were screaming.

What Finley was witnessing was known as the falling exercise. It was a kind of violent fainting spell that would come over people at the height of their religious transports. The Reverend Barton Stone, who participated in many camp meetings, described it in his autobiography: "The falling exercise was very common among all classes, the saints and sinners of every age and of every grade, from the philosopher to the clown. The subject of this exercise would, generally, with a piercing scream, fall like a log on the floor, earth or mud, and appear as dead." They might remain that way for minutes, or for hours; at some meetings, areas were set aside where the fallers could be laid out and not be trodden on. When they revived, they would often sob uncontrollably, or scream out for God and proclaim the glory of the gospel in what Stone described as "language almost superhuman. . . . I have heard them agonizing in tears and strong crying for mercy to be shown to sinners, and speaking like angels to all around."

Those who didn't become fallers might instead experience the jerks. This was a convulsive movement that would begin in the arms, shoulders, or legs and then spread through the whole body. "When the head alone was affected," Stone said, "it would be jerked backward and forward, or from side to side, so quickly that the features of the face could not be distinguished. When the whole system was affected, I have seen the person stand in one place and jerk backward and forward in quick succession, their head nearly touching the floor behind and before." The wandering preacher Lorenzo Dow wrote that he saw one camp meeting where they had prepared the ground ahead of time for the jerks: "Fifty to one hundred saplings left breast high . . . for the people to jerk by. . . . They had kicked up the earth as a horse stamping flies." When people recovered from the jerks, Stone reported, they could not account for what had happened to them, "but some have told me that those were among the happiest seasons of their lives."

Related to the jerks was the rolling exercise. People would start by twisting their heads from side to side and rapidly nodding and snapping their heads back. Then they would hurl themselves to the ground and begin rolling over and over in the mud and dirt like dogs. Sometimes they writhed and screamed as though they were being stabbed with hot pokers. Then they would bounce up and down and shake convulsively as if they were flying apart.

Others performed the dancing exercise, a weird, somber sequence of steps and retreats. While smiles of radiant supernatural bliss played across their faces, the dancers would keep it up for hours, sometimes very rapidly and sometimes with an unearthly slow-motion grace, until they dropped from exhaustion. There was also the laughing exercise ("The subject appeared rapturously solemn, and his laughter excited solemnity in saints and sinners") and the singing exercise, which Stone said was "more unaccountable than anything else I ever saw. The subject in a very happy state of mind would sing most melodiously, not from the mouth or nose, but entirely in the breast, the sounds issuing thence. Such music silenced everything and attracted the attention of all. It was most heavenly." Then there were those who would grunt and bark and howl like dogs. Others would, as Finley did, begin to run wildly, shoving people aside, trampling on the fallers, racing deep into the forest until they tripped or slid or dropped in exhaustion. Many in the crowd got roaring drunk—and the drunks at their most extreme were hard to tell apart from the fallers and the jerkers and the howlers. Others gave in to the general mood of riot and began fighting and beating each other up over nothing. But what made the camp meetings truly infamous were the orgies.

The meetings were always intensely erotic experiences. In the pervasive atmosphere of extreme excitement, people weren't all that careful to make a distinction between religious ecstasy and sexual hunger. The campgrounds were notoriously good places for prostitutes to do business; among the tents of the hawkers and peddlers around the margins of the camp would often be full-service brothels. But at the height of their religious transports, many campgoers would simply go off into the woods together, day or night, in complicated and impromptu combinations. According to one scandalized report from a vigilance committee, a woman at one camp meeting invited six men to meet with her in the woods at the same time. It was a standard joke that the local population invariably spiked nine months after any meeting. Those children were known throughout the river valley as camp meeting babies.

The rumors of what went on around the margins of the grounds were what eventually led to the taming of the camp meeting tradition. Toward midcentury, vigilance committees began to police their local meetings; gradually the events became more staid and tedious. Preachers were still expected to be wildly dramatic—it was often said that a preacher who didn't end a sermon by falling to the ground and rolling around in a fit was simply being lazy. But more and more, the congregations tended to listen with polite attention and only gave in to the falls and the other exercises at controlled and ritualized intervals. The religious authorities that dominated American churches later in the century regarded the boredom of the new camp meetings as one of their greatest moral triumphs.

8

The Cosmopolitan Tide

THE FIRST STEAMBOAT CAME DOWN the Mississippi in 1811—in fact, it was swamped and almost sank in the backwash of the Great Shakes. By the end of that decade, around a dozen steamboats were on the river system. In the 1830s, the steamboat population was estimated to be around five hundred. By the time of the Civil War, it was four thousand.

There was a simple explanation for the ascendancy of the steamboats: they could move upriver almost as easily as they did down. This gave them a decisive advantage over every other form of river transport. They rendered the old, ornate, impractical keelboats obsolete—no need for bushwhacking or cordelling when the steamboats could churn their way up against the strongest current. Keelboats disappeared from the river by the 1840s. By the 1850s, even the flatboat population was in decline. The only serious competition the steamboats had left was the great rafts and barges—they survived because the steamboats didn't have their bulk carrying capacity.

The rise of the steamboats also wrecked the old river etiquette. The river had never been policed, but there had always been a logic to its traffic flow, one dictated by practical necessity: the downriver traffic ran in the channels, while the upriver traffic stuck to the shallows. The steamboats put an end to all that. They cut in and out of the channels no matter which direction they were traveling. Their pilots were notoriously indifferent to the chaos they could leave in their wake. The steamboats routinely swamped the smaller boats as they passed; often they ran right over them and blasted them to splinters. And if the boat people were injured or drowned, if their boats were destroyed and all their possessions were sunk, there was no recourse. It wasn't uncommon for the boat people, when they saw a steamboat approaching—particularly one with a reputation as a channel hog—to bring out their rifles and take shots at the pilothouse.

The steamboats were glamorous—everyone agreed on that. The sight of these gigantic white-tiered wedding cakes grandly gliding up the channels, pennants flying and smokestacks churning, never failed to dazzle the watchers onshore. In many towns along the river, the arrival of a steamboat was practically a public holiday. The boys of the town would be in a frenzy of excitement at the sight. They'd often paddle their canoes out to the levee, where they would caper and deliberately capsize, in hopes that the ladies and gentlemen watching from the cabin deck would laugh and throw them pennies. If the steamboat stayed docked long enough to allow the passengers to go for a stroll, the boys would pester them with souvenir trinkets, with Indian arrowheads and pieces of ancient French flintlocks they'd dug up along the riverbanks. They'd also—as George Merrick recalled—show off their exhaustive knowledge of steamboat design:

> Was she a side-wheel or stern-wheel? Was she large or small? Had she trimmings on her smokestack, or about the pilot house, and if so of what description? Had she a "Texas," or no "Texas"? Were the outside blinds painted white, red, or green? What was the sound of her whistle and bell?

The steamboats generally ran three kinds of routes. There were the packet boats that shuttled between two ports on a regular schedule. There were the transients that did one-shot hops to wherever their largest load of cargo was bound. And then there were the great lines that covered long swaths of the river and made countless stops along the way. A company that ran a major line might at any given time have ten or twelve boats in transit somewhere in the river system.

Passage on a line from New Orleans to the upper valley cost around a hundred dollars, which included a bed in the cabin and three meals a day. Fifty dollars more paid for a private stateroom. (For contrast, a crewman might earn fifty dollars a month; apprentices were lucky to be paid twenty.) Poorer passengers had a cheap alternative available: they could sleep outside on deck and take their chances with the weather. Those who did so were called deckers. For around five dollars, deckers bought the right to whatever space they could find among the barrels and hogsheads and crates and the pens of lamenting livestock; they could work down the fare or pay for meals by helping the crew load or unload cargo at each stop.

The boats were generally designed to carry about 250 passengers, plus crew and cargo. But they were routinely oversold. A boat on a popular line was likely to have at least four hundred passengers on board between the most heavily trafficked ports—fifty to a hundred people in the interior cabin and the staterooms, a couple of hundred deckers, and another hundred or so people who were making short hops and day trips. This endlessly shifting throng through the public rooms and the decks was a source of constant fascination to many travelers. Herman Melville, in his novel *The Confidence-Man: His Masquerade,* described the scene:

> As among Chaucer's Canterbury pilgrims, or those oriental ones crossing the Red Sea towards Mecca in the festival month, there was no lack of variety. Natives of all sorts, and foreigners; men of business and men of pleasure; parlour men and backwoodsmen; farm-hunters and fame-hunters; heiress-hunters, gold-hunters, buffalo-hunters, bee-hunters, happiness-hunters, truth-hunters, and still keener hunters after all these hunters. Fine ladies in slippers, and moccasined squaws; Northern speculators and Eastern philosophers; English, Irish, German, Scotch, Danes; Santa Fé traders in striped blankets, and Broadway bucks in cravats of cloth of gold; fine-looking Kentucky boatmen, and Japanese-looking Mississippi cotton-planters; Quakers in full drab, and United States soldiers in full regimentals; slaves, black, mulatto, quadroon; modish young Spanish Creoles, and old-fashioned French Jews; Mormons and Papists; Dives and Lazarus; jesters and mourners, teetotallers and convivialists, deacons and blacklegs; hard-shell Baptists and clay-eaters; grinning negroes, and Sioux chiefs solemn as high-priests. In short, a piebald parliament, an Anacharsis Cloots congress of all kinds of that multiform pilgrim species, man.

For Melville, the crowd made the steamboat the soul of the river: "Here reigned the dashing and all-fusing spirit of the West, whose type is the Mississippi itself, which, uniting the streams of the most distant and opposite zones, pours them along, helter-skelter, in one cosmopolitan and confident tide."

The interior cabin was a dream of luxuriousness. It had gleaming brass railings and tasseled arras and porcelain doorknobs; there were framed oil paintings on the walls and doors; the dining rooms had sparkling chandeliers and stained-glass skylights that cast colored motes across the carpeted floors. But at close contact the glamour wore off. The cabin sometimes seemed to be occupied by livestock worse than that found on deck—as Frances Trollope wrote about the typical steamboat cabin, "I would infinitely prefer sharing the apartment of a party of well-conditioned pigs."

Trollope found the cabin at its worst at mealtime. The steamboats would lay on a lavish banquet at every meal, and the ladies and gentlemen would descend on it like a locust swarm, devour it loudly without a word of small talk, and then bolt from the table fifteen minutes later. Trollope remembered a "total want of any of the courtesies of the table," and was particularly appalled by "the loathsome spitting, from the contamination of which it was absolutely impossible to protect our dresses," and "the frightful manner of feeding with their knives, till the whole blade seemed to enter into the mouth."

Other travelers were horrified by the behavior in the public rooms. The British geologist George Featherstonhaugh recalled "noise, confusion, spitting, smoking, cursing, and swearing, drawn from the most remorseless pages of blasphemy." The French traveler Marie de Grandfort was offended by the whistling—at the boat's theatrical performances, the audience would express its approval with a chorus of wolf whistles, which she found inconceivably vulgar. But even worse, she thought, was another habit: whittling.

Provided with a large or a small knife, they lay hands on the first bit of stray wood that falls in their way, or the branch of a tree, or a cane, or an umbrella left in a corner. If they are deprived of these, they attack the furniture; they pitilessly cut into counters, window sills, doors, chairs, sofas, billiard tables, church pews; in fact, nothing nothing is sacred against their knife-blades. The railings of the guards on certain boats on the Mississippi have been transformed into gigantic saws by this Yankee process.

The one thing everybody agreed on about steamboat travel was that it was loud. The river and the passing landscape were almost uncannily silent. "The prevailing character of the Mississippi," one traveler wrote, "is that of solemn gloom." But the steamboat was a great puffing, cranking, grinding, hooting, rattling contraption; people in the cabin could barely sleep at night because of what another traveler described as "the constant whizzing of the steampipe, and the ceaseless rumble of the machinery and paddle-wheels." But the noise of the passengers themselves was loud enough to drown all that out. The main deck, Melville observed, was like "some Constantinople arcade or bazaar." The people were in a continual uproar. There were furious political arguments—Frances Trollope said that "the respective claims of Adams and Jackson to the presidency were argued with more oaths and vehemence than it has ever been my lot to hear." There were the inevitable drunken fights; there were countless touts and hawkers; there were hustlers pitching land deals and charitable trusts and patent medicines; there were singers and fiddlers and actors and buskers at their trade. To the strangers caught up in the crowd, everybody seemed perpetually boorish, rude, rowdy, exuberant, quarrelsome, and drunk.

They all had one great recreation: gambling. The passengers played dice games and card games in endless varieties—rondo and keno and faro, roulette and chuck-a-luck, monte and euchre, rouge et noir and seven-up and old sledge. It was quite probable that at any given moment, every single steamboat on the river had at least one high-stakes game going in the interior cabin and several penny-ante games on deck.

Most often they played poker. Poker was the trademark game of the Mississippi. It had been invented by some anonymous genius in New Orleans sometime around 1820; within the decade it had spread everywhere from the delta to the North Woods. The principal games then were draw poker and stud poker, in essentially the same forms they're played now (although in their first versions, four kings and an ace beat a straight flush). The memory of their origin lingers to this day: the last card dealt in a hand is still called the river card, and betting on it is still "living by the river"; if you lose, it is sometimes said that you have "drowned at the river" or else simply that you have been "rivered."

But the gamblers didn't need poker or any other formal game. They'd bet on anything at all. On the steamboats, they'd bet on the speed of their passage, and the afternoon's weather, and the depth of the river bottom at the next sounding. In the port towns, they'd stagger off roaring drunk to hit up the casinos and gambling houses; if they couldn't find a good game, they'd make any bet they could with a local, even a footrace to the end of the levee. One professional gambler, George Devol, bet a hundred dollars once on whether a fish for sale in a New Orleans market was a catfish or a pike.

They'd bet on anything; they cheated at everything. The professional gamblers routinely used marked cards, either ones they'd marked themselves or decks they'd bought commercially (these were blandly advertised as "advantage decks"), and they had dozens of dizzying ways of stacking clean decks (it was then known as stocking a deck). The gamblers' fancy suits were as tricky as a magician's false-bottomed box. There were whole decks concealed in the sleeves and vests, fanned out in sequence and memorized so that the necessary card could be discreetly fetched to fill a hand. The gamblers also wore mirrored rings and jewels, and they took their snuff from mirrored snuffboxes; they flashed and twinkled and glittered as they played, and every stray reflection off a silver pitcher or a glass behind the bar gave them a glimpse of their opponents' cards.

When they weren't cheating, they were conning. The presence of con men on every steamboat was a given: guidebooks even warned tourists to beware of any stranger striking up a conversation, because it was almost certainly going to be a con. There were con men soliciting subscriptions to orphanages and schools; there were hustlers trading in land claims and in benefits for resettled Native Americans. But probably the most vigorous and inventive of the hustlers were the medicine men. They had an endless array of products for sale: Clark's Famous Anti-Bilious Pills, Great Worm Lozenges, Carmody's Tonic Pills, Radway's Ready Relief for Toothache, Wolcott's Instant Pain Annihilator, Derby Condition Powder,

Piso's Cure for Consumption, and (a particular favorite in New Orleans) Dr. Vandeveer's Medicated Gin and Genuine Scheedam Schnapps, which was advertised as "a wholesome beverage, and an invaluable family medicine, particularly beneficial in all cases of Dysentery, Dyspepsia, Diarrhea, Rhumatism, Gout and Fever." It was, the bottle said, "peculiarly adapted to the use of females and children." As a satirical poem of the time put it:

> For us, new countries are the best,
> Hence we perch down in this far West;
> This is, despite of your attacks,
> A famous stamping ground of quacks.

The poem was "Letter from a Thompsonian Doctor" by James M'Chonochie. Thompsonian doctors—the steam doctors—were a big presence on the river. On the steamboats they couldn't hustle their famous saunas and hot baths; instead they had whole traveling stores of herbal remedies. Their placards read, "If you wish genuine poisons, call at a Genuine Mineral Drug Store; but if you wish genuine Botanic Medicine, call at a genuine Anti-Poisoning Botanic Drug Store." Since orthodox doctors actually were feeding people poisons then (primarily arsenic and mercury), the Thompsonians had a point; in fact, they would have been the most valuable health providers on the frontier if their treatments had only worked. Unfortunately what they were selling were random herbal mixtures, in vials labeled with cryptic numbers, that left people either untreated or worse off than before. Their general efficacy was all too justly summed up by M'Chonochie:

> Our numbers Six, and One Two Three,
> Are drugs of sovereign potency,
> They cure complaints of every name—
> At least, we say so—'tis the same;
> The grave will not disgorge its dead
> To chase our slumbers from our bed.

The con men, of whatever persuasion, generally called themselves sharpers; everybody else they called suckers and greenhorns—there was no greater insult on the river than to refer to somebody as green. The sharpers were so plentiful that they had to work out a quick-and-dirty way of sorting out who was who, so they didn't waste time trying to con each other. That was how they came to use a kind of shorthand code, a password; when they met a stranger on deck, they'd immediately ask, in a tone of idle curiosity:

"Do you live on the river?"

Among the landsmen, the talk wasn't of sharpers and greenhorns but of green thumbs and black thumbs. The green thumbs were the farmers and the builders, the ones who were actually doing the work of planting and cultivating and civilizing the valley; the black thumbs were the river people. But not just the boatmen and the voyageurs and the gamblers: the black thumbs were anybody who made their money by way of the river, because on the river there was no honest business. It was a place, one travel writer observed, where "the very order of civilized society was reversed, and a disorganization of principle, of men and manners, prevailed, to which, or approaching to which, I had never seen a parallel in the whole of my former experience."

The rule in any commercial transaction was that each party was out to cheat the other. People routinely lied and stole with impunity; they took for granted that commerce was indistinguishable from swindling. False weights, ersatz or fraudulent goods, and bait-and-switch sales were the norm. The first thing that apprentices learned on steamboats was how to judge the true weight of a load of wood, because the employees of every wood yard along the river would do everything possible to cheat the steamboats of their fuel. They were particularly fond of hollowing out the interior of a woodpile (which was sold by volume) and hoping the trick wasn't discovered until the boat had pulled back into the river again.

The phantasmal nature of business on the river was best reflected in the money used to conduct it. Honest money was the major issue of the river economy. The only currency generally trusted was specie—the gold and silver coinage of the U.S. Mint. But specie was a rare commodity, partly because people tended to hoard it, but also because the valley's economy was growing so fast that the demand for coin tremendously exceeded the supply. Without specie, most transactions involved barter or some equally rare commodity—coffee or salt, for instance, which were both so scarce in the upper valley that they were more prized than gold.

As a last resort, people could use the paper currency issued by private banks. This was known as commercial money, and it came in a rainbow of dubious and peculiar forms. There were bills known as greenbacks and redbacks and bluebacks, blue pup and red horse, rag tag and stump tail. People across the valley skirmished through deals involving paper money with the same fantastic ingenuity shown by the arbitrageurs and derivatives traders of the modern world. Word might come into a river town by way of a steamboat that a particularly well-known form of commercial money was now trading at substantially below face value in New Orleans or St. Louis; all over town, people holding it would immediately rush to spend it, preferably at stores where the clerks hadn't yet heard the news. But if they got hold of specie, they would keep it until they could make a deal to sell it. Specie routinely traded for much higher than face.

Knowing what varieties of money could be trusted was an unending hassle. Paper issued by banks of uncertain solvency or legality was generally called wildcat money. It was a major challenge to avoid taking wildcat money—or, if you had it, to lay it off on somebody else as fast as possible. Meanwhile, the paper from known and respected banks was rated almost as highly as specie. This naturally led to another problem: it spawned hordes of counterfeits. Counterfeiting came to be regarded on the river as a particularly heinous crime. Anybody suspected of passing counterfeit money was immediately arrested, brought before a lynching court, and flogged; anybody found in possession of blank paper that could possibly be used to print fakes was branded; anybody who had plates etched with currency patterns would most likely be put to death.

The long-range movement of the steamboats greatly facilitated the spread of wildcat and counterfeit currency, adding to the constant tension between the river and the shore. By midcentury, periodicals known as detectors had sprung up to help businessmen on both sides assess the legitimacy of the paper currently in circulation and identify the telltale marks of known counterfeits. The most trusted detector on the river was *The Western Bank Note Reporter and Counterfeit Detector,* a weekly periodical published in St. Louis and distributed by steamboat. Every store and business in the large towns had a subscription; well-prepared traveling businessmen invariably brought a copy along to potential sales. Sooner or later all transactions would come down to a long, suspicious session of scrutiny and negotiation and reconsultation with the current issue of the detector, as the notes were passed around, examined, questioned, argued about, and fought over.

Melville describes such a scene in *The Confidence-Man*. Two characters, with the aid of a detector, exhaustively inspect something that "looks to be a three-dollar bill on the Vicksburgh Trust and Insurance Banking Company." As they argue, the elusiveness of the bill in front of them starts to make the whole concept of the genuine seem like a will-o'-the-wisp:

> "The Detector says, among fifty other things, that, if a good bill, it must have, thickened here and there into the substance of the paper, little wavy spots of red; and it says they must have a kind of silky feel, being made by the lint of a red silk handkerchief stirred up in the papermaker's vat—the paper being made to order for the company."
>
> "Well, and is—"
>
> "Stay. But then it adds, that sign is not always to be relied on; for some good bills get so worn, the red marks get rubbed out. And that's the case with my bill here—see how old it is—or else it's a counterfeit, or else—I don't see right—or else—dear, dear me—I don't know what else to think." . . . "Stay, now, here's another sign. It says that, if the bill is good, it must have in one corner, mixed in with the vignette, the figure of a goose, very small, indeed, all but microscopic; and, for added precaution, like the figure of Napoleon outlined by the tree, not observable, even if magnified, unless the attention is directed to it. Now, pore over it as I will, I can't see this goose."
>
> "Can't see the goose? why, I can; and a famous goose it is." . . .
>
> "Then throw that Detector away, I say again; it only makes you purblind; don't you see what a wild-goose chase it has led you? The bill is good. Throw the Detector away."

9

A Pile of Shavings

WHEN TRAVELERS ARRIVED at the Mississippi by way of the Gulf of Mexico, the first sign of human habitation they came to was a town of sorts known as the Balize. It was a ramshackle cluster of half-collapsed wooden shanties and lean-tos standing knee-deep in the brackish water of the estuary and linked by a jerry-rigged tangle of rotting piers and pontoons. It served as a station for the river pilots who would take over the wheel of the tall ships for the last tricky leg of their journey through the delta upriver to New Orleans. The population consisted of around a hundred pilots, maybe fifty or so of their wives and children, and twenty or thirty prostitutes. Frances Trollope called it "by far the most miserable station that I ever saw made the dwelling of man."

There were better places ahead. Early in the nineteenth century St. Louis was a vision of loveliness: a small cluster of ornate stucco buildings in the Spanish and French styles standing on a high bluff at the confluence of the Mississippi and the Missouri. There were towns like Alexandria and Keokuk, Davenport and Dubuque—towns like collections of white clapboard dollhouses, with skylines of spiky church steeples and picturesque scatterings of steamboats and flatboats bobbing on the blue waters below. Their streets were laid out in neat checkerboards. Their business districts had brick storefronts. Many residences had windows of glass—a reliable mark of middle-class prosperity (the basic frontier cabin window was a sheet of parchment paper rubbed with bear grease to make it translucent). Some towns even had statues of their founders in their public squares.

But such places were never the norm. The average river town, as seen from the deck of a steamboat, was a graceless, muddy, purely functional place—no more than a huddle of shoddy buildings knocked together out of the local lumber, standing at one of the innumerable river junctions. It served as a supply depot or a transshipment point for the river traffic, and it was inevitably dominated by a row of hulking warehouses along the levee. The only retail business of note was a general store, where boatmen could stock up on basic supplies—dried meats, beans, flour and sugar, bolts of coarse fabric, tubs of lye soap—and which always stank from the open barrels of vinegar and kerosene. Behind the levee, on the straggling backstreets, there was inevitably a bunch of saloons, and up the back stairs behind any one of them was certain to be a brothel.

Travelers found these places wearying and depressing. "I thought all the little towns and villages we passed," Frances Trollope wrote of her steamboat trip upriver, "wretched-looking in the extreme." They seemed to merge into one enormous shantytown that stretched all the way from the delta to St. Louis and beyond. They were dreary, anonymous, filthy, and disease-ridden—and they were firetraps.

John Bunyan's *Pilgrim's Progress*—the only book that any literate person in the river valley was sure to have read—is about a man's desperate search for a town where the buildings are fireproof. Most readers take this as an allegory, and with good reason: the hero is named Christian, he lives in the City of Destruction, and the fireproof refuge he ultimately finds is the Celestial City. But the readers on the Mississippi felt Christian's dilemma on a much more visceral level. Their towns really were at the edge of fiery ruin; the threat of death in a blazing inferno was a daily terror. But there was no journeying to a safer place. The city that wouldn't burn was as remote as heaven.

Every building in the average river town was made of wood; stone and brick construction didn't become common until much later in the century. The buildings were heaped on top of each other with little planning and were built to no particular standard. The result was a maze of shanties set at irregular and unpredictable angles, strewn with spidery staircases and connected by rickety walkways. The heating, when there was any, was provided by woodstoves with spindly flues that exhaled still-glowing cinders that would fall into neighboring yards and blow through nearby windows. One unlucky spark and in moments the whole edifice was in flames.

There were so many fires in the river towns that people refused to believe they could have an innocent explanation. Stories were constantly circulating about mysterious gangs of incendiaries at work in the river valley who were setting the fires for some occult purpose of their own. The most common theory, particularly in the years leading up to the Civil War, was that they were disgruntled slaves and infiltrating abolitionists trying to foment a revolution. But these gangs proved to be elusive spirits—never caught, never even identified. Only once did the people of Natchez corner somebody they believed to be a member: a local loudmouth who'd been heard offering to bet that a particular downtown block would be on fire within a week. The man was almost put to death. But the townspeople concluded at the last minute that he wasn't an incendiary at all, merely a drunken fool.

What made the threat of fires particularly nightmarish was the absence of professional firemen. Towns had volunteer night watches, and all able-bodied men were required by local ordinance to respond whenever the night watch raised the alarm. Some towns did have fire engines—horse-drawn wagons equipped with ladders and buckets and hand pumps. But these rarely went to good use. After a major fire in St. Louis in 1825, a newspaper report found "buckets broken and without handles, and not half enough of these; the engines unfit for service; everyone gaping at the fire instead of forming a line to convey water."

St. Louis eventually became the first city on the river to hire and train a professional fire department. The local authorities had no choice. Fires were becoming a major threat to the city's survival. By the 1840s St. Louis was the largest city in the American interior: a maze of wood shanties and factories, infamous for the inferno of heat on its streets in the summer and the storms of fiery cinders blown down from the smokestacks that blackened the snow all winter. Frederick Marryat wrote that St. Louis "approaches the nearest to the Black Hole of Calcutta of any city that I have sojourned in." Some longtime residents called it "the city built above Hell."

But it was also a rich and progressive city; some boosters claimed that it would inevitably replace Washington, D.C., as the capital of the new American empire. It was particularly renowned for its levee, a long promenade where more than a hundred steamboats arrived and departed each day. On May 17, 1849, a small fire broke out at the levee's north end, on a steamboat called the *White Cloud*. The night watch spotted it almost immediately. But by then it was already too late. The steamboat was built entirely of white pine, and, as the official history of the St. Louis Fire Department later noted, once on fire anything made of white pine "is as impossible to save as a pile of shavings."

There was barely even a need for the night watch to sound the alarm: the boat burned so fiercely that the glare could be seen all over the city. The fire department hurtled to the docks in their nine fire engines. They found that there was little they could do. The fire had already reached the *White Cloud*'s waterline and the boat was a dead loss. But that was not the end of it. The moorings burned through, and the burning wreck drifted downriver with the current and began bumping against the other steamboats lined up along the levee. They, too, caught fire; their moorings also burned, and they were set loose. They in turn started fires on other boats, and soon there were twenty-three steamboats burning.

Then the fire jumped to the warehouses along the levee. The fire department had been attempting ineffectually to prevent the last of the steamboats from catching fire; now they had to watch helplessly as the flames fanned out into the riverfront. Over the next several hours the fires burned their way through the warehouse district and into some of the oldest residential neighborhoods before reaching the central commercial district. By dawn hundreds of downtown buildings were on fire, including three of the city's largest banks and the central post office.

The fire department then made a move of desperation. They planted gunpowder charges and blew up a long row of commercial buildings to form a firebreak. One of the lead firefighters, Captain Thomas B. Targee, was throwing a powder keg through the window of a music store when it ignited; the fire department history says "he was blown to atoms." (He was later honored as the first professional fireman in America to die in the line of duty.) But the plan worked: the firebreak held. To the incredulity of the whole city, the flames didn't jump the gap. By midafternoon some of the worst fires were burning out. The area around the riverfront was a smoking ruin—the burned stumps of the buildings went on smoldering for weeks and the levee was devastated (though within days, its docks were rebuilt and steamboats were stacked three deep in the river waiting for their turn)—but the city had been saved by its firemen.

The St. Louis fire became famous around the world. It wouldn't be displaced in the public consciousness till the great fire in Chicago two decades later. It led to the formation of professional fire departments in cities across America, and it inspired ordinances throughout the river valley requiring all new buildings to be constructed of brick or stone. St. Louis itself passed the first such ordinance, and the city began its transformation into the monstrous hulk of sooty red brick that it had become by the end of the century.

Even the most gracious and beautiful towns on the river, one writer observed, showed "to much the greatest advantage at a distance." No traveler enjoyed the experience of a river town close up. They were notoriously squalid. They had no indoor plumbing; people simply emptied their night soil into the alleys and waited for a rainstorm or a flood to wash it away. In summer the stench and the swarms of flies were unendurable, and it was said that you couldn't walk a few feet down any block without treading on the putrid corpse of a dog or a pig half buried in the mud of the unpaved streets.

The concept of public health was still in embryo. Most communities on the river had nothing more than a few ordinances concerning cleanliness, and these were usually about the selling of tainted food. But even these were useless, because the origin of food contamination was almost always unknown. In the 1810s and 1820s, a mysterious illness killed thousands of people in the central valley (one of those who died was Abraham Lincoln's mother): it was known by a variety of vivid names, including the shakes, the slows, and puke fever. But it was most often called the milk sick, because it was believed to be caused by tainted cow's milk. People blamed the taint on the bite of a (nonexistent) insect known as the milk-sick fly; another theory was that the cows were poisoning themselves by licking the dew off the meadow grasses (everybody knew that dew was poisonous). In fact, the cows were being poisoned by eating white snakeroot, which grew abundantly in the meadows of the central valley. Although this was discovered independently several times, decades passed before farmers learned to weed out white snakeroot from their pasturage—and in the meantime, they were still selling the milk to the river merchants, who were carrying it as far downriver from the areas of known infection as they could before putting it up for resale.

That was another source of resentment between the river and the towns: the river traffic scattered diseases everywhere just as casually as it dispersed counterfeit money. All the conditions of the valley—the squalor and overcrowding of the towns, the absence of basic sanitation, the ignorance of fundamental principles of medicine (particularly antisepsis), and, most of all, the free movement up and down the river of the steamboats—made the river the perfect environment for the rapid spread of disease. The Unitarian minister Theodore Clapp wrote in his memoirs that in his thirty-five years in the river valley, he lived through twenty major epidemics.

The outbreaks came in great recurring waves: smallpox, diphtheria, measles, mumps, influenza, malaria, typhus. Several other diseases showed up only once, killed thousands of people, and disappeared without a trace—some leaving names behind, but no real clue as to what they were. People were reported to have died of dew poisoning, ground itch, woods fever, dog fever, locked bowels, the summer complaint, and congestion of the brain.

These epidemics were the ceaseless subject of conversation everywhere on the river—particularly in the hot weather, when outbreaks tended to be at their worst. The talk was always of what towns were afflicted with something new and terrifying, and of where there were sudden quarantines, and of which were enforced by armed committees. Herman Melville wrote about the season's current epidemics as though he were a gossip columnist passing on the latest about local affairs:

> At Cairo, the old established firm of Fever & Ague is still settling up its unfinished business; that Creole grave-digger, Yellow Jack—his hand at the mattock and spade has not lost its cunning; while Don Saturninus Typhus, taking his constitutional with Death, Calvin Edson and three undertakers, in the morass, snuffs up the mephitic breeze with zest.

Calvin Edson was a kind of performance artist, a man with a mysterious wasting disease who toured the country as the Living Skeleton. That made him a natural associate for this sinister crew: fever and ague (usually seen together), typhus ("Don" because it was believed to have originated in Spain; "Saturninus" because infected people were known for their air of sluggish gloom), and, perhaps the most ominous figure of all, "Yellow Jack."

Yellow jack is what the river people called yellow fever. It was consistently the most dreaded disease in the valley. It was endemic in the Caribbean and the Gulf of Mexico—which is why Melville described it as "Creole"—and it tended to ebb and flow up the river valley according to how hot and wet the summers were and how far north the mosquitoes that carried it were hatching. People didn't know that yellow jack was connected to the mosquitoes (that wouldn't be established until the twentieth century), but they did somehow sense it. In many towns, there were pioneering public health campaigns to drain all stagnant ponds and pools during yellow fever outbreaks. Their reasoning was faulty, since they believed that night mist from the pools was the cause of the disease, but the impulse was right, because the mosquitoes were breeding in the standing water. There was also a widespread custom of warding off yellow jack by taking a big jolt of rye whiskey just before bedtime. This was sometimes called a mosquito dose because it was thought, or hoped, to prevent mosquito bites.

The other epidemics came and went, disappeared and then roared back after decades of quiescence out of some forgotten river pesthole; new diseases like cholera burst out of nowhere and panicked the entire river valley; yellow jack remained. People never failed to regard it with dread. Of all the plagues that visited them, Theodore Clapp wrote, "there is none more shocking and repulsive to the beholder." He cataloged the signs of yellow jack at its peak: not only its unmistakable black vomit from blood in the lungs, but "profuse hemorrhages from the mouth, nose, ears, eyes, and even the toes; the eyes prominent, glistening, yellow, and staring; the face discolored with orange color and dusky red." Then there was the sight of a yellow jack corpse, which Clapp grew to know intimately. The expression on the face was "sad, sullen, and perturbed"; the skin was "dark, mottled, livid, swollen, and stained with blood and black vomit"; and even after death "the veins of the face and whole body become distended, and look as if they were going to burst."

The river people would fly flags to warn off other boats during epidemics: red was a general announcement of a quarantine, yellow meant yellow jack. Sometimes a steamboat would come around a bend and find that the town ahead was flying yellow flags from every church steeple and rooftop and sheets of yellow were fluttering from the warehouse windows along the now-deserted levee. In the boat cities, everyone was constantly scrutinizing strangers for the telltale early signs—the yellow skin and eyes, the hint of a nosebleed or a drop of red brimming from an eyelid. Every encounter was a tense standoff when Old Yellow Jack was abroad on the river.

Nobody had heard of cholera in North America before 1832, when there was an outbreak in Montreal. It was a terrifying plague even for a population used to plagues: extraordinarily contagious, it had a high fatality rate and progressed through the body with stunning rapidity. People in perfect health at noon could be torn apart by convulsive and violent diarrhea in the late afternoon and be dead by nightfall. There were many cases where the interval between first symptoms and death was three hours.

Cholera is transmitted by the fluids expelled by an infected person and can be contracted from clothes, sheets, raw foods, and drinking water. None of this was known until much later—but, as with yellow jack, people did obscurely sense the connections. It can be seen in this urgent public health warning posted at the height of the outbreak:

BE TEMPERATE IN EATING AND DRINKING! Avoid Raw Vegetables and Unripe Fruit! Abstain from COLD WATER, when heated, and above all from Ardent Spirits, and if habit have rendered them indispensable, take much less than usual. SLEEP AND CLOTHE WARM! DO NOT SIT OR SLEEP IN A DRAUGHT OF AIR! AVOID GETTING WET!

By late spring, the epidemic had spread down the East Coast and was beginning to show up in the American interior. There was a particularly bad outbreak among Irish immigrants crossing the Great Lakes on packet steamboats bound for Indiana and Ohio. A few weeks later, some of those

Poling a keelboat against the current, circa 1800
(Pittsburgh History and Landmarks Foundation)

A drawing of a houseboat by Alfred Waud, a British-born illustrator of
Civil War and frontier themes
(Louisiana Digital Library)

The Great Earthquake at New Madrid, Missouri. A nineteenth-century woodcut from R. M. Devens's *Our First Century.* The 1811–12 New Madrid earthquakes were the strongest recorded in the continental United States.

Fog on the Mississippi, circa 1840. Note the flatboat in the foreground about to be struck.
(Center for Louisiana Studies)

A broadside advertising a lecture by Montroville Dickeson. During the nineteenth century, Dickeson excavated and lectured about hundreds of sites along the Mississippi, including those of the Native American Mound Builders.
(Courtesy of the University of Pennsylvania Museum Archives, Dickeson Collection)

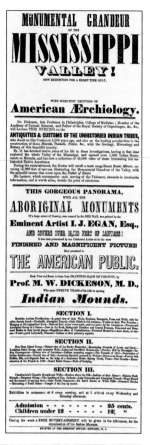

Huge Mounds and the Manner of Opening Them. A scene from the *Panorama of the Monumental Grandeur of the Mississippi Valley,* which the Irish-born artist John J. Egan painted from Montroville Dickeson's sketches.
(Saint Louis Art Museum)

Murder of Woods, the South Carolinian. An illustration showing the outlaw John Murrell and an associate disposing of a victim, from *The Life and Adventures of John A. Murrell, the Great Western Land Pirate, with Twenty-one Spirited Illustrative Engravings,* 1847.

Our Peculiar Domestic Institutions. Life in the lower valley: duels, brawls, slave torture, and the lynching of the Vicksburg gamblers during the insurrection hysteria. From the *Anti-Slavery Almanac* for 1840, New York.
(Library of Congress)

The Shirley in Vicksburg—known as the White House to soldiers on both sides during the Civil War—circa 1863. The caves served as bombproof shelters for the Forty-fifth Illinois Regiment.
(Library of Congress)

A Currier and Ives lithograph of Admiral David Porter's fleet running the Rebel blockade of the Mississippi at Vicksburg, April 16, 1863
(Library of Congress)

A newspaper depiction of the Mardi Gras celebration in New Orleans, March 6, 1867
(Library of Congress)

The Champions of the Mississippi: A Race for the Buckhorns. A lithograph by Currier and Ives of a steamboat race, 1866.
(Library of Congress)

The ill-fated *Sultana,* in Helena, Arkansas, on its last voyage, April 27, 1865
(Library of Congress)

The *Sultana*'s end. This illustration first appeared in *Harper's Weekly* on May 20, 1865.
(Library of Congress)

A photograph of the great levee at St. Louis, by Hoelke and Benecke circa 1860
(Library of Congress)

The construction of the Eads Bridge in St. Louis, Missouri, early 1870s
(Library of Congress)

same steamboats were requisitioned by the federal government for a military convoy: thirteen hundred troops were on their way to Illinois to put down a fierce resistance movement that had sprung up among the Native American nations along the Mississippi. (The fighting became known, after the resistance leader, as the Black Hawk War.) Conditions on board were suffocatingly close and casually filthy. The steamboats hadn't been cleaned since the cholera outbreak—nobody had a clue that this mattered. By the time the convoy crossed into Lake Michigan, there was a full-blown epidemic.

The military commanders of the convoy understood the rudiments of quarantine. They ordered the pilots to keep the boats in the deep waters, and when they came into port, there were armed guards posted to make sure the soldiers remained belowdecks. But the boats also had to make frequent stops to refuel at the wood yards along the Lake Michigan shore. Every time the boats got anywhere near the beaches, the soldiers began jumping overboard. Once they were on land, it was only a few steps until they were hidden within the dense forests that grew down to the shoreline. Few of them were ever recaptured. Meanwhile, the death toll was rising on board, and the bodies weren't being quarantined; they were simply thrown into the lake, and they were washing up onto the beaches all the rest of that summer.

By the time the convoy reached Fort Dearborn, on the western shore of Lake Michigan, the expeditionary force had been obliterated. Of the thirteen hundred troops, only two hundred were still fit for combat. The rest were sick or had died or jumped ship. The surviving force was kept in quarantine and never saw any action in the Black Hawk War. The commanders' one consolation was that they had prevented the epidemic from reaching the river valley.

The rest of that summer, there were no reports of outbreaks anywhere in the western Great Lakes. In fact the cholera was simply out of sight; it had been carried inland by the deserters and by the infected corpses washed ashore. But the new cases were still confined to remote and isolated fishing communities deep in the wilderness country. Whole villages could be wiped out and it would be months before the outside world even noticed.

Then that autumn, cholera erupted down the length of the Mississippi.

In the first few weeks of the outbreak, tens of thousands of people died—orders of magnitude greater than the casualties of the Black Hawk War. Quarantines were set up, and sometimes violently enforced, all the way to the delta. But they were useless. At the first signs of infection, people bolted. Thousands scattered from St. Louis when the epidemic reached it; many of them were already infected, and the ones who fled up the Missouri brought cholera into the Great Plains. (The following year, it spread beyond the Rockies and into the Pacific Northwest.) Those escaping downriver carried it to New Orleans. Within days, the city had turned into a ghost town. All the stores were shut, the commercial district and the levee were deserted, and everybody who could afford to leave the city was gone. "There were no means, no instruments for carrying on the ordinary affairs of business," Theodore Clapp wrote in his memoirs, "for all the drays, carts, carriages, hand and common wheelbarrows, as well as hearses, were employed in the transportation of corpses."

The epidemic rapidly overwhelmed New Orleans's frail infrastructure of public health. Hospitals were packed; one hospital was found abandoned by its staff, with every bed occupied by a bloated and putrid corpse. (By order of the mayor, the bodies were carried out to a yard next to the hospital grounds and burned.) The scenes at the cemeteries were chaotic. People were simply bringing in their dead and leaving them without ceremony, uncoffined, to await disposal. "Words cannot describe my sensations," Clapp wrote, "when I first beheld the awful sight of carts driven to the graveyard, and there upturned, and their contents discharged as so many loads of lumber or offal, without a single mark of mourning or respect." At one cemetery he found that the bodies were being stacked up in layers, "like corded wood." Periodically, whenever there were around a hundred bodies in the pile, a work crew would shovel them into a trench and cover them over with dirt, and start a new pile.

The city officials of New Orleans did have an emergency plan to halt the epidemic: it was to attempt to purify the atmosphere of its poisonous vapors. To accomplish this task, they positioned big barrels of tar and pitch on the street corners and set them ablaze. They also ordered the military to fire off cannon around the city at steady intervals—this would, they believed, disperse the worst of the river fog (which was thought to be particularly deadly). The sparks from the burning barrels set off major fires throughout the city; the noise of the cannon, Clapp observed, was so nerve-shattering that he suspected many people were dying of sheer fright.

Clapp himself wandered the streets nightly, visiting hospitals and sick houses. By then the epidemic had spread to every quarter of the city: the shanty districts were the hardest hit, as ever, but soon even the richest mansion districts were in mourning. "Many persons," Clapp wrote, "of fortune and popularity, died in their beds without aid, unnoticed and unknown, and lay there for days unburied. In almost every house might be seen the sick, the dying, and the dead, in the same room." Meanwhile, the city had taken on a hellish splendor at night. The skyline was silhouetted by the endless flickerings of the artillery fire, and from every direction came thunderings and rumblings as though from dozens of battlegrounds. The barrels of tar were burning at the intersections; along the levee, so many phalanxes of barrels were on fire that the river and the low-hanging clouds were lit up bright as day. The glare of the fires flooded the endless rows of windows along the streets. Within, Clapp wrote, "could be seen persons struggling in death, and rigid, blackened corpses, awaiting the arrival of some cart or hearse, as soon as dawn appeared, to transport them to their final resting place."

It might have been the end of the world—except, of course, that it wasn't. It was just another epidemic. As the bodies went on accumulating through the nightmarish days of that autumn and winter, the living had no choice but to resume their business. The river traffic kept arriving. The big ships came in daily from the Balize. Gradually, unobtrusively, the cemeteries caught up with the backlog of corpses. And then in the spring everyone was suddenly worried about outbreaks of measles along the Gulf Coast, and by the next summer Old Yellow Jack was on the move again.

The terror receded, but it never went away. Cholera remained endemic on the river and flared up again spectacularly several more times. New Orleans saw an even worse outbreak in 1853, and another in 1866. But by then they were taken as normal, part of the expected routine of horror in the place that one writer called "the city of pestilence and death."

10

The Coasts of Dark Destruction

NEW ORLEANS WAS A SQUALID CITY, even by the standards of the river valley. The sewer system was a network of open trenches perpetually backed up with dead animals, putrid water, and rotting refuse. Garbage built up into hills and festered in the alleys and in the middle of the streets. Trash was collected in some districts, but it was merely carted off to what were known as nuisance wharves and thrown into the river, and it immediately washed back onto the levee. (Eventually the city obtained "nuisance barges" to carry the garbage a hundred yards or so into the river before dumping it.) New Orleans, one British traveler wrote, "affects painfully the olfactory nerves of all who prefer the odors of the rose to those of the cesspool."

It was also an extraordinarily violent city. Duels, rare elsewhere in the lower valley, were daily occurrences; manslaughter and murderous assaults were common. "A frightful deluge of human blood flows through our streets and our places of public resort," said an editorial in *The New Orleans Bee* in 1836. "Whither will such contempt for the life of man lead us?" An anonymous pamphlet writer noted a few years later: "We have just been looking over a broken file of Louisiana papers, including the last six months of 1837 and the whole of 1838, and find ourselves obliged to abandon our design of publishing even an abstract of the scores and *hundreds* of affrays, murders, assassinations, lynchings, etc, which took place during that period."

The violence was fueled by the desperate overcrowding, by the wild currents of wealth running through the economy, and by the waves of immigrants arriving daily. The city had Creoles, Cajuns, Germans, Spaniards, Italians, Mexicans, Danes, Portuguese, Belgians, and free people of color from the West Indies and South America—all of whom were at various times feuding with at least one of the other groups. The longest-running tensions were between the Americans and Northern Europeans on the one side and the Spaniards and Creoles on the other; there were skirmishes and sometimes full-scale riots on the streets until the Civil War.

But it was also a beautiful city. The graceful crescent of white-pillared buildings along the levee was said to be the loveliest urban vista in the New World. The salt air from the Gulf rotted the stucco in curious and delicate ways; buildings only a few years old looked as mysterious as Roman ruins. The skyline was shrouded in fogs and river mists, and the shifting play of tropical light across the pastel-painted walls, with their weatherings and peelings and blotchings, was perpetually alluring and magical. The surrounding landscape added to the air of a dream. The mass of domes and cupolas and steeples floated within a maze of impassable bayous, alligator-haunted sloughs, and dim, receding forest halls of cypress cloaked in Spanish moss; the remote, sinister lagoons glimpsed from the arriving boats looked like the sunlight hadn't penetrated them for generations.

The thing that most struck travelers arriving at the harbor was the sound. "Astonishing," the architect Benjamin Latrobe described it in his diaries: "a sound more strange than any that is heard anywhere else in the world." It came floating past the turmoil of boats and ships along the levee: "a most incessant, loud, rapid, and various gabble of tongues of all tones that were ever heard at Babel." The French traveler Marie de Grand-fort described it as "a strange concert of oaths, questions, cries, and savage noises." She heard "the *by God* of the Yankee, the *per la madona* of the Italian, the *carumba* of the Spaniard, the *Diou bibant* of the Gascon, the gutteral *Goddam* of the Irish." Latrobe wrote: "It is more to be compared with the sounds that issue from an extensive marsh, the residence of a million or two of frogs, from bullfrogs up to whistlers, than to anything else."

The sound came from the great market on the levee. Between the river and the warehouses, there were hundreds of booths, stalls, and tables in a line more than a mile long. Latrobe described the sellers: "White men and women, and of all hues of brown, and of all classes of faces, from round Yankees to grizzly and lean Spaniards, black negroes and negresses, filthy Indians half naked, mulattoes curly and straight-haired, quadroons of all shades, long haired and frizzled, women dressed in the most flaring yellow and scarlet gowns, the men capped and hatted." Their goods, laid out in the shade of ragged canvas tents and awnings or set on palmetto leaves fanned out on the ground, formed a garish collage of strange colors and textures and smells. There were fresh fish in endless profusion and cuts of what Latrobe thought "wretched" red meat (a lot of it had arrived in port already butchered and in the hot climate was getting rank). There were wild ducks and other game fowl, shellfish and poultry and eggs, Irish pota-toes and sweet potatoes, root vegetables of all sorts, pyramids of oranges, heaps of bananas and ears of corn, oozing stacks of sugarcane, and all manner of dry goods and tinned goods, curios and trinkets—there were, Latrobe said, "more and odder things to be sold in that manner and place than I can numerate." Latrobe was particularly surprised to find book-stalls; something of a collector, he was delighted to turn up, among the saints' lives and the deeds of notorious criminals, a rare set of bound vol-umes of political pamphlets from the Revolutionary War.

But large and garish as the market was, it was only a pocket curio itself amid the immense movements of cargo through the port. The harbor was swarmed: there was an armada of schooners and freighters from the Gulf, and of rafts and barges and flatboats and keelboats from upriver; the steamboats clustered in such mobs that they were sometimes stacked four deep waiting for a turn at the levee. All around the levee crews unloaded cargo. The warehouses were overflowing with the harvest of the river val-ley and with the manufactured goods coming in from the North and from overseas. In the shadowy coolness of the arched warehouse interiors were mountain ranges of barrels and crates and tuns and hogsheads: fine silk from China and crude ingots of lead from Iowa, handcrafted furniture from France and raw pine lumber from Minnesota, perfumes from the Middle East and rye whiskey from Pennsylvania. All kinds of basic goods were waiting for transport up the river—coffee, salt, flat-head nails, vine-gar, whale oil, rolls of gingham, and crates of window glass. There was also quite a lot of food coming in, not only tinned delicacies from Europe but staple foods—flour and grains and legumes, enormous barrels of beef and pork—and corrals and pens were crammed with livestock. And spilling out from all the warehouses were the goods for export—the cotton bales, the raw sugarcane, the sheaves of tobacco. Millions of bales of cotton were transshipped through New Orleans every year, along with hundreds of thousands of hogsheads of sugarcane and tens of thousands of hogsheads of tobacco. Almost all of it was bound for New York for consignment sale in New England and in Europe. The planters of the lower valley dealt exclusively with brokers, factors, and commission men in New York City and had no direct dealings with their ultimate buyers around the world. The outflow of cotton and sugarcane was growing every year, making New Orleans and the lower valley enormously rich—but also building up destabilizing pressures in the regional economy that would shortly prove catastrophic. No one cared much, as long as the money was pouring in. But there was a reason why the levee was groaning under that weight of imported food and livestock. Even though the lower valley had some of the most fertile agricultural land in the world, so much of it had been planted with cotton and sugar that by midcentury the region was no longer self-sufficient in food.

If there was a heart to the city, it was down from the old French Quarter, behind the warehouse district at the southwest curve of the waterfront crescent. This was the American Quarter. Its great landmark was the St. Charles Hotel, a neoclassical construction with an enormous dome—the first sight of the city skyline for travelers coming downriver. It was the hotel of choice for planters in town to meet with their local brokers and factors. It was also where buyers went when they were in the market for cheap slaves. A regular auction was held in the hotel rotunda. The slaves sold there were the most defiant, the most recalcitrant, the sickliest, and the feeblest in New Orleans; the bidding would start at two or three hundred dollars and rarely went much higher. But then, the buyers weren't particular. Most of them were looking for fresh fodder for the sugarcane plantations of the lower delta, where conditions were notoriously brutal and where slaves didn't have a long life expectancy. It was largely because of these sugar plantations that the New Orleans public auctions were universally viewed by the slaves with such horror: all through the valley, the threat of being "sold down the river" was seen as tantamount to a death sentence.

Most of the slaves who passed through New Orleans weren't sold at auction, though, but at the slave yards. The big yards were mainly clustered in the side streets around the St. Charles. They were called yards because they were old-style French buildings with open-air courtyards. They were decorated and maintained with dignified good taste. When customers arrived, the slaves for sale would be brought out into the court-yard (or, if the weather was foul, into a long interior hall or ballroom) and arranged in rows so they could be inspected. The mood was generally low-key, even pleasant. The slaves were well dressed—the women in gorgeous calico dresses with rainbow-spattered bandannas, the men in dark blue suits with ties and vests and dignified beaver hats. On sunny days when there were no customers, they would be sent out to the sidewalk, where they would tease and laugh and pass the time of day with passersby.

Not all the customers were charmed by the show. The Swedish traveler Fredrika Bremer toured several of the yards near the St. Charles. She found them to be civilized-seeming institutions—the slaves all appeared happy and well treated—not resembling at all the sadistic hellholes described by the most rabid of the Northern abolitionists. "I saw nothing especially repulsive in these places," she wrote, "excepting the whole thing."

The geniality of the atmosphere was of course a charade. Henry Bibb, who was sold at one of the yards, described in his autobiography how the slaves were prepared to play their part. By ten o'clock each morning they had to be spiffed up, their hair combed and their faces washed. "Those who were inclined to look dark and rough, were compelled to wash in greasy dish water, in order to make them look slick and lively." Slaves who slouched when they were in line, were sullen, or didn't answer questions cheerfully and promptly were punished as soon as the buyers left. The instrument of their punishment was a paddle—a whip would leave marks. Bibb became an authority on this:

The paddle is made of a piece of hickory timber, about one inch thick, three inches in width, and about eighteen inches in length. The part which is applied to the flesh is bored full of quarter inch auger holes, and every time this is applied to the flesh of the victim, the blood gushes through the holes of the paddle, or a blister makes its appearance. The persons who are thus flogged, are always stripped naked, and their hands tied together. They are then bent over double, their knees are forced between their elbows, and a stick is put through between the elbows and the bend of the legs, in order to hold the victim in that position, while the paddle is applied to those parts of the body which would not be so likely to be seen by those who wanted to buy slaves.

On average, a slave sold at the yards for somewhere between seven hundred and twelve hundred dollars. Skilled slaves—blacksmiths or coopers, for instance—cost more, usually at least fifteen hundred dollars. Slaves who were known to be able to read and write (they often kept their literacy secret) went for far less, sometimes for closeout prices, five hundred dollars at the most. They were considered highly undesirable, since they were believed to be the smartest and therefore the biggest flight risks.

The most expensive slaves for sale in New Orleans couldn't be obtained at either the auctions or the yards. These were the slave girls sold for sex. They were called fancy girls, and they went for thirty-five hundred up to five thousand dollars. The dealers in fancy girls had their own private showrooms, some of which were by invitation only. But others were advertised openly on street-corner placards and in newspapers. The British traveler Robert Everest, on his way downriver, spent a night in Baton Rouge and discovered that fancy girls were the ordinary talk among gentlemen in the public room of his hotel. One group was "discussing the merits of the different dealers in 'fancy girls' at New Orleans, and their respective stocks, with as much gusto as amateurs of pictures or race-horses."

Fancy girls were bought mostly by plantation owners; the gentlemen of the town made other arrangements. There was an elaborate social network in place by which they would take young women of color as mistresses. The caste system was based on proportions of African blood: from white through octoroon, quadroon, mulatto, and griffe to full Negro. Girls who were octoroon or quadroon were considered suitable as mistresses; the others were fit only to work in the brothels. The men would select these mistresses at formal social affairs known as quadroon balls. They were lavish events. The travel writer Edward Robert Sullivan attended one; admission was a half-dollar, and he was politely asked to check his "implements"—knives, pistols, and other weaponry—at the door. "You leave them as you would your overcoat on going into the opera," he wrote, "and get a ticket with their number, and on your way out they are returned to you. You hear the pistol and bowie-knife keeper in the arms-room call out, 'No. 46—a six-barrelled repeater.' 'No. 100—one eight-barrelled revolver, and bowie knife with a death's-head and cross-bones cut on the handle.' 'No. 95—a brace of double-barrels.' All this is done as naturally as possible, and you see fellows fasten on their knives and pistols as coolly as if they were tying on a comforter or putting on a coat." Sullivan himself had to submit to a search by a policeman who refused to believe that he was unarmed.

Inside, Sullivan reported, all was glamour. The beauty and charm of the young women, their social skills, their lovely gowns, and the elegance of their dancing were all intoxicating. "I had heard a great deal of the splendid figures and graceful dancing of the New Orleans quadroons," he wrote, "and I certainly was not disappointed. Their movements are the most easy and graceful that I have ever seen. . . . I never saw more perfect dancing on any stage." It was a pity he wasn't himself in the market for a mistress—but then he was a transient, after all, and a quadroon girl wouldn't have made a suitable companion back home.

Strangers found New Orleans a threatening city—particularly Southern strangers, who were disturbed by how little was done to keep the races apart. Free Negroes and slaves were allowed to gather in large numbers in the public squares, and they were known sometimes to mock and taunt white passersby. That was unheard of anywhere else in the lower valley or the South. Prosperous men of color were openly invited into the homes of white aristocrats. The Catholic Church maintained separate parishes for the Creoles, the Irish, and the Germans; black Catholics could attend any service they liked. There were even notorious brothels with both black and white prostitutes. Respectable brothels everywhere else in the South were strictly segregated.

The most sinister sight was the presence of African culture on the streets. Voodoo and other West African religions were in fact widespread throughout the slave states, but they were practiced surreptitiously; while every plantation had its witches and conjure men, and the plantation owners routinely used their slaves' medicines, it was all done out of sight.

In New Orleans there were voodoo shops openly advertising for business. The most celebrated was on the old Bayou Road on the outskirts of town. It was run by a black African who called himself Dr. John. He was an imposing figure: invariably dressed in formal suits with frilled shirts, and his face fantastically tattooed. His shop was stocked with glass jars and phials filled with odd swamp weeds, wildflowers, dried lizards, insect eggs, bird feathers, and an assortment of carved bones and amulets. Dr. John practiced astrology and cartomancy; he was a healer and a skilled mind reader; he performed divination with pastel-colored pebbles and curious seashells. "One would stand aghast," one observer wrote, "were he to be told the names of the high city dames who were wont to drive in their own carriages, with thickly veiled faces, to this sooty black Cagliostro's abode, to consult him upon domestic affairs."

By the 1850s, Dr. John had been eclipsed by Marie Laveau, who became known as the Voodoo Queen. She, too, dealt in herbs and medicines, and she sold charms to guard against curses, spells, and maleficences. She discreetly consulted with her wealthiest clients by paying them house calls as their hairdresser—and she was reportedly an excellent hairdresser. She was also, according to some, an excellent procuress. After a long career, she hit upon a kind of early version of the franchised brand: she secretly retired and set her daughter up in her place. Many people late in the century assumed that the woman they knew as Marie Laveau was the same preternaturally young Voodoo Queen who had been practicing her craft since before the Civil War.

Marie Laveau was usually cited as the one who did the most to popularize (vulgarize, some said) voodoo among New Orleans's white society. Local politicians bought Laveau's charms before elections, and gamblers would carry them on their watch chains when they went out to the racetrack. But in fact there was a large trade in magical tokens throughout the city. People everywhere left poisoned crosses under pillows and trickled the dirt from graveyards around doorways. They bought, or concocted themselves, powders and poisons, which were known as gris-gris: combinations of black and white pepper, arrangements of carved bones stolen from mausoleums, cursed chicken feathers. They attended midnight ceremonies on the shores of Lake Pontchartrain that often ended up as orgies.

These were supposed to be secret, but Marie Laveau would invite police-men, reporters, politicians, and the ladies of high society to ensure that the forces of law and morality left her unmolested.

There was a well-attended public event on Sundays in a park known as Congo Square. During the afternoons the atmosphere was gaudy and fes-tive. Slaves, free people of color, and whites mingled in the shade of tow-ering old sycamores while in the central square hundreds of dancers exuberantly performed the Calinda and the Bamboula. The spectators bought ginger beer and wine, lemonade and lime soda water, vinegar pies and ginger cakes, at tables set below long awnings draped with streamers. But then at dusk, the tourists drifted off to the restaurants and the opera houses; the staid citizens went back to their homes; the students from the local university, already tipsy, would usually depart singing old Creole lul-labies and calling out *"Soleil, couche."* The remaining revelers, both blacks and whites, now unobserved, would take "the oath to the serpent." The oath was, according to one observer, nothing but "a string of barbarous epithets and penalties." What followed was something like a camp meet-ing, except that the eroticism was wholly overt. The king and queen of the ceremony would caress a large snake representing the god and begin to tremble; the other celebrants would touch them and begin to tremble as well. Gradually everyone's movements became more violent and convul-sive. They would sing, tear off their clothes, scream, and writhe around and grind against and bite at each other until they at last collapsed in exhaustion—waking the next morning, one observer said, "retaining but one thing firmly fixed in their minds, the date of the next meeting."

The life of New Orleans was always at its lowest ebb in the late summer. That was the season for cholera and yellow jack: anybody who could afford to leave was gone. Then, too, the harvests in the valleys up north hadn't come in yet, and the Mississippi ran the shallowest in August and September. Few boats were arriving from upriver, and the levee was some-times deserted for days at a time. The traffic picked up in the fall, and by November and December the harbor was jumping. It got quiet again in midwinter after the upper Mississippi iced over, but by then the deals had been made, the warehouses were stuffed with goods, and on the streets the money was flowing easily. That was the start of the Carnival season.

Today Carnival in New Orleans means Mardi Gras—Fat Tuesday—the traditional tourist draw that marks the beginning of Lent. But the city's organized Mardi Gras celebration, with the famous parade, dates from around 1860, and tourists began showing up for it in large numbers only after the Civil War. Before then Carnival was strictly for the locals. It was a wilder, more diffuse event that went on throughout the winter. According to one count, there were a thousand masked balls each year between Twelfth Night and Ash Wednesday. A few of these events were lavish minuets of aristocratic glamour; most were wild gatherings overflowing into the streets. At a celebrated ball held each year in one of the city's best-known brothels, the partygoers wore masks, had guns and knives strapped to their arms and thighs, and otherwise danced entirely naked.

As Lent approached, the celebrations gradually coalesced into one sprawling masquerade that took over the whole city. By the night of Fat Tuesday everyone was in costume: men and women, whites and blacks, free people and slaves. The masks were ornate and astonishing. The British traveler George Augustus Sala described "an eruption, a lava-flow, an inundation of masks." There were sea monsters, gargoyles, alligators, snakes, mermaids; there were fairy-tale figures from Perrault and the Brothers Grimm; there were kings and queens, nuns and monks, Indians and slaves, a scattering of angels and great mobs of red-horned devils. Always there were confusions of race and age and sex, a perpetual scramble of reversed identities: whites in blackface and blacks in whiteface, boys made up as old women in calico dresses, and young women swaggering through the streets as swashbuckling pirates. One procession in 1839 was led by what a guidebook later described as "an immense cock over six feet high, riding a carriage and delighting the crowd with its stentorian crows."

The city seemed swallowed up in chaos. But there were a few focal points. One of them was an ornate theater in the French Quarter, which kept its doors open all night on Fat Tuesday for the revelers to drift in and out. Onstage was enacted a series of lewd tableaux based on Milton's *Paradise Lost*. The big attraction for most of the spectators was *The Expulsion from Paradise*—it was hard to tell by gaslight, in the uproar and hilarity of the crowd, but Adam and Eve appeared to be naked. The most spectacular scene, though, was *The Building of the City of Pandemonium.* It began with a big crowd of red-masked demons (almost as many demons as there were among the maskers in the audience) lying unconscious on the stage after their expulsion from heaven. They shook off their stupor and pantomimed amazement and dismay as a narrator declaimed the description of their new land from Milton:

> Rocks, caves, lakes, fens, bogs, dens, and shades of death,
> A universe of death: which God by curse
> Created evil, for evil only good;
> Where all life dies, death lives, and nature breeds,
> Perverse, all monstrous, all prodigious things,
> Abominable, inutterable, and worse.

Then, with a great roar of defiance, they set to work rearing up a home for themselves—the great city of Pandemonium. This was done in a bustle of hammering and forging and lifting and carrying, while painted flats were raised and lowered and kettledrums and flutes sounded from the orchestra pit. In the hubbub were demons flashing glimpses of flesh beneath their swirling robes, and other demons in hot pursuit. The demons were mostly the horned and red-faced gargoyles of folklore, but some were ornate apparitions more directly inspired by Milton: figures of bejeweled and regal power who radiated glamour and ambiguous sexuality (as Milton himself had written, "Spirits when they please / Can either sex assume, or both"). On a platform above, Satan presided over it all, taking in the demons onstage and the demons in the audience, urging his subjects to go on with their great work of taming the wilderness while he flew out from hell in search of Eden:

> Go therefore, mighty powers,
> Terror of Heaven, though fallen: intend at home
> While here shall be our home, what best may ease
> The present misery, and render Hell
> More tolerable.
> .　.　.　.　.　.　.　.　.　.　.　.　.　.　.

> While I abroad
> Through all the coasts of dark destruction seek
> Deliverance for us all.

Only a few areas of New Orleans had streetlights. All through the Carnival nights the streets were a storm of flying lights and shadows. Masqueraders lined up along the wrought-iron balconies holding candles in paper flowers like wavering stars, and the windows of all the stores were aglow with countless paper lanterns. Down the backstreets were masked revelers carrying torches, and in the crumbling alleyways there were wild skirmishes of shadows like swirling black robes. Within this seethe of confusion people gave way to strange impulses. The custom in those days was to throw flour down from the balconies to pelt the maskers thronging the streets, so that by dawn most of the costumes were streaked white and clotted with wet flour. The maskers would shed them (but not the masks) as they became fouled, getting steadily closer to full nakedness. One year a group of unseen pranksters on a rooftop threw not flour but quicklime, and left a whole street filled with maskers writhing in agony. A mob quickly gathered and began breaking into the houses along the block to catch them, but the pranksters escaped across the roofs into the night and were never found.

Most of the violence was more impulsive. Amid the ceaseless turmoil of masks were assignations made and broken, identities guessed and mistaken, feuds erupting at the wrong targets, wrongs secretly revenged, a year's worth of scores and resentments anonymously settled, passersby left beaten in alleyways because they'd made an ill-judged joke to a prowling gang of maskers, innocents murdered because they'd worn the wrong mask to the wrong party. There were some sections of the city—including a zone of cheap brothels and gambling houses known as the Swamp, into which the police were afraid to go—where the masquerade turned every year into a riot. The most urgent duty on the first morning of Lent was the burial of the dead.

The first settlers of New Orleans had sensibly built their town on the hilltops. The French Quarter stood on the highest land and was the only part of the city that generally survived the floods. The later waves of construction spread down into the lowlands. By the middle of the nineteenth century, most of the city was below sea level and even below river level: passengers coming in by the river were amazed to look down over the sides of the levees and see rooftops gliding below them. The ground in the lowlands was so thoroughly saturated with river water that it wasn't particularly habitable—at least, the conditions caused a number of fundamental problems in the city's conduct of ordinary life. Burials, for example, were difficult, because any hole dug more than a few inches deep would immediately fill up with water.

"Strictly speaking, there is no architecture in New Orleans," Mark Twain observed, "except in the cemeteries." The cemeteries were elaborate and fantastic constructions. Burial in the earth was a last resort only for the poorest citizens: everybody else was laid to rest aboveground. The cemeteries were crammed with ornate crypts and freestanding mausoleums lined up along stone streets like habitations of the dead. As the grounds became more crowded, the tombs grew taller and narrower; to stand out from their neighbors, they were loaded down with garish statuary and sometimes were extravagantly decorated with harlequin-patterned tiles. The epitaphs were a jumble of mourning tongues. Sometimes it was hard to make out exactly what language they were in or even if they were in an earthly language at all. A representative example (apparently composed, one later writer said, "in the language of the Jabberwock") read as follows:

> Alas that one whose dornthly joy had often to trust in heaven should canty thus sudden to from all its hopes benivens and though they love for off remore that dealt the dog pest thou left to prove thy sufferings while below. Sacred to the memory of Robert John, a native of this city, son of Robert and Jane Creswell died June 4, 1845 age 26 years, 7 months.

The funerals were often just as mysterious. Benjamin Latrobe came across a funeral procession as he was returning home one evening. Around two hundred Negroes, all dressed in white and carrying candles, were making their way through the twilight streets and singing a hymn of mourning. Latrobe couldn't resist following them into the cemetery. They threaded through the aisles between the grand mausoleums until they reached the outskirts of the necropolis, where weeds began poking up through the flagstones and there was a patch of grassy ground. Here were the plots set aside for the poor citizens. The gravedigger was at work. It was a sweltering night, and he was naked except for a pair of ragged breeches. Latrobe guessed that the grave was around three feet deep, and it was already halfway filled with river water.

As the mourners waited, five priests entered the cemetery; they were preceded, as was traditional, by two boys bearing urns and one boy bearing a large crucifix. They began their prayers while the women crowded in around the grave and cried out their lamentations. The coffin was let down into the grave. It immediately bobbed up in the water. The gravedigger began shoveling earth onto the coffin to weigh it down. One of the mourning women (who seemed, Latrobe noted, "particularly affected") hurled herself into the grave. She hit the water with a great splash, and the coffin popped up out from under her. The gravedigger used his shovel to lever her up. Some of the other mourners reached down to grab her arms and legs and pull her out of the grave.

Meanwhile, the young boys in the group were getting bored. Beside the hole was a big heap of skulls and bones that had been unearthed by the gravedigger; the boys began tossing the skulls around and using the leg bones for a sword fight. One of the skulls hit the coffin with a loud, melancholy, reverberant thud. The adults all froze in shocked silence; then some of them began to laugh. "The whole became a sort of farce after the tragedy," Latrobe wrote. The boys went on tossing the bones and skulls at each other, and the mood of hilarity spread until all the mourners were laughing.

PART THREE

THE COURSE OF EMPIRE

11

The Mound Builders

WHEN THE EARLIEST EUROPEAN EXPLORERS came down the Mississippi in the seventeenth century, they had been startled to find, everywhere they went, evidence that somebody else had been there before them. The evidence was cryptic but irrefutable: it took the form of gigantic earthen mounds, some of them more than a hundred feet tall, piled up in the open land along the riverbanks. Some mounds stood in clusters like mushrooms; others were posed in solitary isolation against the prairie sky; many had been worn down by the weather and were half covered by the wilderness, barely distinguishable from natural forms. The farther the explorers went, the more of the mounds they found. There were hundreds of them and then thousands and then tens of thousands, all along the Mississippi valley to the delta and up the Ohio to the Alleghenies.

But what were they? Monuments? Observation posts? Funeral mounds? Nobody knew. The only thing that seemed obvious to the explorers was that they couldn't possibly have been the work of the Native Americans. The Indian nations of the river valley had no contemporary large-scale works like these, no lasting constructions of any kind; they lived in small transitory villages and in nomadic camps. Then, too, the mounds were clearly the product of a unified culture, and the Native Americans were fractured into hundreds of warring splinter societies with no common language. (By one count there were two hundred mutually incomprehensible languages spoken in North America when the Europeans arrived.) And lastly, none of the Native American societies laid claim to the mounds; in fact, they professed to be just as baffled by them as the whites were.

But the Cherokee did tell one story. They said that when they had first arrived in the river valley, it had been inhabited by strange beings with milky white skin and eyes like moons who could do many cunning things in the dark but couldn't see in the daylight. They were long gone, the Cherokee couldn't say where—maybe they were the ones who had made the mounds.

Inevitably they came to be called the Mound Builders. In the nineteenth century, people along the frontier began excavating the mounds systematically to see whether the builders had left any traces of themselves behind. What was found was strange and tantalizing. The Mound Builder culture had plainly been enormous: it had thoroughly explored the Mississippi River system out to its remotest tributaries and beyond. A single mound along the banks of the Ohio proved to contain silver pieces from Lake Superior, alligator teeth from the Gulf of Mexico, chalcedony from North Dakota, and volcanic glass from the foothills of the Rocky Mountains. The Mound Builder craftsmen had been remarkable and subtle artists: the mounds contained exquisitely carved statues and pieces of jewelry. The Mound Builders had had a peculiar religion of their own: there were ritual masks in which human faces were fused with those of hawks and wolves, as though illustrating some form of spirit possession. And, most sinister of all, there were signs that the Mound Builders had been practitioners of human sacrifice: some mounds held rows of human skeletons, each with a puncture wound at the base of the skull.

But in none of the mounds was there any writing: not a symbol or a hieroglyph; nothing to indicate who the builders of the mounds were, what they'd called themselves, where they'd come from, or where they'd gone.

There were countless theories. The Mound Builders had come to America from across the Pacific—from China or from India: they were Siberians, or else Tatars, or possibly Mongols. Or they had come across the Atlantic: Vikings from Greenland or Irish who had migrated during the Dark Ages. Or else they might have been a branch of the Toltecs or Mayans or Aztecs who had come up from South America. Maybe—and this theory was especially popular—they were the lost tribes of Israel. Or—an even more popular theory—they were refugees from the sinking of Atlantis.

Whoever they were, they had to have resembled the Europeans more than they did the Native Americans. A story that some of the skeletons were holding cross-shaped objects suggested that they might even have been Christian—or if not Christian exactly, then proto-Christian, or quasi-Christian. Maybe, as one writer put it, "some stray fragments of the holy structure [had been] obscurely delivered over to them by paternal or patriarchal hands."

As for what had happened to them, there were still more theories about that. Were they destroyed by a plague, or an earthquake, or a volcano? Or was it some deep cultural malaise, some collective loss of will, like the spiritual decadence that was believed to have brought down the Roman Empire?

A novel published in 1839 offered a particularly garish solution to the mystery. It was called *Behemoth: A Legend of the Mound-Builders*. The author, Cornelius Mathews, was a well-known poet and editor. He took his inspiration from the gigantic bones of prehistoric creatures that were often found in the river valley. He imagined that one of these monsters had been the leveler of the Mound Builder civilization. *Behemoth* describes how a woolly mammoth of unimaginable size, a kind of proto-Godzilla, appears out of the mountains of the Far North and comes rampaging down through the river valley, trampling everything before it into the ground. The Behemoth is so large that "the whole region trembled as when a vast body of waters bursts its way and rolls over the earth, ocean-like, wave shouting to wave, and all crowding onward with thunderous tumult." Nothing can stand up to him: "In vain was the solid breast-work; the piled wall was in vain; in vain the armed and watchful sentry." Soon whole cities are falling before him: "Like some stupendous engine of war, he bore down on them, rendering human strength a mockery and human defences worse than useless. . . . He swept through the towns and villages, the tilled fields and pleasure gardens of the Mound-builders—desolating and desolate—none daring to stand before his feet thus dreadfully advanced."

But what proves to be far worse than the physical destructiveness of the Behemoth is the psychological damage he leaves in his wake. His nightly stampedes break the will of the Mound Builders; they can see no point to going on when their proudest achievements are being so casually smashed down all around them:

The voice of joy died away into a timid and feeble smiling; proud and stately ambition fell humbled to the earth, and love and beauty trembled and fled before the gloomy shadow of the general adversary. Men shunned each other as if from a consciousness of their abasement, and skulked away from the face of day, unwilling that the heavens should look in upon their desolation and shame.

In the later sections of the novel, a lone hero rises up and inspires the Mound Builders to one last supreme effort: they capture and kill the Behemoth. But the damage to their civilization is irreversible, and they go down into oblivion, brought to their ultimate ruin by their own failure of spirit. Their great mounds become their mass graves, and the rest of the works of their civilization disappear.

Behemoth the novel is itself forgotten, pretty much on its merits. (Edgar Allan Poe once reviewed a book of Mathews's poetry and pronounced it, not unfairly, "gibberish.") The only influence it may have had on American literature is indirect and speculative: Mathews happened to know Herman Melville, and it's conceivable that *Behemoth* provided an initial stirring of inspiration for Melville's world-shaking Leviathan. But as ephemeral a novel as it was, its premise was not that far removed from what the most respected scholars of the time were actually saying. They, too, assumed that the Mound Builders must have been done in by some dark and mysterious power. Not a woolly mammoth, but one they regarded as quite as sinister: the Native Americans.

The way it was imagined, the Mound Builder civilization at its height had been as rich and profound a culture as ancient Greece. The Mound Builders had cultivated the land, built monumental cities, created a sophisticated society that was spread out all down the river valley and throughout the forests of the eastern seaboard—but they had proved helpless before the danger of the primitive and cunning Indians. There had been, centuries before the Europeans arrived, a vast war across America, in which the Mound Builder civilization had at last been overrun and all its great works, except the mounds, wiped off the face of the earth.

The story can be found in a poem by William Cullen Bryant called "The Prairies," first published in 1832. This is the section about the mounds:

A race, that long has passed away,
Built them;—a disciplined and populous race
Heaped, with long toil, the earth, while yet the Greek
Was hewing the Pentelicus to forms
Of symmetry, and rearing on its rock
The glittering Parthenon. These ample fields
Nourished their harvests, here their herds were fed,
When haply by their stalls the bison lowed,
And bowed his manèd shoulder to the yoke.
All day this desert murmured with their toils,
Till twilight blushed, and lovers walked, and wooed
In a forgotten language, and old tunes,
From instruments of unremembered form,
Gave the soft winds a voice. The red man came—
The roaming hunter tribes, warlike and fierce,
And the mound-builders vanished from the earth.
The solitude of centuries untold
Has settled where they dwelt. The prairie-wolf
Hunts in their meadows, and his fresh-dug den
Yawns by my path. The gopher mines the ground
Where stood their swarming cities. All is gone;
All—save the piles of earth that hide their bones.

The great masterpiece about the fate of the Mound Builders, though, wasn't a poem but a work of art: Thomas Cole's series of five paintings known collectively as *The Course of Empire.* They trace the rise and fall of an unknown civilization deep in the American wilderness. The civilization is never named; there are no markings or inscriptions or hieroglyphs on their buildings; the citizens are seen only at a great distance, so that it's impossible even to say what race they are. The only clue to their identity is in their style of architecture: a wild, classical jumble that simultaneously recalls Rome, Carthage, the Aztecs, and Atlantis—just the same chaos of origins attributed to the Mound Builders.

The first painting, titled *The Savage State,* shows the American land-scape in its primeval desolation. There is a wigwam village in a hollow shel-tered from an autumnal storm, figures are paddling a canoe up a creek, and in the foreground a hunter with a bow and arrow pursues a deer. The second painting, *The Arcadian or Pastoral State,* shows the same scene now in the springtime of civilization: the land is tamed and cultivated; there are shipbuilders at work along the shore; the village has been supplanted by a fuming stone temple resembling Stonehenge; in the place of the hunter is an old Socrates-ish philosopher scratching some sort of calculation in the dirt with a stick. The third painting is called *The Consummation of Empire,* and the scene is now a summery high noon. The pastoral world has been wholly covered over by a kind of classical version of urban sprawl: instead of the serene meadows and forests there is a fantastic clutter of colonnaded marble buildings and towering monuments; the water of the harbor is swarming with sailboats, keelboats, triremes, and gondolas; the bridges and promenades are thronged by citizens in a riotous festival. In the foreground a general is seen making a victory procession across one of the great arched bridges, surrounded by solemn priests dressed in white. The fourth painting is the inevitable crisis: *The Destruction of Empire.* The harbor city of the third painting is shown in the midst of a vast disaster. The great palazzi are in flames, the bridges are collapsing, the sky is congealing into a furious storm. The throngs have become stampeding mobs; soldiers are everywhere, looting, torching the buildings, grabbing at fleeing women. It's an invasion, an uprising, a natural disaster—maybe all of the above. The last painting is the dark and tranquil epilogue: *Desolation.* The imperial city is gone; the wilderness is reclaiming the land. In the background, over the placid ocean, the moon is rising into a clearing sky. A fading twilight plays over the deserted ruins that line the estuary; the broken arches of the bridges and temples are being overgrown by weeds and ivy. A lone pillar on the shore is home to seabirds. The people have all vanished, and the land will soon erase their last traces.

These paintings caused a tremendous stir when they were first exhibited in 1836. "A great epic poem," James Fenimore Cooper called them. "The highest work of genius this country has ever produced." While Cole never explained exactly how his paintings should be interpreted, few of the original spectators seem to have had any trouble decoding them. They were a rebuke to the idea that America had no history, that the land was a clean slate, that the new civilization the pioneers were building was its first. The truth was, the same grand historical cycles were playing out here just as they had in Europe or Asia. A great civilization had once risen up in the American wilderness, had reached the crest of the wave, and had toppled over into destruction and disappeared. And even as the spectators gawked at Cole's paintings, far away, in the depths of the American interior, the whole story was happening again.

12

A Young Man of Splendid Abilities

ONE WINTER AFTERNOON in the mid-1830s, two men met on a deserted Tennessee road near the Mississippi. One was a young man who said he was looking for a lost horse. The other, who was several years older, said he was a commercial traveler on his way to the ferry to cross into Arkansas. After a brief conversation, the older man offered to delay his journey and help the young stranger in his search.

To an onlooker it would have all seemed quite innocuous. But this was the river valley: neither man was what he appeared to be. In fact, both were taking part in an elaborate masquerade. The exact nature of this masquerade wasn't clear then, and it may not be clear even now—but one thing about it can be said for sure: no other such meeting by the Mississippi has ever stirred up anywhere near as much trouble.

The men spent the rest of the day meandering through the winter landscape in the general direction of the ferry. All the while, they were engaging in the sort of idle chatter that American men have always gone in for when at loose ends: blunt, earthbound spitballing about the sorry state of the country. "What is it that constitutes character, popularity, and power in the United States?" the older man asked at one point. The answer was obvious: "Sir, it is property; strip a man of his property in this country, and he is a ruined man indeed—you see his friends forsake him; and he may have been raised in the highest circles of society, and yet he is neglected and treated with contempt. Sir, my doctrine is, let the hardest fend off."

As the two men ambled on, their talk drifted to the exploits of a celebrated local horse thief and slave stealer named John Murrell. With typical bravado and cynicism, the men agreed that Murrell was a true hero of the age: admirable for his courage, his daring, his cleverness, his rebellious spirit. The young man was so caught up in enthusiasm that he compared Murrell favorably with Alexander the Great and Andrew Jackson—they were "little and inconsiderate" next to him, since "he is great from the force of his mental powers, and they are great from their station in the world."

That was when the older man confessed: he himself was Murrell.

The young man was astounded. "Is it possible," he asked, "that I have the pleasure of standing before the illustrious personage of whom I have heard so many noble feats, and whose dexterity and skill in performance are unrivalled by any the world has ever produced before him: is it a dream or is it reality? I can scarce believe that it is a man in real life who stands before me!"

Murrell, flattered and impressed by the young man's attitude, invited him to forget about the missing horse and cross the Mississippi with him to Arkansas, where he had "a thousand friends." The young man accepted at once. He introduced himself as Arthur Hughes, and never mentioned the horse again. But this was hardly an act of neglect. The horse didn't exist, nor, for that matter, did Hughes—the young man, whose real name was Virgil Stewart, had made up the story as a way of introducing himself to Murrell. He had in fact been hired by one of Murrell's victims to track him down and bring him to justice.

Murrell suspected nothing. He was so taken by Stewart that, as they went on together toward the ferry, he launched into a detailed account of his life and past crimes. He told how he was instructed in villainy by his mother; how by the age of sixteen he'd become so expert a sharper that he could walk into a clothing store, order a new suit, and have it charged to the son of the richest man in town. He'd since become a master of disguise who could pass himself off as both a Catholic priest and a Protestant minister (he was especially good at the falling exercise). But his most lucrative career was as a slave stealer. He claimed that "fifteen minutes are all I want to decoy the best of negroes from the best of masters." Some slaves he would trick into throwing in with him; he would sell the slave to somebody else, and the slave would escape again. Sometimes they did this five or six times. He would promise the slave a share of the profits—but sooner or later would kill him instead, bury him in the swamps, and keep all the money for himself.

Several times in the course of this confession, Murrell intimated that he had a larger design. It took very little coaxing on Stewart's part for him to reveal it. For many years, Murrell said, he had been engaged in a vast and secret project to organize all the thieves, murderers, and pirates in the river valley into one overarching criminal organization, which he called the Mystic Clan. The clan had two major components. The large outer circle of around a thousand men, called the Strikers, consisted of conventional lawbreakers who thought the purpose of the clan was simply to commit crimes more efficiently. Only the inner circle of four hundred men, called the High Council, knew the clan's true purpose: to foment a slave insurrection throughout the South. Even as Murrell and Stewart talked, this plan was moving toward the crisis point—the moment when, Murrell said, "every state and section of the country where there are any negroes, intend to rebel and slay all the whites they can."

The insurrection had been surprisingly easy to set up. It relied on Murrell's skill at tricking slaves into betraying their masters. He laid out the technique in detail to Stewart. "We do not go to every negro we see, and tell him the slaves intend to rebel," he cautioned. Instead the clan had to find "the most vicious and wicked-disposed ones on large farms." The first step was to "poison their minds by telling them how they are mistreated, and that they are entitled to their freedom as much as their masters, and that all the wealth of the country is the proceeds of the black people's labor." Next, lessons from current events: "We tell them that all Europe has abandoned slavery, and that the West Indies are all free; and that they got their freedom by rebelling a few times and slaughtering the whites." From there it was a quick route to the ultimate prize: "If they will follow the example of the West India negroes, they will obtain their liberty, and become as much respected as if they were white; and that they can marry white women when they are all put on a level." And to seal the deal, they were told they had the backing of the world at large: "We get them to believe that most people are in favor of their being free, and that the free states in the United States would not interfere with the negroes if they were to butcher every white man in the slave-holding states."

Of course, Murrell was careful to stress, this was all nonsense. He didn't believe in abolitionism at all. The slave uprising was only a diversion. His real motive was larceny. In the midst of the chaos, the Mystic Clan was going to loot simultaneously all the banks in the slave states. "We have set on the 25th December, 1835, for the time to commence our operations," he told Stewart. "We design having our companies so stationed over the country, in the vicinity of the banks and large cities, so that when the negroes commence their carnage and slaughter, we will have detachments to fire the towns and rob the banks while all is in confusion and dismay."

It was a dizzying and nightmarish prospect for Stewart. But that was not the worst of it. As Stewart listened, he began to realize that there was something much darker at work in Murrell's soul than greed. He was really a visionary. His ultimate motive was a kind of satanic spite. As he put it to Stewart: "I will have the pleasure and honor of seeing and knowing that my management has glutted the earth with more human gore, and destroyed more property, than any other robber who has ever lived in America, or the known world. I look on the American people as my common enemy. They have disgraced me, and they can do no more; my life is nothing to me, and it shall be spent as their devoted enemy."

At the end of this monologue, Murrell invited Stewart to join with him in the Mystic Clan. As a sign of good faith, he offered to supply Stewart with a complete list of the clan's membership, both the Strikers and the High Council, including addresses. "I consider you a young man of splendid abilities," he declared. "Sir, these are my feelings and sentiments towards you."

This story is told in a pamphlet, first published early in 1835, that caused a tremendous stir in the lower river valley. The pamphlet's full title is *A History of the Detection, Conviction, Life and Designs of John A. Murel, the Great Western Land Pirate; Together with His System of Villany, and Plan of Exciting a Negro Rebellion, Also a Catalogue of the Names of Four Hundred and Fifty-five of His Mystic Clan Fellows and Followers, and a Statement of Their Efforts for the Destruction of Virgil A. Stewart, the Young Man Who Detected Him; to Which Is Added a Biographical Sketch of V. A. Stewart, by Augustus Q. Walton.* Several things about it are peculiar. There is the putative author, for instance: Augustus Q. Walton is a name otherwise unknown to literary history. There is the style, which mixes self-consciously poetic prose ("It began to grow late in the evening, and the sun shone dimly as it was sinking below the western horizon, and reflected a beautifully dim light from the sleet which shielded the lofty young timber of Poplar Creek bottom") with crude phonetic spellings ("Murel" for "Murrell," "Hues" for "Hughes"). And then, of course, there is the very odd story it's telling.

The story does go on. Murrell and Stewart cross the Mississippi together. Murrell presents the young man to the High Council, Stewart makes a long extempore speech that immediately convinces the council that he is a kindred spirit, and they welcome him into their most secret deliberations. (A sample of the speech: "The conspiracy of four hundred Americans, in this morass of the Mississippi river, will glean the southern and western bank, destroy their cities, and slaughter their enemies.") Stewart then manages to make his getaway, carrying enough proof with him to have Murrell arrested, convicted, and sentenced to the penitentiary.

For a modern reader, there isn't much question about how to assess all this. It's flagrantly absurd. It's absurd not simply because of the wooden speechifying of the characters or the ridiculous melodrama of the action; there isn't anything about the basic situation that seems even remotely plausible. How could Murrell have concocted such an enormous conspiracy, and how could he have kept it so secret? And why, if he had done all this, would he casually confess it to a total stranger—and then offer to supply the stranger with the names and addresses of every one of the conspirators?

But these weren't doubts that troubled the original audience. People then had a different standard for judging the truth of what they read. Newspaper stories, and even formal histories, routinely recorded people making impossibly high-flown speeches to each other at moments of dramatic crisis and revealing all their dread secrets in ornate soliloquies. The overall effect was somewhere between Gothic melodrama and the oratory of Cicero. Readers did not find it necessarily implausible. They would have found a modern reader's objections to be niggling and irrelevant. Even if Stewart's account wasn't a naturalistic rendering of how people actually behave, that didn't mean the underlying substance wasn't, in all the most important senses, true.

And besides, there were many things about the pamphlet that were already known to be true. There really was a man named John Murrell (or possibly Murel, as the pamphlet spelled it, or Murrel, as some later writers favored) who had been put on trial in Tennessee for slave stealing. He had been convicted, and in the spring of 1835 he was in a Tennessee penitentiary. Virgil Stewart was also a real person, and it was a matter of public record that he had been a witness against Murrell at the trial. And then, too, there was that list Murrell had promised Stewart of all the members of the Mystic Clan. The pamphlet reproduced it in full. It was disturbingly plausible; it carefully mixed vague and not-quite-traceable names (somebody called Williamson in Kentucky, a D. Harris in Georgia) with the real names of some of the most prominent citizens in Tennessee and Kentucky. No wonder that the original readers found it so convincing—in fact, wholly terrifying.

In the spring of 1835, Virgil Stewart went on a speaking tour on the lower Mississippi. At each stop along the way, he repeated the charges made in the pamphlet: that the Mystic Clan was real, that it was organizing a slave insurrection, and that the entire South was in imminent peril. The arrest of Murrell hadn't put an end to the plot; in fact, it had accelerated it. The original target date for the uprising had been Christmas Day of that year; now it had been pushed forward to the Fourth of July.

Stewart caused a sensation everywhere he went. He impressed everybody with his demeanor: despite the desperate urgency of his message, he was in all respects modest and dignified, the model of a respectable young man. He told the most hair-raising stories about the Mystic Clan's campaigns to kill or otherwise silence him, and yet he was never boastful, never arrogant; he was decorous, even prim. (The credited author of the pamphlet, Augustus Walton, remained out of sight—the widespread assumption was that Stewart had written the pamphlet himself.) Only a few people failed to be won over. In Vicksburg, for instance, Stewart was introduced to the celebrated lawyer Henry Foote (the defender of the Horace-reading highwayman Alonzo Phelps), who had read the pamphlet and found it "fearfully exciting and inflammatory." But Stewart himself seemed somehow troubling; Foote described him as "sagacious and insinuating," a rather ambiguous compliment. But then Foote thought it would be a bad idea to express any doubts, given the enthusiasm of Stewart's supporters. "Those who dared even to question the actual existence of the dangers which he depictured," Foote wrote later, "were suspected by their more excited fellow-citizens of a criminal insensibility to the supposed perils of the hour, or were denounced as traitors to the slaveholding interests of the South."

In June 1835, Stewart gave his speech to the citizens of Madison County, Mississippi, deep in the plantation country northeast of Vicksburg. One person in the audience was especially alarmed. She is identified in the published records only as a Mrs. Latham, from the small town of Beatie's Bluff. In the days after Stewart's appearance, Mrs. Latham grew progressively more worried about the behavior of her slaves. "Her suspicions were first awakened," reported a pamphlet entitled *Proceedings of the Citizens of Madison County,* "by noticing in her house-servants a disposition to be insolent and disobedient." The situation rapidly became worse: "Occasionally they would use insulting and contemptuous language in her hearing respecting her." Soon she was convinced that "something mysterious was going on, from seeing her girls often engaged in secret conversation when they ought to have been engaged at their business." Naturally she began eavesdropping. Her worst fears were confirmed: they were discussing—cryptically but, she thought, unmistakably—the coming insurrection. Here was the giveaway: she overheard one girl say that "she wished to God it was all over and done with; that she was tired of waiting on the white folks, and wanted to be her own mistress the balance of her days, and clean up her own house."

Immediately Mrs. Latham set out to raise the alarm. There wasn't much in the way of official authority available in Beatie's Bluff, so she consulted with the most respected gentlemen of the town. They heard her out and decided to investigate for themselves. At her house they closely examined the girls she had overheard. The finding of these gentlemen, according to the pamphlet, was that the statements of the girls "corresponded in every particular with the communication of the lady." The gentlemen came to a simple and terrifying conclusion: there was indeed reason to believe that an insurrection of the slaves was imminent. They made urgent recommendations: that new committees of vigilance and safety be immediately formed and that the system of slave patrols be reinstated. The slave patrols, the author of the pamphlet observed, "had been entirely neglected heretofore."

It may seem odd that the slave owners had been so lax about security up until then. But their guiding principle had always been to make as little effort as possible—and, in particular, to spend as little money as possible—to keep the system of slavery going. Most of the plantations in central Mississippi had absentee owners who hired the absolute minimum number of white employees they could get away with—a few overseers (usually noted for their unyielding cruelty), a bailiff, and sometimes a doctor, or at least someone who purported to have a little medical training. By the 1830s, the ratio of slaves to whites in some rural counties of Mississippi was reaching fifty to one. The owners were trusting geography to do the work of security: their thinking was that since the slaves knew they were trapped in the middle of an entirely hostile country with no way of ever returning home, they would give up, accept their situation, and settle in to being docile and obedient laborers.

The news that this might not be true galvanized the white community. A committee of vigilance was immediately formed in Madison County. It set to work questioning slaves with ferocious speed and determination. The interrogation technique was straightforward: the slaves would be flogged until they confessed something. Sometimes a slave was given dozens of lashes; sometimes it was hundreds. The interrogation went on for hours or days. But sooner or later the committee heard what it wanted to hear. Then the slave would immediately be hanged.

Most of these confessions were vague. A slave would admit to having heard some sort of indistinct talk about trouble coming. The talk would usually be attributed to some other slave—most often a known troublemaker on another plantation. That slave would be brought in and flogged, and would then admit to having heard something about the trouble from some other slave on yet another plantation. The committee relentlessly followed this trail from plantation to plantation until, eventually, one of the slaves would admit that there had been some talk concerning the insurrection with a white man.

The committee wasn't looking for any specific white man. Sometimes they heard about a nameless stranger who'd been loitering along a country road; other times it was one of the disreputable locals known to consort with slaves at the darky parties. But most promising were the odd hints about a group of shadowy white instigators making grand promises, the way the Mystic Clan was supposed to be doing. One slave, surely realizing that he was a dead man no matter what he said, came out with a particularly garish confession that might have been straight from Stewart's pamphlet: he claimed that it was the plan of the slaves "to slay all the whites, except some of the most beautiful women, whom they intended to keep as wives; said that these white men had told them that they might do so, and that he had already picked out one for himself; and that he and his wife had already had a quarrel in consequence of his having told her his intention."

After several such confessions the committee believed that the situation was now clear. *Proceedings of the Citizens of Madison County* summarized the committee's findings:

> They ascertained that they were not to contend alone with a few daring and desperate negroes, and such of their deluded race as they might enlist in their daring and bloody enterprise, but that these negroes were instigated and encouraged by some of the most wicked and abandoned white men in the country; highway robbers, murderers, and abolitionists, who were to supply them with arms and ammunition, and lead them on to the work of massacre and carnage, conflagration and blood.

What was the next step in preventing this disaster? The committee believed that was obvious: they had to root out the white conspirators in their midst. By late June they had taken several suspects into custody. There was no thought about turning them over to the official legal system—the crisis was too urgent, and the testimony of the slaves (even assuming they'd been kept alive) wouldn't have been admissible in court anyway. The committee carried on with the interrogations themselves. They made a great show of following the procedures of the legitimate courts: the anonymous author of the *Proceedings* pamphlet insisted (with considerable passion) that where the white suspects were concerned, the committee members conducted themselves in an appropriate legal fashion, with full respect for the rights of the accused. Henry Foote witnessed one of the interrogations and came away with a different opinion: "The examination was conducted in a very rapid and informal manner, and without the least regard to the established principles of the law of evidence."

In each case, there was only one piece of direct evidence: the confession of a slave obtained through torture. But, as the pamphlet author was careful to point out, there was plenty of supporting evidence and corroboration. There was one Joshua Cotton, for instance: he was a suspect because it was well known that he was "in the habit of trading with negroes." Then there was a William Saunders, suspected because he was unemployed and because "his deportment was such as to induce his employer to discharge him." There was an Albe Dean, who had several strikes against him:

He was known to associate with negroes, and would often come to the owners of runaways and intercede with their masters to save them from a whipping. It was in evidence before the committee that he was seen prowling about the plantations in the neighbourhoods of Vernon, Beatie's Bluff, and Livingston, ostensibly for the purpose of inquiring for runaway horses, which he did with great particularity—sometimes inquiring for a black, bay, gray, or other color that suggested itself at the time. It was evident that horse-hunting was not his business, but that he was reconnoitring the country, and seeking opportunities to converse with the negroes.

All of these men were tortured; some of them did confess. Joshua Cotton finally admitted that he and the others were following "the plan laid down in Stewart's pamphlet." All of them were hanged.

Then there was the case of Reuel Blake, a local gin wright (that is, one who built and repaired cotton gins). A slave of Blake's had been named by several other slaves as belonging to the conspiracy. When this slave was brought before the committee, Blake was as a courtesy allowed to take part in the interrogation. It did not go well. The slave refused to talk, and the committee invited Blake to whip him until he disclosed his part in the conspiracy. Blake was reluctant; he carefully informed the slave about the situation, explained what the flogging was for, and, as the *Proceedings* author remarked with incredulous italics, "*requested* him to tell all he knew about it."

Then Blake began flogging his slave. It was obvious to everyone that Blake's heart wasn't in it; he only lashed weakly, "occasionally striking a hard lick to keep up appearances." The committee called a halt and asked him to step aside. Then they began the interrogation in earnest. Blake, standing a little off from the group, grew increasingly agitated. As the flogging reached a peak of intensity—and just as the committee believed the slave was about to confess—Blake burst back into the center of the action and proclaimed that if they were going to touch his slave again, they'd have to flog him first. The committee member doing the flogging immediately raised the whip to oblige him, and they got into a fistfight. The spectators broke it up and "from the best of motives," according to the pamphlet, urged Blake to flee. He did so, and as he ran away from the committee, some of the boys in the crowd ran along with him for a few hundred yards, hooting and mocking him.

Once Blake was out of sight, the committee talked over what had happened. At first everyone assumed that Blake was merely some kind of perversely softhearted sentimentalist. But as they went on talking, their views changed. Soon they all began to say that there was just something about the man they'd never trusted. They didn't like the looks of him, for one thing: "He was of a cold, phlegmatic temperament," the pamphlet writer explained, "with a forbidding countenance." He had been living in Madison County for two or three years, and had never tried to fit in— preferring instead more suspicious company. "He kept himself almost aloof from white society, but was often seen among negroes." He looked worse and worse the more they thought about it. "His character, as known to the citizens, was one of the darkest die. He was noted for cold-blooded revenge, insatiable avarice, and unnatural cruelty; had been detected in several attempts to swindle his fellow-citizens, who, if they exposed his rascality, were ever after the objects of his deadly hatred." Lastly, he had said that he had gone to sea in his youth. "From vague hints he would occasionally drop, it was the general impression that he had been a pirate." The case was closed.

Blake was no fool. He understood from the outset how things were going. By the end of the afternoon, the committee had decided to try him on the grounds that he was likely a member of the conspiracy—but when they went to his house to arrest him, he was gone. He'd already gotten out of Madison County and was making his escape to Vicksburg.

There he hid out in the boat city off the levee of Vicksburg Landing. He passed himself off as a boatman from Indiana. The disguise didn't work for long. The Madison County vigilance committee offered a reward of five hundred dollars for him and posted it up and down the river; somebody in the boat city saw it and ratted him out. The committee arrived soon afterward and put him under arrest.

Blake was brought back to the town of Livingston in Madison County under heavy guard. A mob surrounded him on his arrival and he was almost killed then and there, but the committee held the people at bay long enough to put him on trial at the lynching court. Unlike most of the other accused, he never made any kind of confession or admission. But he was found guilty and he was hanged.

The approach of the dread Fourth had the whites of rural Mississippi in a panic. That was a day when the plantation slaves of the lower valley were traditionally granted a certain amount of liberty. They weren't required to work and were permitted to hold their own holiday celebrations with little or no interference from their overseers. On some plantations these parties were enormous events that slaves from other plantations were allowed to attend unsupervised. These were ideal conditions for the breeding of revolt.

But even if all those celebrations were canceled, what good would it do? The interrogations of the committee had established, if nothing else, that slaves were already moving around the countryside with impunity and were in constant and casual contact from plantation to plantation. There was also the whole problem of the maroons, as they were called—escaped slaves who hadn't fled north but were still living secretly in the plantation country and the wilderness. Nobody knew how many maroons there were, possibly thousands. Maroons were living in all the riverfront districts of the valley; there was known to be a sizable clandestine maroon community in New Orleans; maroon encampments were believed to be scattered through the wild country from the Everglades through the sea islands along the Gulf and up through the river delta. There were persistent rumors about a large and flourishing maroon city in the trackless bayous somewhere north of New Orleans, possibly led by a notorious escaped slave known as Squire. (Squire was finally caught and executed in 1837, but the city was never found.) If there were any maroons in Madison County, they were surely in touch with the slaves in the plantations—and were perfectly placed to help organize the revolt.

By the beginning of July the towns of Madison County were on full alert. No one stayed alone after dark. At sundown, the women and children gathered in a central location—usually the public square—while the men formed posses and patrolled the outskirts of town and the surrounding countryside. There were no streetlights in these towns, so people built bonfires at the intersections. The stillness of the night would be broken by sporadic gunfire as the posses, deceived by the wild shadows cast by the bonfires, took shots at each other. Meanwhile, the women and children kept scanning the sky above the treetops, watching for the telltale glow that would mean the arsonists had set to work in the neighboring towns and the insurrection had begun.

In Vicksburg, the Fourth of July was celebrated as it always had been, with a huge open-air barbecue. This was a gay and colorful event—the citizenry in their Sunday best, the militia in full uniform, the local band playing, and cannonades and fireworks at sundown. Nothing was any different that year: the disturbances in the rural counties had so far made little impression on the cosmopolitan river towns. (The governor of Mississippi had issued a proclamation on July 3 urging all citizens to be on the watch for any uprisings—he, too, blamed the threat on "lawless base villainous white men"—but in Vicksburg it was ignored.) Then something unpleasant happened on the picnic grounds. People were sitting at ease at the long tables set out under the trees when a man named Cabler, a gambler from Vicksburg Landing, "insolently thrust himself into the company" (as one newspaper later put it). He insulted one of the militia officers and took a swing at another guest. He was quickly and forcibly ejected.

That was all. It should have been immediately forgotten. On the Fourth, as with all big public occasions, there were inevitably a lot of drunken quarrels and fistfights that blew over as quickly as summer squalls. But Cabler was unwilling to let the incident go. Later that afternoon, the militia officers moved into the town square and put on a public demonstration of their close-order drilling. Cabler showed up spoiling for a fight. He shouldered his way into the middle of the militia company and confronted the officer he'd earlier insulted. The two were immediately surrounded by the whole company. Cabler was seized and searched: he was found to be carrying a knife, a dagger, and a loaded pistol. Several officers carried him off into the woods. There they whipped him, tarred and feathered him, and ordered him to leave town.

The parties resumed. Formal balls began in the mansions, and after sunset there were fireworks shows. Sometime that evening, the crowds of revelers scattered around town were swept by a rumor: Cabler's gambler friends in Vicksburg Landing were planning revenge. Nothing overt had taken place—there was no sign of a war party coming up from the landing. But around midnight, as the celebrations were beginning to break up, a large group of citizens held an impromptu meeting at the courthouse to decide what to do about the threat. They agreed that it was time for drastic action. The waterfront district of Vicksburg Landing needed to be cleaned up once and for all. The crowd passed by voice vote a public declaration ordering all professional gamblers to leave the landing within twenty-four hours.

As it happened, there were a lot of gamblers in Vicksburg Landing. Its reputation had grown almost as bad as that of Natchez-Under-the-Hill. People up and down the river had started calling it the Kangaroos, after its largest and rowdiest gambling house. Shock and consternation spread throughout the Kangaroos the morning of July 5, when its inhabitants woke late to find the walls and doors on every street and alley nailed with hastily printed posters announcing the resolution the townspeople had passed the night before. The Kangaroos was in a turmoil all day: Would the gamblers obey the order and leave? By nightfall some of the waterfront's most notorious gamblers were in fact seen departing—at least as far as the boat city, just as a precaution.

Meanwhile, a new rumor was riling Vicksburg. Up until that point, the squabble with Cabler and his fellow gamblers had been seen as a strictly local affair. But somehow during that day a connection was made: people started saying that this whole business had something to do with the stories emerging from the plantation districts about John Murrell and the slave insurrection. By nightfall on July 5, people all over Vicksburg were quoting from Stewart's pamphlet and saying the gamblers were members of the Mystic Clan.

There was no evidence, not even a single coerced confession, but from that point on, the rumor was regarded as a proven fact. As one writer noted a few years later, "It was known that the gamblers as a body belonged to, or were cognizant of, the conspiracy."

On July 6, the local militia moved into the Kangaroos to enforce the resolution. They were accompanied by a mob of citizens determined to put a stop to the Mystic Clan. As the militia began rounding up the gamblers, the mob fanned out swiftly through the tangle of streets and alleys. Soon they were breaking into every gambling house and saloon. They stampeded the residents; they dragged out the faro tables and everything else connected with gambling they could find. They smashed it all and burned it; there were bonfires on every corner of the Kangaroos.

The mob met with little or no resistance. But then they came to Cabler's house by the wharves. A large, well-armed group of gamblers had barricaded themselves inside. The mob surrounded the house. The back door was forced open. The windows had all been blocked off by the gamblers, and the interior of the house was pitch-black. The scene rapidly grew confused. People began shooting. One of the shots struck and killed a leader of the citizenry, Dr. Hugh Bodley, one of the most well-regarded men in Vicksburg. A newspaper obituary the next day called him "universally beloved and respected"; Henry Foote, who knew him, said in his memoirs that he was "a most intelligent and high-spirited young gentleman, of great professional promise." Bodley's death put the mob in a frenzy. They stormed the house, seized five of the gamblers, and immediately hanged them.

Over the next several days, the news about the hangings and the mass expulsion of the gamblers spread up and down the river. It caused an immediate wave of excitement. In river towns all through the valley, the committees of vigilance and safety were joined by new "anti-gambling societies" that took the events in Vicksburg as their model. They were guided by Stewart's pamphlet and by the now-universal belief that the river gamblers as a class were connected to the Mystic Clan. They were also galvanized by the sudden appearance of the gamblers themselves in their midst: those who had been expelled from Vicksburg were scattering along the river and were showing up in alarming numbers in other river-front districts. The anti-gambling societies made a great point of deploring the hanging of the five men in Vicksburg Landing—but they also put up posters announcing that any gamblers found in their communities "will be used according to the Lynch Law."

The weeks that followed were chaotic. As more towns purged undesirables from their riverfront districts, the Mississippi was suddenly swarming with a flood of displaced gamblers and prostitutes. They all were wandering from town to town, looking for any place without an anti-gambling society. Mostly they traveled by steamboat, but there were some large groups of gamblers who'd dawdled too close to a town's deadline and found themselves unhappily thrashing through the forests on foot while pursued by hunting parties. Many of the gamblers drifted down to New Orleans, where anybody could be hidden; others showed up as far away as Texas.

Meanwhile, in the rural counties the campaign against the insurrection was intensifying. Even though the July 4 deadline had passed with no signs of trouble from the slaves, nobody thought the danger was over. The committees in fact regarded the situation as so urgent that they dispensed with the trials before the lynching courts. Those who were arrested were simply hanged where they'd been caught. Sometimes their bodies were left dangling from the eaves of their houses or suspended from a high tree branch in a prominent place on the roadside, as a warning to the others. By mid-July every stranger found in the interior of Mississippi was being detained. Commercial travelers, itinerant craftsmen, wandering preachers—they were all caught up by one or another committee. One man hunting in the woods was arrested for possession of a shotgun and gunpowder. The vigilance committee found the evidence against him not completely conclusive—so they sentenced him to a flogging. But a mob had gathered outside the building where the committee was meeting, and when they heard the verdict, they were so outraged by its leniency that they stormed the building, seized the prisoner, and hanged him.

The net of suspicion was wide. Since one of the original victims of the Madison County committee was a Thompsonian doctor, all Thompsonians were automatically suspect. Henry Foote, traveling in the Mississippi countryside that summer, came upon a dire scene in a small town east of Vicksburg: a crowd had tied a man to a tree and was flogging him. He had been put on trial by the local committee and, in a rare move, had been found entirely innocent, but the townspeople weren't satisfied. It wasn't that they were certain he was guilty of anything in particular. "He was, unfortunately, a Thompsonian doctor," Foote wrote, "and on that ground it had been thought that he ought at least to be decently scourged."

Also included in the sweep were any locals the people had never much liked. One of these in Madison County, a William Benson, "was considered by the committee a great fool, almost an idiot"; the committee took pity on him and simply ordered him to leave town. Another was held in the local jail because he was deemed a "rascal." He was visited by the committee after sunset and was flogged until long after midnight; when they came for him again in the morning to pass sentence on him, they found he had hanged himself. Others, where there was inconclusive evidence of their guilt, were treated with what the committee viewed as mercy. First the accused would be given a thousand lashes. Then he would be stripped naked, bound at his wrists and ankles, dumped into a boat, and set loose on the local river—to work himself free, or to fall overboard and drown, or to die of sunstroke as the boat floated through the furnace of the summer day on its way downstream toward the Mississippi.

Meanwhile, the story of the Murrell excitement went on spreading, until it reached the world beyond the river valley. The people who had taken part in putting down the insurrection were shocked to discover that outsiders did not view the events in the same light they did. In fact, in the rest of the world, the valley's response to the danger was seen as somehow worse than the danger itself. The hanging of the Vicksburg gamblers was regarded as an especially heinous injustice. There were outraged editorials condemning it in newspapers in the North and even in Europe. It became the subject of protest ballads and pamphlets and broadsides; ultimately there was even a touring panorama, a full-size version of the storming of Cabler's house in the Kangaroos, with a sinister tree dangling with nooses in the background, awaiting the victims of the mob. The hanging of the gamblers was said to have been the event that first taught the rest of the world about the existence of the courts of Judge Lynch; it was the reason why "lynching" became a dirty word outside the South.

The story of the summer became increasingly garbled as it circulated. The retellers outside of Mississippi and Louisiana were never altogether clear what happened when. The way it was most often told, the Murrell excitement had actually started with the anti-gambling riot in Vicksburg, and then had spread back to the plantation country. At least that was the version Abraham Lincoln heard. In 1838, Lincoln spoke at the Springfield Lyceum about "the increasing disregard for law which pervades the country; the growing disposition to substitute the wild and furious passions, in lieu of the sober judgment of Courts; and the worse than savage mobs, for the executive ministers of justice." Here was how he summarized the summer of 1835:

> In the Mississippi case, they first commenced by hanging the regular gamblers. . . . Next, negroes, suspected of conspiring to raise an insurrection, were caught up and hanged in all parts of the State: then, white men, supposed to be leagued with the negroes; and finally, strangers, from neighboring States, going thither on business, were, in many instances subjected to the same fate. Thus went on this process of hanging, from gamblers to negroes, from negroes to white citizens, and from these to strangers; till, dead men were seen literally dangling from the boughs of trees upon every road side; and in numbers almost sufficient, to rival the native Spanish moss of the country, as a drapery of the forest.

After the worst of the frenzy had passed—after the interrogations and the hangings had petered out, after the committees had largely disbanded, after the scattered gamblers had resumed their old ways (many of them

had discreetly returned to the Kangaroos by the autumn of 1835), after the
people in Madison County had started sleeping in their own beds again at
night—a second edition of Stewart's pamphlet appeared.

It was a curious production. The original author, Augustus Walton,
vanished from the title page, never to be heard from again. John Murrell's
name was pushed far down into the subtitle as well: the pamphlet was now
called *The History of Virgil A. Stewart, and His Adventure in Capturing and
Exposing the Great "Western Land Pirate" and His Gang.* There was also this
new epigraph:

> *I am not willing to admit to the world that I believe him.*
>
> —*A bitter enemy*

> *I care nothing for his jealous animosity. He may vent his poisonous spleen. I
> am sustained before the world by evidence that shall chain his envenomed
> tongue.*
>
> —*Stewart*

There had always been a certain amount of skepticism about Stewart's
original pamphlet. This wasn't so in the lower valley, where the pamphlet
had been universally accepted at face value, but it was especially true back
in Tennessee, the site of Murrell's arrest and trial. There John Murrell had
been a known quantity. A lot of people had had dealings with him personally, and the notion that he was some kind of Mephistophelean master
conspirator struck them as preposterous. They'd never heard anything
about this "Mystic Clan," and they didn't believe it existed. To them, Murrell was a small-time horse thief, slave stealer, and swindler—nothing
more.

So how to account for Stewart? The skeptics pointed to one highly suspicious fact. When Stewart had been a witness against Murrell at his trial
for slave stealing, he'd never said a word about the Mystic Clan or about
the slave insurrection. Why not? There was an obvious explanation: he
hadn't thought any of it up yet. He'd waited until Murrell was safely convicted and thrown in prison, and then he'd spun the whole thing out of
thin air, just to cash in on Murrell's notoriety.

There was another and darker theory. This was the version favored by people with a grudge against Stewart—in particular, those whom Stewart had identified in the pamphlet as members of the Mystic Clan. Their theory was that Stewart was lying about his entire relationship with Murrell. The initial meeting on the river road had never happened; Stewart and Murrell had actually known each other all along. Murrell really did run some kind of gang of horse thieves and slave stealers—and Stewart had been one of them. He had invented his story about being a secret infiltrator so he could dodge his complicity in Murrell's crimes.

Stewart responded to these rumors and insinuations with fury. The second edition of his pamphlet was substantially longer and more elaborate than the first because it was primarily concerned with fending off these attacks against his good name. He (or whoever was the now-anonymous author) sometimes talked as though the insurrection was only a minor sideline for the clan; their real business was the persecution of Stewart himself. Page after page of the pamphlet recounts the ongoing malevolence of the clan and Stewart's own indomitable courage and fortitude in standing up to it. Stewart (still described only in the third person) is surrounded at all times with a halo of sanctimony; he is said to be "of untiring perseverance, and well schooled in the disposition of man; and possessed of an inordinate share of public spirit." His critics, meanwhile, are "murderers, thieves, and refugees, brandishing their envenomed weapons of destruction." Particular rage is reserved for "a certain Mr. A. C. Bane, who has been calumniating Mr. Stewart by means of abusive and slanderous letters, in which he has endeavoured to produce the impression on the mind of the public that Mr. Stewart was an accomplice of Murrell's in villany."

The second edition of the pamphlet didn't do anywhere as well as the first. Stewart blamed the poor sales on his critics, who he said were all secret members of, or at least sympathizers with, the clan. As one admirer of Stewart, the writer Philip Paxton, put it a few years later:

His enemies, the yet undiscovered members of the clan, in a thousand ways sought to poison the public ear. They denounced him as a member of the clan, induced by hope of reward, by cowardice, or a spirit of revenge, to betray the plot. When a man has hundreds of secret enemies thrusting their stealthy but fatal daggers into his character, with but few friends who can but ward off the more open blows, his chance for obtaining even-handed justice from any community is small, and so it proved with our hero.

Stewart's response was defiance: in the next election he ran for Congress. He did so, Paxton said, "to test his popularity and the strength of his enemies." He was badly defeated. He then capitulated: "Justly disgusted and indignant at the ingratitude of those for whom he had sacrificed so much, he left the state and country."

There were a lot of stories about where Stewart went after that. Back east somewhere, Henry Foote heard; or maybe it was out west; or maybe he'd gone undercover again with the clan. According to one story, he'd gotten rich. At the height of the original excitement, he'd been offered a ten-thousand-dollar reward by the Mississippi state legislature for alerting them to their danger—and he'd respectfully, even nobly, turned the money down. Now some people were saying that he'd somehow gotten hold of that money after all and was living in luxury in Europe. But Philip Paxton claimed to know the real story firsthand. According to him, Stewart moved to a barely settled region of Texas, where he lived in an isolated cabin in the desolate hill country along the Colorado River.

Stewart still insisted that he was in danger from the Mystic Clan. He was so certain the clan had him under surveillance, Paxton wrote, that he "did not dare to venture out from his cabin after dark, to have a light in his room, or to sleep in the same chamber as his wife." He let his hair and his beard grow wild, and if he had to go into town, he wore a disguise. He believed that the only reason the agents of the clan didn't attack him directly was that they had been ordered to hold off by John Murrell himself. Murrell was still in the penitentiary in Tennessee, after his original conviction for slave stealing—but the moment he was free, according to Stewart, he was going to come west and take his revenge.

In the spring of 1845, the news came that Murrell had finally been released. There were rumors in Texas—possibly started or encouraged by

Stewart himself—that Murrell was coming, that he had been spotted at this or that railroad depot or stagecoach way station somewhere west of the Mississippi. Stewart grew extraordinarily frantic. But the weeks passed, and Murrell mysteriously failed to appear. And by summer, even if Murrell had arrived, he would have been sorely disappointed. Stewart was already dead.

Some said it was natural causes—that was the version Paxton gave. Others said he'd been poisoned by persons unknown. According to another story, Stewart had been fatally shot in a saloon fight a short time before Murrell was expected to arrive in Texas. The man who shot him was a complete stranger, and nobody ever found out what they'd been quarreling about.

As for John Murrell himself, he was never charged with anything connected with the insurrection. He served out his ten-year sentence for slave stealing. He had a tough time in the penitentiary, even by the standards of those days. In his first months, he had made a daring escape but had been recaptured a few weeks later; as punishment he'd spent the rest of his sentence chained to a stone block in his cell. Some said he eventually converted to Christianity and became a model prisoner. Others said he went insane. In any case, he never said a word about Stewart, the pamphlet, or the clan.

After his release from the penitentiary, Murrell disappeared from public view. There were stories that he was spotted in this or that river town along the Mississippi—a gaunt, pale, sickly street preacher who'd cough up blood as he harangued passersby about damnation and Judgment Day. He is reported to have died of tuberculosis in Memphis, a year or so after his release, in the squalid back alleys of the riverfront district.

Over the next few years, as more writers took up the story, a fuller image of Murrell and the Mystic Clan emerged. Many questions left unanswered by Stewart were addressed. There was, for instance, the great practical mystery of how Murrell had managed to co-opt all the criminals of the lower Mississippi into his conspiracy. Philip Paxton described it as a feat worthy of Eugène Vidocq, the famous French master criminal turned private detective. Murrell had formed a kind of cordon of criminal police the length of the Mississippi, and anytime a crime was committed by somebody not in their lists, they would immediately investigate, identify the criminal, seize him, and bring him up before the clan for judgment. "The criminal was astounded," according to Paxton, "on discovering that deeds which he supposed none but his God and himself to be cognizant of, were known by numbers, whose mandate he must obey implicitly, and among whom he must enroll his name, or be immediately exposed to the world. . . . All . . . were fish that came to Murrel's net; the low gambler and the rich villain were equally received with open arms."

Other writers considered the extent of the clan and speculated on which celebrated criminals had been secret members. What about Alonzo Phelps, for instance, the backwoods highwayman and reader of Horace? His lawyer, Henry Foote, recorded his belief that Phelps had certainly been a member, or at least an associate. After all, hadn't he called for the emancipation of the slaves, even threatening to start a rebellion himself? Then there was James Ford of the Ford's Ferry Gang: a history published early in the twentieth century, Otto Rothert's *Outlaws of Cave-in Rock,* examined the matter of Ford's possible membership in the clan at length but found the evidence inconclusive.

As for the ultimate goal of the conspiracy, Stewart had taken it no further than the apocalyptic night of the insurrection, but others carried the story onward. In the version Frederick Marryat heard in 1839 (and the way it was told and retold in pamphlets and dime novels for decades afterward), the clan's real objective had been to overthrow the governments of the slave states and establish a new empire, with its capital at New Orleans and Murrell as emperor.

But was that still the plan? What was the clan up to? It didn't seem to trouble anybody that the clan was proving to be very elusive. None of the members identified on the master list in Stewart's first pamphlet were ever arrested or tried; nobody else ever came forward to confess membership; no intrepid adventurer ever followed Stewart's lead and infiltrated the group to find out about its current status. In the years after the initial excitement faded, the clan appeared only in fitful, ghostly traces here and there in the lower valley and the South. The abolitionist Cassius Marcellus Clay, for instance, wrote in 1845 that the lynched gamblers remained unavenged and that he had heard that the clan was continuing to look for payback: "It is said that this fraternity have sworn eternal enmity against Vicksburg." In 1853, the *Texas Ranger,* a newspaper in Galveston, Texas, ran a long story headlined THE MURRELL GANG IN WASHINGTON COUNTY, the gist of which was that a still-flourishing branch of the clan was up to its old tricks:

Passing counterfeit money, stealing negroes, cattle, and other property, were the principal branches of business followed by this extensive association. A correspondent of the *Ranger* says, the number of negroes stolen from the counties named is very considerable. Two of the gang, Short and McLaughlin, were tried for murder in 1848, but by means of their associates on the jury got clear, and afterwards boasted that they had followed one of the state's witnesses to take his life for giving evidence against them, which it is thought they succeeded in doing. The same correspondent says, the gang is composed of ministers of the gospel, merchants, lawyers, farmers, traders, and also that some editors of newspapers are inculpated, as having aided by their advice and support.

But nothing more followed from this report—perhaps those "inculpated" newspaper editors hushed it up.

Gradually the clan evanesced into folklore. John Banvard, artist of the "Three-Mile Painting" of the Mississippi, described in the pamphlet accompanying his panorama how he'd once been set upon by members of the clan. There'd been a furious gun battle, he said, and he'd left one of the villains dead—while he himself had rowed away with a souvenir line of bullet holes along the bow of his canoe. The actor Noah Miller Ludlow claimed in his memoirs that he'd first heard of the Mystic Clan during his earliest days traveling in showboats on the Mississippi, in the 1810s—when the real John Murrell was still a child.

Mark Twain was fascinated by Murrell. In *The Adventures of Tom Sawyer,* the gold that Tom and Huck Finn find at the end is said to have been left behind by "Murrel's gang." In *Life on the Mississippi,* Twain recalls with a certain kind of nostalgic pleasure how Murrell used to masquerade as a preacher (Twain always liked tweaking church people), and he indulgently compares Murrell's villainy with that of a current, highly celebrated outlaw, Jesse James:

> Murel was his equal in boldness, in pluck, in rapacity; in cruelty, brutality, heartlessness, treachery, and in general and comprehensive vileness and shamelessness; and very much his superior in some larger aspects. James was a retail rascal; Murel, wholesale. James's modest genius dreamed of no loftier flight than the planning of raids upon cars, coaches, and country banks. Murel projected negro insurrections and the capture of New Orleans; and furthermore, on occasion, this Murel could go into a pulpit and edify the congregation. What are James and his half-dozen vulgar rascals compared with this stately old-time criminal, with his sermons, his meditated insurrections and city-captures, and his majestic following of ten hundred men, sworn to do his evil will!

Among the whites of the lower valley and the delta, there had never been any serious doubt about Stewart's story. The consensus was and remained that Stewart had been telling the truth and the insurrection had been a real threat. Frederick Marryat wrote in 1839 that while Stewart had recently been savagely vilified, his critics "no longer attempt to deny that his revelations were correct." The actions taken by the committees and the courts of Judge Lynch may have been regrettable—even illegal—but however much the rest of the world condemned them, they had been necessary to stave off the ultimate catastrophe.

Why were they so certain the story was true? Stewart had been, as Henry Foote called him, an "insinuating" man, and his masterstroke of insinuation had been his claim that Murrell was secretly allied with the Northern abolitionists. The way his pamphlet tells it, the abolitionists were a worse evil than the clan itself. The pamphlet offers Stewart's vision of that awful day when the clan and the abolitionists would emerge from the shadows together and wreak destruction on the South—"the fertile fields and smiling scenes of his native land, destined to be deluged in the blood of his fellow countrymen; its cities and villages laid waste by the desolating march of a lawless and murderous band of ruffians and robbers, led on by a poisonous swarm from the 'great northern hive' of fanatics and incendiaries."

Passages like this went over very well in the lower valley. They were essentially how people pictured the abolitionists already: as a swarm of insects bent on destroying the South for some insane, inscrutable reason of their own. The fury against the abolitionists can be seen all through the Murrell excitement. The author of *Proceedings of the Citizens of Madison County* loses all sense of decorum when he comes to one of the white accused—the unfortunate A. L. Donovan of Kentucky, who had been "repeatedly found in the negro cabins, enjoying himself in negro society." The author reports incredulously that Donovan was once heard saying that he couldn't be a plantation overseer because "it was such cruel work whipping the poor negroes." No wonder the local vigilance committee was so easily convinced that Donovan was what the author calls "an emissary of those deluded fanatics at the north—the *Abolitionists*." He was immediately hanged. "Thus died an *Abolitionist*," the author remarks with satisfaction, "and let his blood be on the heads of those who sent him here."

The source of this venom was generally unstated, but not hard to deduce. It was an article of faith in the South that the slaves were basically well-treated and that any cruelties they suffered were rare aberrations in an essentially humane system. It followed that any resentment the slaves might feel at their situation was being deliberately encouraged by outside troublemakers acting out of sheer malice. In the wake of the Murrell excitement, a large organization of Northern abolitionists made an ill-advised attempt to reach out to moderate Southerners and sway them to their cause: they began mailing their pamphlets in bulk to prominent white citizens in the South and in the river valley. The result was a public explosion. Nobody believed that the abolitionists were trying to influence white opinion; it was obvious they were trying to get their propaganda into the hands of the slaves and trigger an uprising. President Andrew Jackson condemned the abolitionists in his annual message to Congress:

I must also invite your attention to the painful excitement produced in the South by attempts to circulate through the mails inflammatory appeals addressed to the passions of the slaves, in prints and in various sorts of publications, calculated to stimulate them to insurrection and to produce all the horrors of a servile war.

Legislation was soon passed making it a federal crime to use the United States mails to distribute abolitionist literature. From then on, postal inspectors routinely opened mail sent from Northern addresses to Southern destinations to ensure that no prohibited writings were passing through. In states throughout the lower valley and the Deep South, possession of abolitionist literature became a felony; any Negro, any person of color, slave or free, found with such literature was immediately put to death.

These actions, drastic though they might seem, did nothing to calm white anxiety. Stronger action was required. In the years that followed the Murrell excitement, more and more laws were passed to stamp out anything that might kindle an insurrection. It became a capital crime to teach slaves to read and write; it was forbidden for slaves to assemble in public for any reason—a prohibition that was soon extended to free people of color as well. In fact, by the 1840s and 1850s, free people of color had come to be seen as one of the main sources of danger, and their lives were increasingly hemmed in by laws designed to keep them down or to drive them out of the slave states altogether. Some states forbade free people of color to move or travel without permission from the government; other states expelled all free people of color who'd been born or emancipated after a certain date; still others retroactively invalidated their emancipations, so that any freed slave who remained in the state would be sold at auction to a new owner. Just before the Civil War, Louisiana passed a law making it illegal for any slave to be emancipated for any reason.

But none of it helped; the dread was unappeasable. There is no solid evidence that slaves anywhere in the South ever attempted to organize a large-scale uprising after the catastrophic failure of Nat Turner's revolt in 1831—three years before the Murrell excitement even began. But the whites saw new uprisings everywhere. In December 1835, after the initial wave of the Murrell excitement had died down, it flared up again, this time in Louisiana. It began when a rural vigilance committee got a slave to confess that the insurrection was back on and was scheduled for its original date, Christmas 1835. (The committee may have been inspired by a play called *The Great Land Pirate,* based on Stewart's first pamphlet, which had just opened in New Orleans.) The committee led a frantic search of all the plantations for miles around; a rumor spread that caches of weapons had been found in many of the slave quarters. New committees immediately sprang up, and regulators and slave patrols spent the rest of that month keeping watch. The plantation owners and their families were evacuated and waited out an uneasy Christmas in New Orleans.

The excitement faded away by January—but two years later, it burst out again. This insurrection was said to have been betrayed before it could begin by a slave who was unwilling to see his beloved master harmed. More than fifty slaves and free Negroes were arrested by the local committees; twelve were executed. Two companies of federal troops were stationed in the region over the next several months to preserve order.

From then on, every few years—sometimes more often than that—the excitement erupted anew in random places throughout the lower valley. It went essentially the same way each time: an overheard conversation among the slaves would be given a sinister interpretation by their owner, and there would be a flurry of interrogations and coerced confessions, then a general panic. After urgent sessions of the courts of Judge Lynch, several people, sometimes dozens, would be left dead. But in the end, the ultimate organizers of the conspiracy remained mockingly out of reach, and the panic was primed to break out again somewhere else.

Anything at all could be the trigger. In New Orleans in 1840, after a few scattered incidents of hostility on the street between whites and disorderly slaves, one newspaper editorialist wrote that "the late repeated attacks of the negro upon the white man in our city should excite our suspicions whether they be not the piquet guard of some stupendous conspiracy among the blacks to fall upon us unawares." By the 1850s, when fresh excitements were sweeping the South, one panic was set off in Virginia by the sight of a line of slaves heading to work in the mines: they were carrying shovels and pickaxes, and people thought they had armed themselves for murdering their masters. Another wave of panic spread through Texas in the summer of 1860 after a number of big fires broke out in the major cities. Texas happened then to be in the middle of a severe drought—but nobody blamed the weather. The fires had to be the work of secret gangs of disaffected slaves and infiltrating abolitionists. There followed a convulsive wave of arrests and lynchings. By early fall, when the rains returned, the situation briefly calmed. It flared up all over again that November, reached a new peak of fury, raged out into the lower valley, and then inflamed the whole South as the news spread that the archfiend of the abolitionists had just been elected president of the United States.

13

The Oracles

IT WAS A CREDULOUS AGE. One reason people were so quick to believe in the Murrell excitement was that they were eager to believe in anything, no matter how strange, as long as it was bad news. They were particularly fascinated by occult portents of doom. Everybody knew that owls and whip-poor-wills were evil omens, that a dog howling in the night meant somebody was about to die, that prudent people had to carry a tuft of wool tied with thread at all times to prevent being ridden by witches. It was a time of séances and mirror divination and spirit rapping—an era when, as Melville observed in *Moby-Dick,* "the rumor of a knocking in a tomb will terrify a whole city."

Many people lived their whole lives in a penumbra of supernatural dread. Calvin Stowe, for example, the husband of Harriet Beecher Stowe, was a down-to-earth and practical man, but he was tormented all his life by visions of weird presences infesting the world. On the streets mingling with ordinary people, he said, was another race "with the human form and proportion, but under a shadowy outline that seemed just ready to melt into the invisible air, and sometimes liable to the most sudden and grotesque changes." These "rational phantoms," as he called them, were hunted by yet another supernatural race, which appeared as "heavy clouds floating about overhead, of a black color, spotted with brown, in the shape of a very flaring inverted tunnel without a nozzle. . . . They floated from place to place in great numbers, and in all directions, with a strong and steady progress, but with a tremulous, quivering, internal motion that agitated them in every part." And then there were the devils—a great many devils, down every street and in every meeting place. They were "very different from the common representations," he said. "They had neither red faces, nor horns, nor hoofs, nor tails. They were in all respects stoutly built and well-dressed gentlemen. The only peculiarity that I noted in their appearance was as to their heads. Their faces and necks were perfectly bare, without hair or flesh, and of a uniform sky-blue color, like the ashes of burnt paper before it falls to pieces, and of a certain glossy smoothness."

People troubled by apparitions like these did not find in the culture at large any kind of reality check. Newspapers in particular were infamous for their shameless romancing of the violent, the bizarre, the occult, and the fantastic. Reporters casually invented the most surreal stories out of thin air; editors hungry to fill blank pages ran them without a second thought. Mark Twain, in his early days as a reporter, was once so desperate for copy that he made up a particularly horrific mass murder; Edgar Allan Poe announced the first successful manned crossing of the Atlantic by balloon. Some of these stories grew into elaborate epics. The journalist Richard Adams Locke became famous for a series of reports describing the remarkable discoveries the astronomer John Herschel had recently made about the moon. Herschel's new telescope, according to Locke, had disclosed that the lunar landscape was a colorful and rich tapestry of crystal valleys, hills of quartz, and basalt mountains covered with red flowers. It was also, Locke announced, swarming with intelligent life—most notably, a half-man, half-bat species with copper-colored fur and yellow faces. They were, Locke said, "doubtless innocent and happy creatures, notwithstanding that some of their amusements would but ill comport with our terrestrial notions of decorum." He discreetly refused to specify what those indecorous amusements might be; he said they were "so very remarkable, that I prefer they should first be laid before the public in Dr. Herschel's own work." (Other newsmen eager for the details sought out the real John Herschel, who happened then to be at an observatory in South Africa; he had heard nothing about the story and reportedly could not stop laughing.)

But the true crowd-pleasers were those romances that involved disaster—the larger the better. The greatest popular upset of those years arose over the predictions of a Calvinist preacher named William Miller, who reviewed all the signs and concluded that the end of the world was at hand. Miller would later insist that he never actually pinpointed a time, but his followers took care of that for him: earth's last day, they announced, was going to be March 21, 1843. By the beginning of that fateful year there were daily newspapers in several cities devoted wholly to discussions, analyses, and proofs of Miller's prophecy. Two of the most prominent of these papers, *Signs of the Times* and *Midnight Cry*, were read all over America. An edition of *Midnight Cry* published for the frontier, *The Western Midnight Cry*, distributed from Cincinnati, terrified people throughout the Mississippi valley. By early March 1843, the writer John S. Robb observed, all the river men's talk on the Mississippi was of "the awful evidences of a general conflagration, the signs of the times, the adding up of the times, the proof of their meaning, and the dreadful consequences of being unprepared—with ascension robes." Miller, it was said on the river, was going to "burn down the world." The belief spread into the remotest corners of the valley. When the feared day of March 21 at last arrived, the diarist Bennet Barrow, who owned an isolated sugar plantation in the bayou country, discovered to his annoyance that his slaves were in an uproar about the Miller prophecy and that no work could be done until he gave his slaves "a lecture on the folly of their belief that the world would end today." Meanwhile, the boat people by the thousands were spending the whole of the twenty-first clustered in fright in the deepest channels of the Mississippi. The deep river, they believed, was the safest place to ride out the firestorm.

While waiting for the disaster—whichever disaster they were currently dreading—the people of the river valley became increasingly bewitched by large-scale distractions and amusements. Commercial entertainment was an enormous business on the river in the years leading up to the Civil War. An ever-growing armada of fun and hoopla came downstream: circus boats and theater boats, opera boats and showboats, medicine shows and solemn lecturers on mesmerism, demonstrators of electricity and phrenology, preachers and barkers and card readers and professors. This invasion was led by P. T. Barnum himself, who conducted an enormously successful tour of the lower river with the superstar singer Jenny Lind in the 1840s. But Barnum had countless predecessors, rivals, imitators, and followers—some of whom put on even grander shows than he did.

The theater boats and opera boats were particularly gaudy. They would come into river towns and send out heralds and trumpeters through the streets to announce their performances. They mostly played melodramas and light comedies; the actors would seize every chance for spectacular sword fights and impromptu dances. They were also adept at improvisation and would often draw the most drunken hecklers into the action just to ridicule them. They regularly staged the classics, too, but the scripts were rewritten to fit the modern taste: there was a popular version of *Hamlet* that made Ophelia the tragic heroine, driven mad by the villainous prince. There were also several adaptations circulating of the great literary sensation of the age, *Uncle Tom's Cabin*—although when the theater boats crossed into the lower valley, they'd prudently put on a version where the slave owners were benign and the slaves happily accepted their lot.

The grandest shows were on the circus boats. Stickney's New Orleans Circus, Dan Rice's Metropolitan and Hippo Dramatic Circus: they would arrive with clowns, slack-wire acrobats, dog and horse acts, amazing gymnasts—one gymnast, highly praised by the local Natchez newspaper in 1837, could do twenty-eight backward somersaults in a row. Spaulding and Rogers's Floating Circus Palace was a showboat more than two hundred feet long that required its own full-size steamboat as a tug. It had chimes, sirens, and a huge pipe organ; as it pulled up to the levee, a brass band played on deck to entertain for free those who came down to watch its arrival. The boat seated more than three thousand people. There was an equestrian act featuring forty horses. There was the Museum of Curiosities, with thousands of odd trinkets and treasures, from rows of exotic seashells to stuffed tigers. The strangest attraction in the museum was an oracle—a brass sphere with four protruding trumpets that hung in the middle of a dark stage. In a sinister and otherworldly voice, it would emit riddles about the future. Some of these were topical jokes; some were references to local affairs, which always startled the spectators (the show people would have gone into town that morning and eavesdropped for the latest gossip); some were so cryptic, and were transmitted in such a thick, garbled accent, that nobody understood what they were about. "If the responses were unintelligible," one of the performers shrewdly observed, "this only added to the mystery."

By the 1850s, the most popular form of entertainment on the river was the minstrel show. Dozens of minstrel troupes went on tour in those years—

groups with names like the Christy Minstrels and the Congo Melodists and the Original Ethiopian Serenaders. Most of them were white men performing in blackface, but there were some all-Negro minstrel shows, too, and a few with female performers. These were highly controversial; in fact, the minstrel phenomenon in general was so upsetting to audiences in the slave states that in the years just before the Civil War, minstrel shows were banned throughout the Deep South and the lower valley.

The shows were alarming and exhilarating. Audiences had never seen anything like them. Their atmosphere was ferociously unpredictable. The performers kept breaking into wild dances without warning: the Buck and Wing and the Cakewalk, the Shuffle and the Buzzard Lope and the Ring Shout and Jump Jim Crow. When they weren't dancing, they were writhing and hopping and twisting into contorted knots as though they were being jolted by an electric current. They told lurid, outlandish jokes and absurd tall tales in a high-pitched, extravagant parody of Negro dialect. They sang, without parody, Negro folk songs and spirituals, which most white audiences had never heard before; the mourning beauty of the melodies and the strange plangent harmonies left people shaken and sometimes in tears. They staged outrageous skits about current events that were mocking, nasty, and maddeningly equivocal—audiences couldn't tell who or what was being made fun of, and often ended up getting into fist-fights to settle which side was which. Almost every performance ended with avalanches of cheers and boos. After his first sight of a minstrel show, George Thatcher, who later became a popular minstrel himself, recalled: "I found myself dreaming of minstrels. I would awake with an imaginary tambourine in my hand, and rub my face with my hands to see if I was in blackface."

The basic minstrel show was in two parts. In the first part, the minstrels gathered onstage in a semicircle and performed a kind of riotous after-dinner banquet of comic speeches and songs. The master of ceremonies, at the center of the stage, was known as the interlocutor; at either end of the semicircle were the two most extravagant jokesters, known as the end men: Mister Tambo and Mister Bones. The high point of this scene was the furiously ornate banter between the interlocutor and the end men, which was punctuated by smashes of the tambourine and the rattle of drums, and which would sooner or later break down into uncontrolled slapstick violence. The second half was slower and more elaborate. It featured skits and parodies and musical numbers. There were a lot of drippingly sentimental love scenes, with heartrending partings and tearful reconciliations. There were often brutal burlesques of celebrities like Barnum. But most of the scenes were about the slaves and slavery.

These scenes were jumbles of discordancy. They mocked the slaves and ridiculed the masters. They travestied the abolitionism of *Uncle Tom's Cabin* and then showed slave owners as sadistic madmen who'd string up slaves to use as scarecrows. There were sketches about the absurd pretentions of free Negroes—often starring the swaggering dandy Count Julius Caesar Mars Napoleon Sinclair Brown. There were other sketches about a wise and cunning trickster slave named Jasper, who always got the better of his owners. There was a song sung by a slave that included these lines:

White man come to take my wife
I up and stick him with a big jackknife.

There were also constant references to Nat Turner's revolt and the Murrell excitement. There was even a long sketch, evidently performed by several troupes, called *Uncle Gabriel the Negro General,* which was a kind of high-speed mock-epic about a slave insurrection. It seems to have been unnervingly ambivalent: Uncle Gabriel was mocked throughout as a grandiloquent clown, and yet there was a sudden swerve into pathos at the end, when his rebellion was inadvertently betrayed by an innocent slave boy, and at the curtain there was a certain distinct regret that it hadn't come off.

If there was an overt message to the minstrel shows, it emerged at the climactic scene: the stump speech. This was a particularly manic satire on current events. Its point was that things—no matter what things—could not go on like this much longer. The stump speech featured one of the minstrels climbing up onto a makeshift podium (sometimes a prop tree stump, hence the name) and launching into a bizarre rant on some fashionable topic—abolitionism, an upcoming presidential election, séances. The other minstrels would gather around, all doing their own distinctive dance steps and gesticulations. As the speech grew progressively louder and impassioned, their movements and responses would grow more spastic and violent, until the whole troupe was barking and squawking and twirling and shaking and grunting and whistling in a wild cacophony. The speech would hit a frenzy of nonsensical eloquence. This example (unearthed by the historian Robert Toll) is on the then-voguish subject of transcendental philosophy:

> Transcendentalism is dat spiritual cognoscence ob psychological irrefragibility connected wit conscientient ademption ob incolumbient spirituality and etherealized connection which is deribed from a profound contemplation ob de irregability ob dose incessimable divisions ob de more minute portions ob subdivided particles ob inwisible atoms dat become anatomcattalable in de circumambulatin commotion ob ambiloquous voluminiousness!

The last part of the speech would be an unintelligible shrieking. Then, as at a camp meeting, the speaker would fall into convulsions, and the whole troupe in response would simultaneously collapse unconscious to the stage floor.

In those years, many in the river valley who had a horror of politics, who never read newspapers, who avoided gossip, who didn't listen to the preachers of the apocalypse, who stayed away from minstrel shows and all forms of popular entertainment, were still dogged by a sense of coming catastrophe. For them there was a ready-made and inescapable symbol: the steamboat. The more dominant the steamboats became on the river, the more they became a byword for imminent calamity. In *Moby-Dick*, Melville casually described a boat in hot pursuit of a whale as shooting "along the water like a horizontal burst boiler out of a Mississippi steamer." When the diarist Mary Chesnut described a near-fatal heart attack, one comparison came instantly to mind: "Have a violent attack of something wrong about my heart. It stopped beating—then took to trembling and creaking and thumping like a Mississippi high-pressure steamboat."

The record of steamboating on the Mississippi grew to be a litany of disaster. Steamboats wrecked on snags; they went hopelessly aground on sandbars and had to be abandoned; some, especially those on the upper reaches of the river where the settlements were sparse, simply disappeared on the long river stretches between stations and left no trace behind. There were even a few found drifting downriver with the crew and the passengers missing and no clue about what had gone wrong.

But the most common mishap was a boiler explosion. Steamboat boilers were ornately cranky devices that needed constant monitoring; preventing catastrophic malfunction was a full-time job for any steamboat engineer. In general the boilers (mostly wood-fired, although the newest models at midcentury used coal) were competently made and under normal circumstances would have run smoothly for years; the problem was that they were designed for pure water, not the murky, muddy, silty, debris-heavy water of the Mississippi. The river water was pumped up directly from the current and poured into the boilers—nobody could be bothered to filter it. The result was only to be expected: the tanks and the ornate lacery of piping were perpetually clogged with glutinous slosh. The clumping and sticking meant that the boilers were always heating unevenly—and whenever the heat and the pressure erratically spiked beyond the tolerances of the metal, the catastrophe shortly followed.

The narrow margin of safety was further compromised by the increasingly reckless way the boats were operated. This became a major issue in the years just before the Civil War, as the steamboat companies were under growing economic pressure from the new railroads. Businessmen and traders along the river, and particularly in New Orleans, were becoming alarmed at the declining numbers of arrivals and departures in their harbors: it was unmistakable evidence that more and more goods were being shipped by railroad to ports on the Gulf and were bypassing the river altogether. New Orleans businessmen were actively campaigning for their city to become a major rail hub, just in case the steamboats joined the keelboats in oblivion. The response of the steamboat company owners was to push their captains and pilots to go faster. This did not mean bringing in a new generation of speedier steamboats; it meant running the existing steamboats at full throttle essentially all the time.

They were, in a way, successful. Early steamboat trips up and down the river went on for months; in the 1830s, the trip from the delta to the northern valley took more than two weeks; by the Civil War, New Orleans to St. Louis was down to four days. In order to draw attention to how fast steamboat travel was becoming, the captains and pilots were encouraged by the owners to stage impromptu races. If two steamboats came around a bend and spotted a wood yard ahead, they'd tear upriver together to see who'd get there first—much to the exhilaration and terror of the passengers, who were not offered the chance to go ashore before the race began, and much to their ultimate horror if an overtaxed boiler blew before the finish line.

By one count, there were more than five hundred steamboats lost on the river between the 1830s and the Civil War. These disasters were recorded in ballads, newspaper stories, broadsheet engravings—and, inevitably, the Mississippi River panoramas. John Banvard's "Three-Mile Painting" included a scene of a steamboat fatally wrecked on a snag; its bottom was stove in and it was upending into the current. John Smith's *Leviathan Panorama* went one better and showed a steamboat after a boiler explosion. This was a scene that invariably made audiences gasp. A newspaper reviewer described it: "The thrilling interest kept up through the whole—the burning steamboat, the pilot burnt at the wheel, the captain tearing the planks off the upper deck, the yawl upsetting, and females perishing, is a sublime and terrible scene."

Steamboat disasters became so frequent that a whole new industry formed around their salvage. This made its way into the panoramas, too: Smith's found room for an up-to-date scene showing the workings of the new diving-bell salvage boats designed and built by a young inventor named James Eads. Eads's bells were submersible vessels that were open at their base so that their occupant could scour the river bottom for the debris fields of wrecked steamboats. (Eads's prototype version was a whiskey hogshead weighed down by lead ingots.) Once the wreckage was spotted, the large pieces would then be secured and winched up to the surface. Eads sometimes did this work on commission for steamboat companies trying to recoup part of their losses, but he also freelanced for older wrecks: the law in most states along the river was that any boat sunk more than five years belonged to whoever salvaged it.

From the late 1840s on, Eads's boats ranged the length of the river, and his diving bells went down under in all of its conditions and moods. Eads once descended in the middle of a catastrophic flood; he didn't find the wreck he was searching for, but he never forgot the sight of the sand and silt "drifting like a snow-storm at the bottom, sixty-five feet below the surface." He claimed that, adding all his dives together, he had walked every mile of the river bottom from St. Louis to the delta.

Eads's boats became the inevitable accompaniment to any big disaster. They did particularly well after the 1849 fire that destroyed the St. Louis waterfront; dozens of wrecked steamboats were there for the picking at the bottom of the harbor. The boats also routinely haunted the stretch of the central river around the junctions with the Missouri and the Ohio—so many steamboats were coming to bad ends in the turbulent waters there that it was known as the Graveyard. In fact, Eads found his supply to be inexhaustible. No matter how many bends of the river he searched for wreckage, there was always some new form of calamity ahead.

The upper river froze over each year, usually sometime in December, and the ice generally didn't break up until early spring. It was always a big moment, the spring day when the river opened up. The ice floe disintegrated in a great grinding jumble: the bergs and shards and scraps would be swept downriver by the current and would gradually dissolve in the warmer waters of the lower valley. Sometimes the current was still so cold that the larger wrecks of ice held together for hundreds of miles, menacing the river traffic almost all the way down to New Orleans. It wasn't typically until mid-April that the central river was clear and the armada of steamboats that overwintered at the St. Louis levee was set free to move down to the delta again.

The winter of 1856 was unusually cold in the central valley. At St. Louis the river froze over to a depth of three feet, and the floe was firm enough so that people could ride teams of horses between the Missouri and Illinois shores. Then, in February, there was a freak thaw in the North Country. An immense volume of meltwater poured into the upper river. The water was still icy cold when it reached St. Louis—far too cold to melt the floe there. Instead the force of the deep current beneath the ice gradually worked the floe loose from the banks and sent it creeping in a single mass downstream.

The movement was first noticed in the early-morning hours of February 27. It was initially so slight that it couldn't be seen by the naked eye. Anybody looking out from the St. Louis levee saw the same monotonous ice plain that had been in place all winter. The evidence for what was happening was more indirect: a cluster of small boats docked at the northern end of the levee was found to have been nudged out of the river overnight and deposited on dry land. Only over the course of the morning did the floe's slide southward become unmistakable. By noon people from all over the city had gathered at the levee to watch it. The scene was eerily silent at first—but gradually, as the movement of the floe increased, there made itself heard a confused murmur of muffled thunder from all directions, punctuated now and then by a colossal boom or bang when the floe split or collided with something along the shore.

Then people saw that the steamboats moored along the levee were beginning to move. There were forty of them that winter: giant white-pillared, black-chimneyed jewel boxes. The crowd watched in helpless awe as, one by one, they were pushed from their places by the floe. It happened like some mechanical process going horribly wrong. First a boat was torn loose from its moorings. Then it was slowly nudged sideways down the levee. Then, in a deafening cacophony of splintering wood and twisting metal, it turned, toppled over, bent into impossible contortions, and smashed into the next steamboat in the row. The whole process, moving down the levee, took about half an hour. In the end not one steamboat was left.

The wreckage spread out in great heaps along the floe, which was still creeping downriver. At the south end of the levee the floe met up with another line of boats, mostly wood rafts and flatboats. Over the next hour, fifty of them were reduced to kindling. Then the river surface began to change. As the floe glided away, it left behind a churn of ice shards and meltwater. One newspaper report described the river as being in "a frothy, crumbled condition, with an occasional solid piece." The current of free-running water strengthened. The shards and boulders and bergs being carried downriver began to pile up along the shoreline. The day was bitterly cold, and the pieces soon froze into place. By evening the levee had been covered over by ice; by morning there was a mountain range of ice twenty feet high. People peering into it could see the wreckage of the steamboats—the railings and chandeliers, the gambling tables and the wine goblets—preserved within the gleaming shadows of the ice mountains, where it would remain until the spring thaw came.

PART FOUR

BEHEMOTH

14

The Sky Parlor

BEFORE THE CIVIL WAR, the gentlemen and ladies of Vicksburg had a private refuge. It was a little park, reserved for the best people, on a grassy hilltop near the heart of town. They reached it by a wooden stairway snaking up from steet level. The stairway allowed the ladies to ascend with dignity, their hoop skirts unencumbered by tangles and their parasols still trim; the gentlemen were able to keep up their gallant banter without losing a step to a jutting tree root or an ill-placed ravine. Slaves followed behind, bearing the picnic baskets—in those days, none of the best people were ever seen in public doing anything so menial as carrying objects.

The hilltop was a small plot of mown grass, set with wrought-iron chairs and tables and a spyglass. In the evenings the tables would be swathed in white tablecloths, and the wineglasses would be brimming. Around the plot were poles drooping with clusters of Chinese lanterns. Sometimes the parties went on long past midnight. By then the lanterns had guttered, and the lights of the town below were out; with the embers of sunset faded, the sky became an ornate drapery of starlight. The view gave the hilltop its name: the Sky Parlor.

Vicksburg stood on a high bluff overlooking the Mississippi about 250 miles northwest of New Orleans. The hilltop offered a commanding view of the town, the river, and the enclosing countryside. To the north and east of the Sky Parlor, past the last rooftops of the town, was a vista of a jumbled wilderness terrain: thickly forested hills and valleys and sloughs and ravines, romantically shrouded in mist, and as wildly lush and overgrown as a tropical jungle. To the south and southeast, the land was flatter and more passable: low hills and wide meadows and—more and more toward midcentury—the ruled fields and parceled-out expanses of the cotton plantations. To the west, across the Mississippi on the Louisiana shore, was a tangle of swampland. Cutting through the heart of the landscape, between the wilderness and the swamp, was a gigantic curve of the river. Vicksburg had been built on the outer bank of a hairpin turn: from the Sky Parlor you could see the river flowing northeast toward the town, and then bending sharply around a narrow tongue of swampland, and then flowing away again to the southwest, where it went on unfolding its slow, shining arabesques out to the horizon.

Vicksburg was a cosmopolitan town. It had always been rich, and in the years before the war, it was getting richer. Immense quantities of cotton from the plantations were passing out through the warehouses of Vicksburg Landing on their way to the delta, to the brokers in New York, and ultimately to the consignment markets of Europe. Coming back in were money and bulk goods and fine products from around the world. Vicksburg's population was only around four thousand, and yet its commercial district was able to support jewelers, custom tailors, portrait photographers, deluxe specialty bakers and confectioners, a grocery store selling fancy tinned goods from Europe, a milliner carrying fabrics from Asia, a perfumery stocked with scents from the Middle East, and a bookstore called Clarke's Literary Depot with the latest and raciest novels from New York, London, and Paris.

The coming of the war was not viewed in Vicksburg with much enthusiasm. There was no significant sentiment for abolition—but neither was there any for secession. That was in fact a common view among the river towns. They lived and died by the free passage of people and cargo up and down the Mississippi, from the northern forests to the Gulf, and whatever else the outbreak of the war meant, it was certain to start with river blockades. In New Orleans, after the state had voted for secession and even as the war began, there was a popular movement to declare neutrality and preserve its status as an open city.

The beginning of hostilities in April 1861 was anticlimactic. There was no great calamity in Vicksburg, not at first. The heaviest fighting was back east, far away from the frontier. The Mississippi blockades did duly appear, at Cairo, Illinois, at the north and at the river mouth in the Gulf, and many of the big steamboat lines did cease running. But the nearby tributaries remained open—most vitally, the Red River, which led west up through Louisiana into Texas—and each night a glittering boat city still assembled on the waters before Vicksburg Landing.

There were also the railroads. The trains from the western states ran to a depot on the Louisiana shore, where an armada of ferries was waiting to shuttle goods and people over the mile-wide water to town. In the east, another line ran through the wilderness country toward the heart of the Confederacy. Over the first months of the war, as more and more of the ocean and Gulf ports were blockaded, the railroad connection at Vicksburg became the main surviving link between the Deep South and the outside world. Jefferson Davis called Vicksburg "the nailhead holding the South's two halves together." Abraham Lincoln told his military commanders: "Vicksburg is the key. The war can never be brought to a close until that key is in our pocket."

About a year after the war began, Confederate forces started arriving in large numbers to defend Vicksburg and keep its railroad lines open. Over the spring and summer of 1862, interminable lines of wagons and troops came winding in from the train depots and the river ferry, and by the autumn of that year, the observers at the Sky Parlor saw enormous earthworks being constructed around the town—mazes of trenches and revetments and redans and barricades. At the same time, Yankee forces were gradually occupying the wilderness areas beyond; at night their countless campfires were brighter than the stars. By the time the Vicksburg campaign was at its height, in the summer of 1863, there were more than 150,000 soldiers contending for the town, and from the Sky Parlor it looked as though there were nothing left in the world but the war.

The Federal campaign on the Mississippi began in earnest in April 1862. That was when a large Federal naval force entered the river mouth from the Gulf. They were greeted by a spectacular gesture of outrage at New Orleans: the citizens had emptied the warehouses and had piled the levee high with bales of cotton and other goods waiting for export, and as the ships of the expeditionary force approached, the mountains of goods were all set on fire. But after that there was little else in the way of overt violence. The Federal force took the city essentially unopposed. Nor did they meet much more resistance as they moved on upriver, to Baton Rouge and then Natchez: both towns surrendered without firing a shot. The river was open all the way to Vicksburg.

The convoy advanced slowly. From the shrouded swamps and bayous on either side there would occasionally be the white puff and the remote sharp report of a sniper's fired rifle; otherwise there was silence. The wide waters of the river were deserted. Above Natchez, the Federal flagship detained two men poling downriver in a skiff. David Porter, a naval lieutenant, questioned the men closely. They claimed to be getting on with their business the way they always had. One of them said, "This is a highway, and I think we have a right to travel it." Porter decided they had a point and let them go.

They passed the big plantations on either bank. Some of them had been abandoned by their owners; the slaves were all gathered at the levee to cheer the convoy on. Other plantations were being guarded by committees of vigilance, who were keeping the slaves confined to their quarters and were sullenly patrolling the docks. Some plantations were shrouded in black billows of choking smoke: their owners, still in residence, had been inspired by the defiance at New Orleans and were burning their cotton. Many of them piled the bales along the levees before setting them afire. As the convoy approached, they would then shove the bales out onto the water. The bales unraveled and scattered in brilliant drifts and shoals and archipelagoes, while sparkling tufts of burning cotton blew with the smoke in thin shreds across the river's surface. The last of the fires would swirl and gutter in the wake of the convoy—harmless, David Porter remembered, but an impressive sight after sunset.

The convoy reached Vicksburg on May 18. By then the first of the Confederate reinforcements were already in place; new artillery batteries bristled from the shoreline and from the town on the high bluff. The expedition's commander, Admiral David Farragut, normally a vigorous and headlong attacker, quailed at the sight of them—much to the contempt of his junior officers. David Porter thought that the Confederate forces were probably still in disarray and that Vicksburg would be as easy a conquest as New Orleans had been. To the end of his life, Porter remained outraged at Farragut's timidity; he believed that if they'd stormed Vicksburg that day, they might have captured the town and put an end to the Confederacy then and there.

Instead they began digging in for a long campaign. Farragut believed that the major strategic problem he faced was to find a way to move his forces up and down the river out of range of Vicksburg's guns. His solution was to excavate a canal across the narrow tongue of swampland inside the hairpin turn of the river. This project occupied the Federal forces the rest of that spring and into the summer. The work crews spent weeks hacking through the overgrown tangle of cypresses and scrub pines and the thick, treacherous walls of grasses and cattails and reeds; then they had to shovel out the oozing, root-woven mud. The air was punishingly hot and muggy, and the swamps swarmed with battalions of mosquitoes and flies. The work progressed by inches, and the Yankees began falling sick. Mostly they suffered from dysentery and malaria, but there were also outbreaks of measles, and by the summer Old Yellow Jack was everywhere. Their pace slowed from a crawl to a snail's creep.

The Federal command then brought in a new army of workers: slaves from the abandoned plantations. The legal status of the slaves was just then at a point of maximum confusion; it was never altogether clear whether the slaves were conscripts, paid labor, or volunteers. But around a thousand of them set to work on the canal, and a few hundred women and children came in with them to cook their meals, take care of their camp, and run messages. The progress on the canal immediately picked up. By early summer there was a complete trench dug from bank to bank. But the work proved to be in vain: the river defeated them. Strong eddies were flowing away from the shore along the hairpin turn, which kept the main force of the current out of the canal trench. No matter how deep the canal was dug, it simply would not draw enough water to allow boats to pass. Then, in late June, the river rose. It was a big rise that year; the hairpin turn and most of the surrounding swampland were flooded out. The walls of the trench collapsed and avalanches of mud overfilled the entire excavation. When the water receded several days later, the canal had been erased and the work crews had to start over from scratch.

But by then several more waves of disease had swept through the Yankee camp and their strength had worn down to almost nothing. Even though they had taken only a handful of casualties in their occasional low-level skirmishing with the Confederates, fewer than half the troops were fit for combat. In late July Admiral Farragut decided to withdraw back to New Orleans.

"The Yankees have called off their gunboats and quit the river in disgust," wrote one local girl, Kate Stone, who lived on a plantation just outside of Vicksburg. "Sometimes now we can get the papers."

The Yankees returned in force at the end of August. A large fleet descended the Mississippi from Cairo, while another, smaller fleet came up from New Orleans. The Yankee naval forces had a new commander: David Porter, who had been promoted to acting admiral. He had none of Farragut's caution. He quickly bonded with his counterpart in the Federal army, General William Tecumseh Sherman, and he hugely admired Sherman's superior, Ulysses S. Grant: both men, he felt, had come to Vicksburg to fight. Grant, wrote Porter, "saw from the first that there was no use in sitting down before Vicksburg and simply looking at it, or bombarding it to bring about a surrender; we would have lost time, and deposited our shell in the hills, increasing their weight in iron, without getting nearer to our object."

But even Porter realized that storming the town was no longer a real option. While the Federal troops had been building their useless canal, the Confederates had so heavily reinforced the town that a direct attack would have been suicidal. Instead the Federal forces were driven to attempt a new strategy: cutting through the wilderness country north of the town in order to encircle it from the rear.

The wilderness proved to be a mysterious place. The hills were steep and impassably overgrown, and they were cut randomly by countless deep ravines. The Federal troops were disoriented by the ceaselessly infolding tangles of trackless underbrush; their supply trains routinely got lost, sometimes for days, just out of sight of their destination. Encounters with Confederate patrols rapidly deteriorated into confused and desperate firefights, with troops on both sides so bewildered by the labyrinths of foliage that they were charging randomly and firing wildly in all directions. They were even more baffled by the strange acoustic properties of the terrain. Sometimes vital reinforcements failed to arrive because they had inadvertently hidden themselves in the sound shadow of a steep ravine and couldn't hear the roar of a battle a hundred yards away. Then the autumn rains came, and the marshy ground turned to soup; wounded men were often swallowed up without a trace in the mud before medics could reach them. The autumn and then the winter passed in inconclusive and deadly skirmishing. Porter one day found Sherman despondent because several hundred men had been wounded or killed in a useless attempt to take a ridge heavily defended by Confederate cannon. Porter told Sherman to cheer up because it was going to cost them ten times that or more before Vicksburg finally surrendered.

Porter himself led one of the most ambitious campaigns of that autumn. The Mississippi always rose again after the low waters of late summer, but that season its rise was so high that its waters were washing back up into its tributaries and flooding the surrounding countryside. It gave Porter an audacious idea. He and Sherman would take a convoy with a large contingent of troops up to the Sunflower River north of Vicksburg. Then the convoy would cross out of the river and try to ride the floodwaters over the drowned bayou country to the south and east, until they reached the Yazoo River. From there they could descend upon Vicksburg from the rear.

The first part of the plan went just as he'd envisioned it. Federal work crews forced a breach in a levee on the Sunflower, and Porter's convoy glided across it, out from the river and into the flooded woodlands. But their progress after that was excruciatingly slow. After four days, they'd barely made forty miles. The forests closed in impenetrably around them. Each day seemed to bring them no closer to the goal. As the boats crept through the endless corridors of half-submerged trees, the crews saw nothing on either side, mile after mile, but hushed glades lit by a few passing shafts of dim sunlight. The leaf canopies were a solid mass overhead, and the thorny bristles of ancient treetops hung down low; the boats were increasingly battered by clanging, crashing, splintering collisions with the heavy, moss-draped branches. By the time they'd cut their way through to the Yazoo, Porter wrote, "most of the light vessels were perfect wrecks in their upper works."

The only chance the plan had of succeeding was through secrecy and surprise. But the passage through the flooded forests had been so slow, and had kicked up such a racket, the Confederates must have known about it almost from the beginning. Porter later wrote: "I am quite satisfied in my own mind that, while we were steaming along and performing naval evolutions in the woods, the President of the Southern Confederacy was reading something like the following dispatch to his Cabinet: 'Sherman and Porter pirouetting through the woods in steamers and ironclads. Are keeping a lookout on them. Hope to bag them all before to-morrow.' "

But at last they emerged onto the Yazoo and began their descent. They quickly found that their worst expectations had been correct: the river was held in force against them. The Confederates had had time to sink a line of boats to form a barricade across the river and had even thrown up a new fort with a battery of cannon trained on the spot upstream where the Yankees were most likely to appear. Porter recognized at once that the situation was hopeless and that he was obliged to order an immediate retreat. That meant executing another, even more awkward pirouette and steaming backward around a river bend before they could figure out a safe plan of escape across the flood lands toward the Sunflower and the Mississippi.

It had been a complete waste of time, like just about everything the Yankees tried that fall and winter. But Porter, looking back, found that he couldn't entirely regret it. At least, he never did shake the memory of that surreal forest passage. It looked, he wrote, "as though the world had suddenly got topsy-turvy, or that there was a great camp-meeting in the woods on board ironclads and transports."

"Today we actually had *cake,*" Kate Stone wrote at the end of September, "a most rare occurrence, due to Mrs. Hardison's sending us a little homemade flour." That was the sort of deprivation that Vicksburg was suffering—not much, and partly voluntary. They could have had flour whenever they wanted it; all through that autumn, there were trading boats from the North, laden with essential supplies and luxuries, passing the blockades with the permission of the Yankee military command. They sold their goods at what Stone noted were "ridiculously low prices." But, she declared stoutly, "of course no patriot could think of buying from them."

Stone even found some things about the situation cheering. She liked how the makeshift informalities of wartime life had cleared away the

stuffiness that Vicksburg's aristocrats had cultivated for so many generations. "We have been a race of haughty, indolent, and waited-on people,"
she observed. "A year ago a gentleman never thought of carrying a bundle,
even a small one, through the streets." But now, she wrote, "one gentleman I saw walking down the street in Jackson, and a splendid-looking fellow he was, had a piece of fish in one hand, a cavalry saddle on his back,
bridle, blankets, newspapers, and a small parcel in the other hand; and
over his shoulder swung an immense pair of cavalry boots. And nobody
thought he looked odd."

(The mood was not so sanguine among the Southerners who'd fled
their plantations and left their slaves behind. In St. Louis, the writer
Galusha Anderson observed, many of the refugees from the lower valley
proved to be spoiled, petulant, and literally incapable of getting into and
out of their clothes without slaves to help them.)

The town bore up well even when the increasingly desperate Federal
forces closed the blockades completely and began training their heaviest
guns on the bluff. Every day that winter, mortars were fired from the Yankee gunboats anchored in the river. The shells came floating up lazily:
most fell short; a few reached the town and punched through roofs or sent
geysers of dirt up from the streets. But they did little to dampen morale,
and strategically they accomplished nothing. After several weeks of incessant shelling, fewer than ten people in Vicksburg had been killed and only
thirty or forty injured. From the Sky Parlor, the attacks had a certain
beauty. "There was a strange fascination," one observer wrote, "in watching these huge missiles at night, as they described their graceful curves
through the darkness, exploding with a sudden glare, followed by the
strange sounds of their descending fragments."

By the beginning of the spring of 1863, people were growing hopeful
that the campaign would soon be over. It had been going on for almost a
year, and the Yankees had gotten nowhere at all. Even in the midst of the
bombardments, Vicksburg was still lively and crowded. The Confederate
command had issued a proclamation that "earnestly recommended" all
noncombatants evacuate, but few had obeyed: instead they dug makeshift
bomb shelters for themselves in the steep sides of the hills to ride out the
mortar attacks. And the long-range strategic position of the town remained
strong. There had been one bad loss over the winter—the Yankees had cap-

tured the depot on the Louisiana shore and had put a stop to the train ship-
ments from the west. But the Red River was still in Confederate hands and
some supply boats continued to come in. While the prices in the stores
were getting astronomically high, at least the shelves weren't bare: the groceries and clothiers and dry-goods stores in the commercial district were
still open for business. People began saying publicly, with something like
confidence, that when the summer came in and brought along Old Yellow
Jack with it, the Yankees were bound to give up and go away for good.

The first weeks of April were unusually beautiful. There was music at
the Sky Parlor and there were midnight hunting parties in the woods. The
nights were cloudless; in the moonlight, the river and the wilderness
looked almost as pristine as they had before the war. While the gunboats
of the Yankees were still squatting in the water out of range of the Vicksburg batteries, there was little sign of movement on the banks. The
thought didn't occur to anyone in town—or, in fact, in the Confederate
command—that the Yankees might be waiting for the new moon.

The Union command had concluded that their attempts to take the
town were accomplishing nothing and that there was no other strategy
open to them but one of sheer desperation: they would have to take the
main strength of their forces downriver, below the town, where they
would then try to encircle it from the open country from the south. This
meant that they would have to run the gantlet of Confederate batteries
massed on the shore and the bluff; it also meant that if the Confederates
managed to mount a counterattack and regain control of the river, the
Yankee force would be cut off in the middle of hostile territory. The
Union command proceeded with extreme caution. They moved their
troops slowly and surreptitiously through the swamps on the west bank of
the river, out of sight of the Confederate spotters. Meanwhile, they massed
their supplies in large transport ships, which they were going to send
downriver once the nights were dark enough to give them some cover.

They did not go completely unobserved. All through those weeks, the
Confederate scouts below Vicksburg were sending in reports of odd Yankee troop movements on the Louisiana shore. Eventually the commander
of the Confederate forces there ordered a detachment across the river to
reconnoiter. This proved to be an almost impossible task. The land was a
trackless swamp at the best of times, and that year the river was rising

early: the Confederate troops had to wade and thrash through mile after mile of icy water and mud. They gave up before they could complete their reconnaissance—but they had seen enough to terrify them. They returned to camp with an urgent warning: very large numbers of Yankee troops were moving south through the swamps. An enormous Yankee force was being secretly built up on the western banks, positioned for a major incursion across the river.

The report was duly sent up the line of the Confederate command, until it reached General John Pemberton, the man in charge of Vicksburg's defenses. Pemberton had already convinced himself that the Yankees were on the brink of withdrawing from Vicksburg and moving on to a new campaign to the east, based in the recently recaptured city of Memphis. He greeted the report of a secret massing of Yankee troops in the swampland with contempt. His only response was: *Much doubt it.* Those three words, it was later said, cost the Confederacy the war.

April 16 was another lovely day. The afternoon was cloudless and the sunset was serene. Mary Loughborough, the wife of a Confederate officer serving on Pemberton's staff, later recalled in her memoirs the beauty of the evening. She and a few friends went on a carriage ride through town and came home early; they took their ease at her rented house, which had a spectacular view of the river. The air was warm and pleasant. They could hear a band playing at a nearby park, and in the ruby glow of twilight, the huge Federal transports out on the water were black silhouettes with a few twinkling lamps.

After dark there was a ball at one of the town's grandest mansions. There young ladies danced with gallant officers from the Confederate headquarters. The girls wore their finest frocks—corn silk with black lace, white silk with blue point, grass-green with white lace. The officers were all in full dress uniform. The party spilled out onto the grounds of the estate, lit up by clusters of paper lanterns beneath a starry sky. It was the night of the new moon. The darkness of the countryside around Vicksburg was flecked here and there by the golden campfires.

On the river, near the Federal transports, a flotilla of small boats had gathered, around thirty in all. They were crowded with Yankee officers, newspaper correspondents, and an assortment of Northern civilians, both men and women, who'd come down with the Federal troops as observers. General Grant was there; so were his wife and children—they'd just arrived from Illinois for a visit. The atmosphere was festive. It often was before a big battle; the custom was for parties of civilians to position themselves out of the line of fire and watch the fighting unfold as though they were attending a sporting event. That night the correspondent for *The New York Times* reported laughter, singing, flirting, and "a running fusillade of champagne corks."

The night deepened; the lights of the town winked out. Everyone in the flotilla waited. Around ten o'clock they fell silent: a huge black shape was gliding past them in the water. It was Admiral Porter's flagship—the first of ten ironclads and large transports that were carrying the supplies to provision the expeditionary force below Vicksburg.

The convoy was seen first by the scattering of Confederate spotters who were perpetually darting around the river in canoes and small boats. They quickly crossed to Vicksburg Landing, where they alerted the sentries patrolling the riverbank. The sentries fired the signal cannon. The alarm rapidly became general. Then the convoy began its passage of the river before the town. That was when, to the amazement of the Yankees, the darkness was suddenly broken. A line of dazzling lights began springing up onshore. The Confederates had prepared for an assault on the riverfront by positioning along the full length of the levee rows of barrels of tar and pitch, interspersed with huge stacks of cotton bales soaked in oil. They had even commandeered all the abandoned waterfront sheds and barns and warehouses and had stacked them with kindling. As soon as the convoy approached and the alarm was sounded, Confederate troops carrying torches raced around the levee and set everything on fire.

The wall of flames towered over the river and lit up the surface of the water for a mile offshore. The slow, lumbering convoy was caught in the glare. It was immediately targeted by the Confederate batteries. The ironclads of the convoy returned fire. The brilliance of the flames along the levee was rapidly intensified by the spangled, crisscrossing fireworks of the cannonades. It was a "terrible" scene, General Grant said in his memoirs, but he conceded that it was also "magnificent."

The river had turned into a panorama of vast visual confusion. The roils of flame, the billows of smoke, and the dazzling lines of the soaring shells so baffled the spectators that some of them began to see strange things in the light. Several of the Northerners watching from the flotilla became convinced that a gigantic illuminated tower was looming above the town. It was most likely just Sky Parlor Hill underlit by the fires on the levee, but reports were solemnly printed in Northern newspapers for weeks afterward that the Confederates had secretly constructed some kind of infernal machine, a beacon tower that normally was hidden underground but could be raised up to a commanding and terrifying height whenever danger threatened.

By then everybody in Vicksburg was awake and was watching the battle unfold. Mary Loughborough remembered being roused by the booming of the signal cannon and going back out to her veranda, where her friends had already gathered. They could see on the blazing surface of the river the black line of the Federal convoy gliding downstream, firing off artillery as it neared the wall of fire on the levee, and they could feel the concussions as the shells landed on the streets around them. Meanwhile, Confederate couriers on horseback were hurtling frantically through the streets, the soldiers on the levee were shouting and running, and the sound of the falling shells was getting closer. Loughborough kept putting off the decision to take shelter. She waited until the flashes of light from the portholes in the Federal ships seemed to be directly facing her. "While I hesitated," she later wrote, "fearing to remain, yet wishing still to witness the termination of the engagement, a shell exploded near the side of the house. Fear instantly decided me."

Elsewhere in town, the fancy ball was still in full swing. Many of the guests drifted up to the Sky Parlor to watch the battle unfold. But as the firefight grew more furious, and shells started falling all over town, the partygoers began to succumb to panic. One of the girls was dancing with a brigadier general, and she asked him desperately, "Where shall we go?" He answered, "To the country for safety." He was joking—there was no time for them to go anywhere at all. But she and a group of her friends immediately started running down a road that led out of town into the forest. One of the gentlemen at the party noticed their departure and ran after them. "As a shell would be heard coming," a witness recalled later, "he would cry, 'Fall!' and down they would drop in the dust, party dresses and all, lying until the explosion took place; then up, with wild eyes and fiercely beating hearts, flying with all speed onward." Their energy and their initiative quickly ran out. They took shelter at the first house they passed, and they remained there until their friends and families sent carriages after them.

Around midnight, Mary Loughborough returned to the veranda, at a friend's urging, "that we might witness a beautiful sight." She found that the river had grown dark again; the convoy had departed, the fires along the levee had all gone out, and there were only long wisps of smoke floating up and vanishing from the shore into the night air above the town. But just off the levee was the "beautiful sight": one of the big Federal transports. Set afire by the shelling and abandoned, it was now drifting aimlessly in the shadows along the bank as it burned down to the waterline. But the sight did nothing to enliven the mood on the veranda. Loughborough's neighbors, she writes, were all "astonished and chagrined" by the events of the evening. They couldn't stop talking about the daring run of the Yankees and speculating on why it had worked. The abandoned transport had been the only one fatally struck; the others had glided through the gantlet and were now safely downriver. How could this have happened? As the guests went on talking late into the night, few were willing to believe that they had simply been outmaneuvered by the Yankees and that their great river defenses were worthless. (They wouldn't start seriously discussing the possibility until a week later, when the Yankees ran another, larger convoy past them and didn't lose a single boat.) Instead they fell back on their favorite explanation for everything that had gone wrong in the war: the confusion and incompetence of the Confederate military command. "Very few of the Confederate guns," Loughborough reported people saying, "had been discharged at all. Several reasons had been assigned; the real one was supposed to have been the quality of the fuses that were recently sent from Richmond, and had not been tried since their arrival. This night of all others they were found to be defective."

In fact, the whole story appears to have been wishful thinking. The Confederate batteries had sent a storm of shells down on the convoy. The real reason the Yankees had succeeded was Admiral Porter's characteristic bravado and willingness to gamble. He had noticed in previous skirmishes that the Confederate batteries had been relatively ineffectual whenever the action got near shore. There were only two likely explanations: either the Confederate gunners were poor shots (which he didn't believe), or else the big guns could not be repositioned so as to fire accurately at close range. He'd therefore ordered the convoy to run as near to the levee as possible. His gamble paid off: while the shells did batter his boats unmercifully, not one took a hit below the waterline, and among his crews, all taking shelter belowdecks, only six were injured and none killed.

But the truth about the Confederate failure probably wouldn't have made much difference in the postmortem taking place on Loughborough's veranda. Everybody was aware that, whatever the reason, the Yankees had scored a tremendous victory. From their new position, and with such a huge convoy of supplies to draw on, they could now cross the river, occupy the open and relatively passable countryside south of Vicksburg, and encircle the town at their leisure. Loughborough listened to the talk with increasing despondency and growing desperation. "The lurid glare from the burning boat fell in red and amber light upon the house, the veranda, and the animated faces turned toward the river," she wrote. "Fair and beautiful, but false, the crimson, wavering light."

The hills and bluffs of Vicksburg were made up primarily of loess, a fine-grained clay soil easy to excavate. In the weeks after the Yankees ran the gantlet downriver, the shelling of the town intensified, and the towns-people grew more and more skilled at digging out deep shelters in the loess slopes behind their houses or along backstreets and alleys. "Caves became the fashion—the rage," one Vicksburg woman remembered. Mary Loughborough had, or thought she had, one of the better shelters: it was around the size of a large drawing room, had several sturdy and comfortable chairs, and was high enough for anyone to stand upright. But her husband thought she deserved better, and paid to have a more elaborate cave dug. This one had a main room about six feet deep that led to two branches—one was her bedroom and the other her drawing room. It seemed luxurious to her, but by the rapidly rising standards of the town, it was still fairly primitive. The cave belonging to the town minister, William Lord, was an enormous excavation with five separate entrances from the alleys and backyards, and a hatchway up to the slope serving as both a ven-

tilation shaft and an emergency exit. A long central gallery that could hold
more than sixty people was flanked by galleries that served as dormitories,
kitchens, and slave quarters. Most nights it was packed with crying children, squabbling parents, and people coughing from the smoke that
poured out of the kitchens. But Lord's son remembered it as "the *Arabian
Nights* made real." He wrote: "The sound of a guitar here, a hymn there,
and a negro melody somewhere else, all coming to us from among swaying
Oriental draperies, sent me off at night to fairyland."

At first people hid out in the caves only in dire emergencies, when the
bombardment was particularly heavy and their own neighborhood seemed
to be the target. But as the Yankees gradually encircled Vicksburg in April
and May and their guns moved inexorably closer, the shells started coming
down everywhere, unpredictably, at all hours of the day and night. That
was when people abandoned their houses and began staying in and around
their caves full-time. They took great care to preserve a feeling of normal-
ity. Neighbors in adjoining caves paid each other formal visits frequently
throughout the day, to trade supplies and to exchange the latest rumors.
The slaves did the cooking and washing just outside the cave entrances,
under the overhang of the bluff, and ducked into the shelter only when the
bombardment was particularly fierce. Gradually the cave came to seem
like an ordinary home. When Loughborough came to write her memoirs,
she titled them *My Cave Life in Vicksburg*.

"The hill called the Sky Parlor," an anonymous diarist wrote that April,
"has become quite a fashionable resort for the few upper-circle families left
here." The ladies and the idle gentlemen would spend hours each day sur-
veying the occupied landscape through the spyglass. The Federal forces no
longer felt any need for secrecy and their movements of men and matériel
took place in the open, in broad daylight. Across the river in the swamp-
lands, long lines of wagons bearing supplies were trundling down newly
cut trails, and there was a continual flurry of couriers riding up and down
the western bank. Tugboats and rowboats shuttled back and forth among
the Union fleet, obviously carrying orders—Mary Loughborough noticed
that every time a tugboat visited one of the gunboats, the gunboat would
shortly afterward shift position. "Altogether," she wrote, "the Federal

encampment and movements were far more stirring and interesting than the quiet fortified life of Vicksburg."

The mood among the watchers at Sky Parlor was somber. Day after day, there was nothing but bad news. The Yankees now held both banks of the river above its confluence with the Red, and that meant that, upriver and down, the Mississippi was now wholly closed to Confederate traffic: no more supplies were coming in by boat. News soon came that they had captured the eastern rail depot. With both rail lines and the river lost, Vicksburg was now entirely cut off from the outside world. To keep up morale, the Confederate military command had spread the word that there were at least sixty days of provisions stockpiled. That was more than enough to last until a promised relief expedition arrived. But at the Sky Parlor one afternoon in the middle of May, Loughborough saw something that made her realize she and the other townspeople were being lied to. Two large rafts crowded with men pushed off from Vicksburg Landing and crossed to the Federal encampment on the Louisiana shore. The men were Yankee prisoners, and they were being released because the Confederates couldn't feed them. "The idea made me serious," Loughborough wrote. "We might look forward truly now to perhaps real suffering."

The encirclement of the town was complete by mid-May. Soon the field hospitals in the countryside were overwhelmed, and after each day's skirmishing along the siege lines, the wagons came rolling into Vicksburg bearing the sick and the wounded. New field hospitals were set up anywhere room could be found. Rows of white tents popped up in the public parks, on estate grounds, down residential streets, in cemeteries; in some of the cemeteries they laid the wounded men out in mausoleums and used gravestones as operating tables. The hospitals were segregated by the patients' condition. By far the majority of the field hospitals were for those with infectious diseases. The Confederate garrison was being devastated by wave after wave of yellow jack, malaria, dysentery, and measles; according to one estimate, by late May more than a third of the soldiers had fallen sick. The remainder of the hospitals were for the wounded.

The procession of wounds was appalling. "Every part of the body is pierced," the minister William Foster wrote after his first visit to the tents.

"All conceivable wounds are inflicted. The heart sickens." Foster saw a man with his hair, eyebrows, and eyelashes blasted off and his face burned to a crisp. A thick river of drool was perpetually cascading from his scalded and charred mouth. Another man had been shot through the jaw. His tongue had been tied back so he wouldn't choke on it. Another man had his jaw torn off; another had a pair of screwdrivers driven into his jaw and temples. "He floods the bed with his blood," Foster wrote. The care the wounded were receiving was minimal at best, and the conditions in the tents were dire—especially as the summer heat deepened and the insects came swarming. Wounds teemed with so many maggots that the delirious victims kept clawing their bandages off to try to get momentary relief from the torment. The flies on one wounded man, Foster wrote, were "like bees in a hive."

Most of the workers in the hospital tents quickly grew inured to such sights. But no matter how jaded they became, there was one place they had a hard time nerving themselves to enter: the surgery tent. Most of the surgeons at Vicksburg had received their training before the advent of chloroform—many were in fact opposed to its use on religious grounds, because the suffering of the wounded had been sent by God. The driving principle of their surgical training had been to get the operation over with as fast as possible before the patient died. This meant that most procedures more complicated than amputation were ruled out from the start (and would have been fatal anyway, without antisepsis), and amputation itself was seen as a move of desperation. William Foster estimated that more than half of the wounded who passed through the surgery tents died.

The procedure was simple. A patient with a wounded limb was given chloroform, as long as chloroform was still available. He was laid out on the surgeon's table and a tight cord was wrapped around the limb. The surgeon took a stiff jolt of brandy to fortify himself; then he quickly cut through the flesh with his knife and pulled back the flap of skin and muscle to reveal the bone. He took up a saw and used it to cut through the bone with one stroke. He looped a cord around the open artery, which was by then gushing out a torrent of blood, tied it off, pulled the flap of skin around the stump, and stitched it shut. The patient was carried to another tent, the amputated part was pushed off the edge of the table, and the next patient was brought in.

Beside the surgeon's table, amputated arms and legs, hands and feet, piled up over the course of the day. In the heat of summer they soon putre-fied. The Confederate command issued orders that the limbs be disposed of in some sort of respectful manner. But one slave assigned the duty later admitted that they were simply loaded up on a cart and dumped into an abandoned well.

By late May, the townspeople and the troops had come to blame their des-perate position on the Confederate military—particularly on General Pemberton. "Our troops," wrote Foster, "have no confidence in either the head or the heart of our commanding general." Everyone viewed Pember-ton—not without justice—as a weakling, as a vacillating and uncertain officer unable to exert authority over his subordinates. What was worse, he was a Yankee: he'd only joined the Confederate cause in the first place because he'd married into a Southern family. As the siege worsened, more and more people in town were saying openly that he was a traitor secretly working with the other side.

Pemberton was acutely aware of the decline in his reputation. As the Yankee lines closed in around the town, the word began to spread that the Confederate troops were going to rise in mutiny. Pemberton issued a pub-lic denial of all the rumors:

> You have heard that I was incompetent, and a traitor, and that it was my intention to sell Vicksburg. Follow me, and you will see the cost at which I will sell Vicksburg. When the last pound of beef, bacon, and flour, the last grain of corn, the last cow and hog and horse and dog shall have been consumed, and the last man shall have perished in the trenches, then, and only then will I sell Vicksburg.

It did little to quell the unhappiness about him, but it did go to show, as things ultimately turned out, that he was a man of his word.

The townspeople came to trust instead in rumors of victory elsewhere. For a while these were centered back east. There was a brief period of wild excitement when a story spread, which someone had supposedly read in "a Northern newspaper," that General Lee, having destroyed General

Meade's army, had advanced out of Virginia and now surrounded and was shelling the city of Washington. Union surrender was expected momentarily. Then it was expected within a few days. And then not at all.

Bitterly disappointed, people began to hope for salvation from closer at hand. These hopes coalesced around the figure of Pemberton's superior, General Joseph Johnston. Johnston was based in the town of Jackson in central Mississippi, and he was said to be gathering troops for a relief expedition to Vicksburg. Johnston was everything Pemberton was not: gallant, impetuous, authoritative, and purely Southern. He was a brilliant military leader—and he was also the sort of chivalrous gentleman for whom honor was everything and defeat was inconceivable.

Johnston's dispatches to Pemberton concerning the relief expedition were supposed to be secret, but Pemberton's staff officers, who accepted them at face value, continually leaked them. Partly this was to keep morale up, but it was also intended to undermine the ineffectual Pemberton by contrasting him with a bustlingly energetic hero. The word went out after each new dispatch that Johnston was getting closer, that he had almost arrived, that he was expected hourly. One townswoman, Dora Miller, heard that "expert swimmers are crossing the Mississippi at night to bring and carry news to Johnston." People gathered on the hillsides and ascended to the Sky Parlor and kept watch for telltale signs of movement in the eastern forests that would mean Johnston was approaching. By June the local newspaper had run out of newsprint and switched to rolls of wallpaper: the first issue in the new format contained the breaking story that Johnston was now expected within three days.

The shells falling on Vicksburg were not as destructive as modern artillery shells. They would detonate with a ferocious bang that would puncture the roof and shatter the windows and turn rooms into avalanches of plaster, but the building would typically remain standing, and people were rarely killed except by a direct hit. The main effect of the shelling was psychological. The bombardments went on remorselessly, all day and all night. There were a few lulls, chiefly to allow the cannon muzzles to cool, around sunrise, noon, and dusk; then the deafening barrage would resume again. One soldier stationed in Vicksburg, Willie Tunnard, recalled the distinct sounds each weapon gave off: "The hoarse bellowing of the mortars, the sharp report of rifled artillery, the scream and explosion of every variety of deadly missiles, intermingled with the incessant, sharp reports of small-arms." It was so loud that the endless low throbbing like thunder could be heard a hundred miles away.

Gradually it frayed and unraveled the will of the townspeople. Mary Loughborough wrote:

> I shall never forget my extreme fear during the night, and my utter hopelessness of ever seeing the morning light. . . . My heart stood still as we would hear the reports from the guns, and the rushing and fearful sound of the shell as it came toward us. As it neared, the noise became more deafening; the air was full of the rushing sound; pains darted through my temples; my ears were full of the confusing noise; and, as it exploded, the report flashed through my head like an electric shock, leaving me in a quiet state of terror the most painful that I can imagine—cowering in a corner, holding my child to my heart—the only feeling of my life being the choking throbs of my heart, that rendered me almost breathless.

Dora Miller fiercely resisted hiding out in the caves and defiantly insisted that she and her family carry on their ordinary life in their house—until the day she was blindsided by a terror she'd never felt before. She called that day "the most horrible yet to me, because I've lost my nerve." A shell came through the roof of the house and exploded in an upper bedroom; debris and dust scattered and ricocheted all the way down to the cellar. A neighbor had her thigh crushed by debris flying out across the yard; a slave girl lost an arm. Afterward Miller discovered that for the first time she was terrified, and she could not force herself to calm down again. "I do not think people who are physically brave deserve much credit for it," she wrote. "I am constitutionally brave, and seldom think of danger till it is over; and death has not the terrors for me it has for some others. Every night I had lain down expecting death, and every morning rose to the same prospect, without being unnerved." But there was one particular fear that hadn't occurred to her until she heard about the slave girl losing her arm: that she might be crippled and not killed. That was all it took to cast her into despair. "Life, without all one's powers and limbs," she wrote, "was a thought that broke down my courage."

By June the daily ration of food in the Confederate garrison had dwindled to one cup of rice and one cup of peas. These were called cowpeas—not true peas but a variety of hard and tasteless bean normally fed to cattle. Cowpeas and corn flour were ground together and baked into bread, which the soldiers called cush-cush. It was impossible to bake evenly; either the peas or the flour came out raw or rock hard. "It presented a black, dirty appearance," William Foster wrote, "and was most unwholesome—as heavy as lead and most indigestible."

Variety in their diet came only through the hazards of war. A mule or a horse killed in battle meant a little meat for the troops. There was a very odd animal at Vicksburg: a camel—one of the last survivors of an experiment the military had conducted in importing camels from Africa to use as beasts of burden. He was considered "a quiet, peaceable fellow" and his death in a shelling was widely mourned—but that did not stop the soldiers from immediately cutting up his corpse for food.

In Vicksburg itself there weren't many bulk provisions left. Soldiers in town would sometimes spend all their pay on the only delicacy still available: sugar. It was ruinously expensive, but they would simply buy fistfuls of it and lick it out of their hands on the spot. Most store shelves were empty, and the few items on sale tended toward the mysterious. GINGER BEER and SWEET CIDER were two signs that Willie Tunnard recalled seeing sticking out from barrels, but "it would have puzzled a scientific druggist," he observed, to determine what the barrels really held.

Beef and pork were unobtainable. They were replaced in butcher shops by mule meat—which several memoirists later claimed wasn't as bad as they'd thought it would be. One jokester printed up a mock menu for a local hotel restaurant offering Mule Tail Soup, Mule Head Stuffed à la Mode, Mule Brains Omlette, and Mule Foot Jelly. Desserts included acorns, nuts, Pea Meal Pudding, and—what may have been the bitterest joke of all—Genuine Confederate Coffee.

There was a near-universal belief that people around town were hoarding. Suspicion fell first on the local plantation owners. They had become notorious for their lack of patriotism—they openly disdained the Confederate government just as much as they had once loathed the Yankees. They wanted the war over on almost any terms (short of abolition) so that they could get their cotton to market again—in fact they were known, or at least were heavily suspected, to have secretly stockpiled their cotton harvest and burned only a token amount of it for show. They also refused to contribute to the defense of the town; they said they couldn't send in their slaves as work crews because it was too dangerous. Everybody took for granted that they were major hoarders of food. By late spring it was remarked that the plantation slaves looked better fed than the townspeople.

As the siege deepened, the rage turned instead on the grocers and other shopkeepers in the commercial district. They were accused of holding back essential supplies so they could price-gouge at will. One night in early June the town was awakened by the sound of alarms and the frantic rattle of the fire wagons: an entire block in the commercial district was burning, and several groceries and dry-goods stores were destroyed. Suspicion naturally fell on what the local newspaper called "spies and emissaries of the enemy in the city"—in particular, on a mysterious man in a Yankee uniform reported to have been wandering around town a few days earlier, asking many questions and being evasive about answering any himself. But for some reason no one had thought to detain this spectral personage, and by the time the military authorities had been alerted, he had disappeared. And anyway the real cause of the fire had already become known. It had been set by some of Vicksburg's own citizens as payback for the price-gouging of the downtown merchants. This would be the single most destructive occurrence in the siege—more damage was done in that one night than in the months of Yankee shelling put together.

The last of the food was running out by the end of June. People were so desperate for salt that they were tearing apart the butchers' smokehouses so they could scrape out the salt from the ancient fat drippings that had soaked into the floorboards. At night, one witness recalled, "an army of rats, seeking food, would scamper around your very feet, and across the streets, and over the pavements." There were constant jokes about how all the local pets were disappearing—by the beginning of July it was no longer clear that they were jokes. The mule meat was gone from the butchers' windows; several memoirs claimed that it was replaced by neatly skinned rat carcasses. Mary Loughborough, who was by then almost helpless with "the languid feeling of utter prostration," recalled that a soldier brought to her cave a jaybird he had caught, and offered it as a pet to Loughborough's daughter, who was sick with fever. But instead, inside of an hour, the girl was presented with "a cup of soup, and a little plate, on which lay the white meat of the poor little bird."

The town had become a shambles. There were barricades at all the intersections—but most of them had been abandoned because so few soldiers were fit for duty. Many soldiers were wandering the streets asking the citizens for food. Here and there, Willie Tunnard wrote, you saw "hunger-pinched, starving and wounded soldiers, or guards lying on the banquettes, indifferent to the screaming and exploding shells." Bombed houses went unrepaired, and many of them had been looted; fences and sheds all over town had been torn down for firewood. The rows of dark and silent houses on every street made the town look like a cemetery—particularly because all their former inhabitants were now underground.

The Yankees had hoped all along for a quick, decisive victory on the battlefield that would force Pemberton and the Confederate forces to accept the inevitable. But it became clear—especially after the Yankees did get exactly the battlefield victory they wanted in mid-May—that the Confederates would not surrender no matter how many battles they lost. So instead the Yankees gradually evolved a new strategy. They kept hearing from the ever-increasing number of Confederate deserters about the labyrinthine cave system under the town, and when they tried their own excavations, they were startled by how easy the loess of the hills was to dig. A Yankee military engineer, Brigadier Andrew Hickenlooper, described the loess as "a reddish clay of remarkable tenacity, easily cut and requiring but little bracing." So in late May they began digging tunnels from beneath their positions toward the Confederate lines.

It was slow, exhausting, dangerous work. "Every man in the investing line," one soldier later recalled, "became an army engineer day and night." They came in at slants and zigzags to provide cover from the Confederate sharpshooters. "The soldiers got so they bored like gophers and beavers," another recalled, "with a spade in one hand and a gun in the other." At each turning they excavated further entrenchments and rifle pits, and cut deeper entrenchments at odder angles around those. Gradually, inexorably, they approached the Confederate lines.

From behind their barricades, the Confederates watched this flurry of new activity with alarm. They couldn't fathom at first what the Yankees were up to, and the alarm only increased when the truth began to sink in. The Yankees were excavating tunnels all along the line, and if they weren't stopped somehow, they'd eventually be burrowing directly underneath the Confederate defenses. The Confederates frantically began sinking countermines to try to puncture their way into the Yankee tunnels. But they could never quite manage to hit any of them. Sometimes the sappers at the bottom of the mineshaft reported hearing the continual muffled thumps of pickaxes and shovels, and sometimes ghostly conversations and laughter, from the Yankee tunnel crews somewhere nearby.

The first of the Yankee tunnels reached beneath the Confederate defensive works in late June. The Yankees stuffed the end of the tunnel with explosives and gunpowder, and then they lit a long fuse. But they had slightly miscalculated their position: the resulting blast took out only a sparsely guarded section of the exterior defenses and didn't cause anywhere near as much damage or as many casualties as they had hoped. They tried again in a different tunnel a few days later. This blast went off directly beneath a Confederate redan. There was a geyser of dirt, of splintered and charred wood, of bodies and body parts and blood, and then a desperate mêlée as the Yankees attempted to force their way into the breach and the Confederates beat them back. The fighting had been so close that many of the Confederate wounded who came streaming into the town had skulls shattered by rifle butts or intestines spilling out from bayonet wounds.

The Confederates technically won that battle. But they knew that the victory was worth nothing: their strategic position had at last become untenable. The Yankees were already digging new tunnels. At least twelve tunnels were currently in progress, and the Yankees obviously had the capacity to excavate as many more as were necessary. If they weren't stopped, they would keep going until they could reach under the bluff and set off enough blasts to send the whole of Vicksburg tumbling into the Mississippi.

———

By the beginning of July, General Pemberton had given up on Johnston's relief expedition. It was inescapable that the Army of Relief, as it was called, was not going to arrive. In fact, it had never gotten under way in the first place. Johnston had been ordered months earlier to relieve Vicksburg, but he'd never had any intention of obeying. He wasn't about to risk his honor or his reputation on a venture that he considered hopeless. All his dispatches to Pemberton—orders to rendezvous at positions that Johnston himself had already abandoned, to rely on reinforcements that Johnston had never sent, to coordinate plans for a major counterattack that was patently never going to materialize—had simply been an attempt to create a paper trail that would prove to his superiors afterward that he'd done everything he could, when all along he'd simply been stalling until Vicksburg fell.

The effect of Johnston's prevarications was to deepen an agony in the town that was already unsupportable. Pemberton was finally left with no options. He smuggled out a message to Johnston saying that if the Army of Relief wasn't coming forthwith, he would have to surrender; the message came back that surrender would be on Pemberton's head. And so, after "the last pound of beef, bacon, and flour, the last grain of corn, the last cow and hog and horse and dog" had been consumed, Pemberton capitulated to the Yankees.

In the first week of July the guns fell silent. One Yankee soldier, Lieutenant Richard L. Howard, later wrote about how startling that silence was after months of continual thunder: "It was leaden. We could not bear it; it settled down so close; it hugged us with its hollow, unseen arms until we could scarcely breathe." The Yankee forces "did not seem to exult much over our fall," William Foster wrote, "for they knew that we surrendered to famine, not to them." As the first Yankees streamed into the commercial district, they broke into the shuttered stores, and they found that the worst suspicions of the townspeople had been correct: there were stacks of barrels and bags and cans hoarded in the basements. The Yankees immediately gave their finds away to the malnourished Confederate soldiers.

That afternoon, Foster wrote: "Sugar, whiskey, fresh fruit in air-tight cans are enjoyed in great abundance." The Yankees as they ransacked the stores also found scads of Confederate paper currency, which they considered worthless; they left it strewn behind them in the street.

The day was July 4, 1863. This procession of Yankee soldiers, heedlessly scattering food and money in its wake, was the only thing passing for an Independence Day parade in Vicksburg that year. And it would prove to be the last parade on that date for decades to come. The Fourth became a day of mourning in Vicksburg: a tradition that would endure until the last survivors of the siege were gone. Vicksburg didn't rejoin the rest of the nation in celebrating Independence Day until after the Second World War.

"At the close of the day," William Foster wrote on the Fourth, "I visit once more the Sky-Parlor. How changed now the scene." The landscape around the town was alive with movement. Line after line of Yankee soldiers, company after company, regiment after regiment, reserve after reserve, emerged from behind the siege lines and marched up the bluff—looking, one watcher at the Sky Parlor said, "like huge blue snakes coiling around the city." At twilight they were still surging through the streets and passing back out into the country again while countless crews of Yankee sappers, working by torchlight and by bonfire, were disassembling the fierce tangles of Confederate barricades.

There was movement on the river, too. The gunboats of the Yankee navy, which had for so many months been lurking like toads out in the shallows, came huffing up to the levee. As they passed the silenced batteries of the Confederacy, they fired off the national salute. Behind them, more boats were approaching. The fall of Vicksburg meant that the Mississippi was now in Union hands from its headwaters to the delta ("The Father of Waters," Abraham Lincoln declared when he got the news, "flows unvexed to the sea"); the Yankees were ending the blockades and the free flow of traffic was resuming. Around the bend in the twilight the first steamboats were already coming downriver: a line of glittering jewels, gliding up to Vicksburg Landing in a whirl of whistles and clanging bells, loaded with food for the starving town.

15

The Alligator

ON APRIL 15, 1865, the steamboat *Sultana* left Cairo, Illinois, for New Orleans. The *Sultana* was a large boat, one of the largest on the river— almost 250 feet long, and rated to carry a maximum of 376 passengers. But on that run it had an errand more urgent than simple transport. Its lines and flagpoles were hung with black pennants and black banners; its railings and portholes were draped in long, fluttering ribbons of black crêpe. It was an amazing apparition to the people of the lower valley. When they saw this vessel of mourning emerge around a bend in the golden afternoon light, or loom out of the river mists at midnight, they all came running down to the levees to greet it. It stopped at every town and village and plantation along the banks, announcing its arrival not with the customary whistles but with a single tolling bell. The passengers along the railings were all dressed in black. When the boat docked, they fanned out through the streets; some of them did no more than stand and silently hold up the black-bordered newspapers they'd brought from Cairo. Then they boarded again and the *Sultana* moved off and vanished downriver, to bring to the next town the news of Lincoln's assassination.

Constructed over the winter of 1862–63, the *Sultana* had been one of the first steamboats to begin making regular runs in the lower valley after the surrender of Vicksburg. Its frequent passengers had gotten an excellent view of the way the reopening of the river had transformed the valley. The landscape still bore the immense scars left by the passage of the war—the craters and slides in the hills, the burned-out forests, the gutted and abandoned plantation houses, the remnants of the immense earthworks constructed along the battle lines—but the riverfronts were thriving and the commercial districts were jumping with new business. The tough times of the blockades had been quickly forgotten. The people on the streets looked healthy and prosperous. In Vicksburg, which had taken the worst of the war, the buildings had all been repaired, the stores had all been restocked, and the flow of luxury goods to the specialty shops had resumed. "You can get anything you want," one townsman reported in amazement barely a month after the surrender.

In the later years of the war, the *Sultana* had also brought in a flood of strangers. They were people with peculiar accents: Northerners, Europeans. The lifting of the blockades meant the resumption of the cotton trade, and brokers and factors from all over the world were streaming into the lower valley to cash in. With most of the great plantations of the Deep South still behind the battle lines, the planters along the Mississippi found that they had a spectacular seller's market. Locals whose livelihood had been ruined by the siege were setting up as cotton speculators—or else were looking to strike it rich by supplying the speculators with whatever else they might desire. As the harvest came in, the various Landings and Under-the-Hills were all springing back to life, more gaudy than they had ever been, with saloons and gambling houses and the fanciest brothels to be found outside of New Orleans.

The river valley was still under the control of the Union military government, and the burgeoning trade was leading to a complicated new weave of bureaucratic corruption. The river commerce was administered by the staff officers of the Union army, who were the only ones authorized to disgorge the most prized document in the occupied valley: a trading license. These licenses were required for any and all cargo carried by the steamboats. The idea was to give priority to items of immediate military necessity or urgent humanitarian need, but in practice those concepts were defined in an easygoing, elastic way, so as to create for the staff officers a thriving business in bribes and kickbacks. Judging by the licenses issued for one Christmas week, the valley had either an immediate military necessity or an urgent humanitarian need for the following: five barrels of brandy, thirty cases of champagne, one hundred cases of assorted liquors, twenty thousand cigars, 420 dozen pairs of women's shoes, fifty dozen pairs of white gloves, fifteen yards of green velvet, fifteen yards of red velvet, and one pound of silver spangles.

The rebirth of the river economy struck a lot of old-timers as a travesty. By the spring of 1865, the most common remark heard around the valley was that you could barely recognize the place any longer, what with all these Yankees and foreigners—and with all the new money pouring in. And of course there was one more enormous social change that the whites of the lower valley were finding impossible to adjust to: emancipation. So far, the worst nightmare of the whites had failed to materialize—they weren't being murdered in their beds by vengeful gangs of ex-slaves. Instead there had developed a new routine of casual, grinding hostility. The old hair-trigger rage of the frontier was back, only now it was almost exclusively racial. Day after day, the whites were stunned and outraged by the lack of deference shown to them by their former property. Every side-long glance between white and black was a potential provocation; every mutter, every bumped shoulder was the pretext for a fight. Public senti-ment among the whites, one Union officer observed, "has not come to the attitude in which it can conceive of the negro having any rights at all."

In the midst of this rising tension came the news brought by the *Sultana*. The reaction among the whites was public silence and private jubila-tion. While in the North, Lincoln's views on slavery had always been a matter of debate (and remain so to this day), in the South there had never been the slightest doubt. To them Lincoln had been the maddest of the abolitionist madmen, the demonic persecutor who had slaughtered their men and destroyed their country for no better reason than sheer spite. One diarist of that time, Sarah Morgan of New Orleans, could only sup-pose that Lincoln had been driven by a kind of psychotic class envy. "Lin-coln's chief occupation," she wrote, "was thinking what death, thousands who ruled like lords when he was cutting logs, should die." But now that had all changed: "A moment more, and the man who was progressing to murder countless human beings, is interrupted in his work by the shot of an assassin." Kate Stone of Vicksburg put it more simply in her diary: "All honor to J. Wilkes Booth, who has rid the world of a tyrant and made himself famous for generations."

On April 23, 1865, the *Sultana,* returning from New Orleans, stopped off at Vicksburg. Its errand of mourning was completed and it was an ordinary steamboat again, carrying a full complement of passengers and cargo. It laid over at Vicksburg Landing for the day while one of its boilers was repaired, a routine procedure for steamboats on the river—the *Sultana's* boilers had already been patched twice that spring. During the layover, arrangements were concluded for it to carry a very large number of Union soldiers upriver to Cairo.

These soldiers were prisoners of war who had been brought to Vicksburg by the Confederate command for exchange with the North. They had been held at the prison camps of Cahaba and Andersonville in the Deep South, and they had arrived at Vicksburg earlier that spring. They were in horrible shape—sick, malnourished, emaciated, scurvied. Many had open and infected wounds; many were limping in on crutches; some couldn't walk at all and were being dragged on pallets by their fellow soldiers. They told horrifying stories of their captivity. Cahaba, where most of them had been held, had been designed for five hundred men and ultimately was crammed with more than three thousand, and their only drinking water was from a fouled stream that doubled as a cesspool. But that was nothing compared with what some of the other prisoners said about Andersonville. Forty-five thousand men had been held there at the war's height, and almost thirteen thousand of them had died; the rest were described as "walking skeletons." One typical story was told by a survivor:

> A large wagon, drawn by four mules, was used in drawing out the dead. They were laid in as we pile cordwood and taken to the burying ground, generally putting fifty in a grave, and returning would bring mush in the same wagon, where worms that came from the dead could be seen crawling all over it; but we were starving, therefore we fought for it like hungry dogs.

Even after the Confederacy had decided to release them, the men had found fresh miseries to endure. The Confederate rail system was a shambles in the later days of the war; one of the transport trains had derailed three times in a hundred miles. Two of those times, rail cars had overturned, and dozens of the prisoners, their bones already brittle from malnutrition, had their rib cages shattered and arms and legs snapped like twigs. When they approached Vicksburg, they learned that the rail lines west ended at Jackson: the last forty miles of track had been destroyed, and the only way forward was on foot.

In Vicksburg they found themselves in a tormenting legal limbo. The arrangement made between the Yankees and the Confederates had been for an even exchange of prisoners—but the Yankees didn't have several thousand Confederate prisoners available for transfer at Vicksburg, and the Federal command, with the war on the edge of being won, wasn't enthusiastic about returning so many troops to the enemy anyway. Meanwhile, the Confederate command was in increasing disarray. Their lines of communication back to the government were broken, and the government itself appeared to be collapsing—by early April there were rumors everywhere that General Lee was about to surrender and Jefferson Davis was on the run. So while the confused and desultory negotiations between the two commands went on, the Yankee prisoners, almost five thousand of them, were forced to wait.

A holding camp had been built for them about six miles outside of town. The men got new uniforms, tents to sleep in, and the first good rations they'd seen in months or years: hardtack, fresh-baked bread, and sometimes beef and pork. Since they were still technically Confederate prisoners, the Union command had agreed to keep them under armed guard. The first guards assigned were newly commissioned Negro soldiers—but this nearly led to a riot. Many of the prisoners were just now catching up with the news of the emancipation, and not all of them approved. White guards were hastily substituted, and the mood in the camp quieted—that is, until the *Sultana* brought the news about Lincoln.

The official reaction of the Confederate command at Vicksburg was muted and respectful. The Confederate officer in charge of the prisoner transfer immediately ordered all Confederate flags to be lowered to half-staff and had his headquarters draped in black crêpe. He wrote an open letter to his opposite number on the Federal side, expressing "sincere regrets upon receipt of the painful intelligence of the assassination of President Lincoln." Speaking on behalf of the Confederate officer corps, he assured him that "no officer of the United States Government regrets more than they this cowardly assault." In all this, he was acting with extreme prudence. He was aware the situation in the camp was on the edge of calamity; among the Union prisoners, the only thought on anybody's mind was revenge. If they knew how gleeful the citizens of Vicksburg were, they were likely to storm out of the camp and burn down the town. But symbolic gestures weren't going to solve anything for long. This was why, in the days following the assassination, the Confederate and Yankee commanders ultimately agreed to forgo the exchange of prisoners and simply get the soldiers in the camp out of the South and on their way home as quickly as possible.

On the morning of April 24, the Yankee soldiers began boarding the *Sultana*. A few hundred of them quickly filled up the main deck—and then a few hundred more came, and still more, until all the decks were filled and then overfilled. "We were driven on like so many hogs," one soldier remembered, "until every foot of standing room was occupied." The cabin deck was packed with men, amid stacks of cargo and corrals holding pigs and horses; the hurricane deck was jammed, as was the roof of the pilothouse; there were men perched between the smokestacks and men squatting on the coal bins belowdecks. Any of the cabin passengers who looked out through their windows would have seen an unbroken wall of flesh and blue cloth pressing in on the glass. The *Sultana* on a crowded run probably had around 450 people aboard; it was carrying at least five times that many when it finally pulled away from Vicksburg after sunset.

Later, there would be a forest of finger-pointing about who had overloaded the boat, why it had been allowed to happen, who had tried to stop it, who had ignored it, who had cashed in. A lot of blame was put on the Union staff officers, the same ones who'd been in charge of the trading licenses—they had already been caught up in several scandals involving sweetheart deals with steamboat companies over fees for transporting soldiers. It was said in expiation that a steamboat had left Vicksburg a few days before carrying more than a thousand Union soldiers, and it had arrived in St. Louis without incident. The owners of the *Sultana* offered the interesting argument that while their boat had undeniably been overcrowded, it hadn't technically been overloaded: a roughly equivalent volume of cargo would have weighed far more than the soldiers did.

But the *Sultana*'s crew had been under no illusions. Some of them were heard to say before departure that it would be a miracle if they ever reached Cairo. The behavior of the captain, a longtime river professional named J. Cass Mason, was particularly telling. Mason was known (according to a newspaper account) as "one of the clearest heads on the river." But he got dead drunk at the departure from Vicksburg and he stayed drunk until the end.

The Mississippi had begun its rise early that season. It was already in full flood by the time the *Sultana* started north. Banks were drowned and levees overtopped all through the central and lower valley. The boat made sluggish progress against the strong, debris-choked surge of current. That first night proved to be a wretched one for everyone crammed on deck. They could barely move; hundreds of them were leaning against the exterior walls and sleeping upright. The night air was clear and bitterly cold. Food was in short supply—mostly bread, hardtack, and salt pork—and there was no way of heating it. The only privies were by the wheelhouse on the lower deck, and this was for most an impossible journey. By morning some enterprising soldiers had hacked out holes in the planking above the paddle wheels to give everyone who needed to relieve himself a shorter distance through the crowd.

But the atmosphere on the deck, people would later agree, could have been a lot worse. There were no fights and hardly even any complaints. Many of the soldiers were so sick and exhausted they could barely register where they were anyway, much less grouse about the conditions. The rest were so grateful to be on their way home that they were prepared to put up with anything. As the night passed, there were songs and jokes going around, and the occasional impromptu performance: among the paying passengers in the cabin was a theatrical troupe from Chicago who'd been touring the lower valley, and they put on sketches and did dances to keep the soldiers amused. The soldiers were also entertained by the discovery of the boat's mascot, a pet alligator kept in a crate in the wheelhouse. One soldier remembered, "It was a curiosity for us to see such a large one. We would punch him with sticks to see him open his mouth, but the boatmen got tired of this and put him in the closet under the stairway."

As the night ended and the morning light grew, the soldiers found themselves deep in a drowned country. The floodwaters had spread out for miles on either side of the banks; the *Sultana* spent the day moving through a wide, shining, featureless sea. It was a radiant April day, and there were dazzling reflections of cumulus scudding across the shivery blue surface of the water. The familiar navigation landmarks were submerged; the pilot had to weave back and forth by trial and error, marking where the current was strongest by the long, unwinding trails of debris languidly drifting down from upriver. The *Sultana* passed fallen trees and drowned animals. It glided through the sodden contents of overrun farms—patched clothes and spinning wheels, brooms and rakes, keepsake albums and sheet music, heirloom bedsteads and ornamental nightstands. It shouldered aside the debris from drowned boats and overrun levees—barrels of salt and coffee and vinegar and wine, hogsheads of salt pork and molasses, tuns of flat-head nails. The men on deck saw engulfed towns where the citizens were casually moving through the streets in rowboats. In some of the towns there were pontoon bridges between the upper stories of downtown buildings; some store owners had moved their stocks up to the rooftops and were selling to the river traffic.

But in that world the *Sultana* was the strangest sight of all: an enormous boat fantastically overcrowded with deckers, like a forest of men, precariously tilting and grinding up through the flood. The *Sultana*'s crewmen were so convinced that the boat was fatally top-heavy that they urged the army officers on board to order the men to keep as motionless as possible. There was a particularly close call as they passed along the Arkansas shore. A photographer rowed out to the middle of the river to take a picture, and as he laboriously maneuvered his camera into position, so many deckers hustled to the railings to be included that the *Sultana* began listing and almost capsized then and there. It was only after a frantic rush to get everyone back spread evenly across the decks that the sickening tilt subsided and the boat steamed on.

Late in the afternoon of the next day, April 26, the *Sultana* reached Memphis. It was a big, crowded city perched on bluffs safely above the flood, and it was doing a thriving business both with the river trade and with the Yankee military occupation. Much of the *Sultana*'s cargo was off-loaded there—most of the livestock, to everyone's relief, and, to their regret, several hundred hogsheads of sugar. (A couple of the hogsheads had cracked open, and the soldiers had been gorging themselves on their contents ever since Vicksburg.) Several of the cabin passengers disembarked at Memphis as well—among them the theatrical troupe, whom the soldiers gave a big cheer of thanks as they descended the gangway. By then the soldiers who were healthy enough to move were getting eager to sneak in a little time onshore themselves. They had been ordered to stay on board, but nobody felt any compelling need to obey. "The moment the boat touched the wharf," one soldier, W. G. Porter, remembered, "the boys began to jump off." Hundreds of them spent that evening carousing around the river district.

The *Sultana*'s whistle sounded its warning around 10:00 p.m. The soldiers straggled back on board. They found that the decks had gotten more crowded: a big new load of coal had been taken on, and those soldiers who'd been sleeping in the coal bins had been evicted. W. G. Porter had been one of them, and he now faced a long, weary scramble to find somewhere else to lie down. He wandered around the cabin deck among a tangle of sleepers; whenever he found an empty place to spread out his blankets, he'd be told it was being held for somebody else. At last he crammed himself onto one of the outside stairways between decks. He was only able to make himself fit onto a step by letting his feet stick out over the edge.

Other soldiers never did get back on board. Some of them had had enough; they couldn't bear the overcrowding and, despite their orders, decided to wait on the levee for the next boat coming upriver. Others had managed to get so drunk during their few hours ashore that they missed the steamboat whistle. One later estimate was that roughly 150 soldiers were left behind in Memphis that night. When the *Sultana* departed, there were probably around twenty-two hundred people still on board.

The *Sultana* pulled off from the levee a little after 1:00 a.m. It continued its wheezing way north through the murky gulf of the river. Some of those watching from the railings guessed that at this point the Mississippi had swollen up more than five miles on either side: in some places the banks were submerged under twenty feet of water.

It was a new moon that night; the *Sultana's* lights were the only illumination. The sky began clouding over. Soon a storm came up from the southwest. Its thunder was inaudible above the rumbling of the paddle wheels and the roar of exhaust from the smokestacks—but the men on deck could see distant flickers of lightning glinting on the surface of the flood, silhouetting the snarl of half-submerged treetops along the drowned banks and the remote peaked islands of farmhouse roofs.

One of the men on the cabin deck was a soldier from Ohio named Joseph Bringman. He was sleeping near the balusters on the port side; he'd barely moved from the spot since Vicksburg. He'd come aboard in bad shape: sickly, weak, and exhausted, and with all his teeth loose (a common result of life in the prison camps). His chief emotion so far had been sheer gratitude that he'd found someplace to lie down. On this night he hadn't even bothered to take off his clothes—partly because of the approaching storm, partly because he was simply too tired.

Sometime around two in the morning, he had a dream. "It appeared to me," he wrote, "that I was walking leisurely on an incline or sloping hill, and when I reached the top there appeared to be a ledge or projecting rock overhanging a river; I seemed to step upon it so as to look down into the water, and just as I took the second step the rock seemed to burst with a report like the shot of a distant cannon. I felt pieces of rock striking my face and head and I seemed to be hurled out into the river."

Another soldier, J. Walter Elliott, remembered at that moment "a report as of the discharge of a park of artillery, a shock as of a railroad collision, and I am sitting bolt upright, straining my eyes and stretching my arms out into the Egyptian darkness; face, throat and lungs burning as if immersed in a boiling cauldron." William A. McFarland "seemed to be dreaming and could hear some one saying, 'there isn't any skin left on their bodies.' I awoke with a start and the next moment the boat was on fire and all was as light as day."

All over the *Sultana,* people were waking into a nightmare of fire and confusion. One of the boilers had exploded, and the concussion wave had caused two of the remaining three to go up as well. Most of the soldiers near the boilers, as well as almost all the cabin passengers, had been killed instantly. The main force of the blast had cratered the midsection of the boat, and the burning debris that had been blown out in all directions was setting off fires from prow to stern.

Immediately around the blast crater there was chaos. One survivor, Commodore Smith, remembered the scene: "At the time her boilers exploded I was lying sound asleep on the lower deck, just back of the rear hatchway to the hold. I was not long in waking up, for I was nearly buried with dead and wounded comrades, legs, arms, heads, and all parts of human bodies, and fragments of the wrecked upper decks." Commodore Smith tried to fight his way to the bow to jump overboard, "but could not on account of the wreckage and carnage of human freight which now covered the lower deck." W. G. Porter, sleeping on the stairs, remembered that when he woke, he first thought that the stairway and the deck had collapsed from being overloaded, "but soon found out different." He wrote: "It was not long before it was all confusion, some singing, some praying, some lamenting, some swearing, some crying, and some did not seem to know anything."

Since the main force of the blast had gone upward, the hull was still intact and the boat wasn't yet sinking. But the fires were spreading rapidly. People were grabbing and hurling into the water everything they could find that they thought might float, and they were jumping in after and praying for the best. Bales of cotton and hay went first, but so many grabbed hold of them that they sank or unraveled into useless tufts. Then the gangway board went, carrying dozens with it. Commodore Smith remained on deck, he guessed for around twenty or thirty minutes, "throwing overboard all the loose boards and timbers and everything that would float to assist those in the water and save them from drowning if possible."

Around him fights were breaking out among those who hadn't yet jumped into the river. One woman fought savagely with two soldiers over a life belt she was trying to put on her child. She succeeded in wresting the belt away from them, but in her panic she put it on incorrectly, and when she let the child go into the water, he helplessly rolled over head down and drowned.

In the river surrounding the burning wreck were people and animals frantically thrashing amid a spreading field of bodies and debris. Everyone was clawing wildly for handholds on the flotsam; they were grabbing on to hands and shoulders and legs and feet to keep from drowning—sometimes several men at a time dragged each other under. Meanwhile, the fires on the boat were raging out of control and were whipping down on the people still on board. There were no railings left around the deck—they had already been torn off and thrown overboard—and the rushing of the crowd back and forth to stay out of the flames forced those closest to the sides to jump into the water. Chester Berry, a soldier from Pennsylvania, recalled looking up from the water and seeing an apparition: a woman still on board, in the midst of the pandemonium, calling to those in the water to stay calm.

Seeing them fighting like demons in the water in the mad endeavor to save their lives, actually destroying each other and themselves by their wild actions, [she] talked to them, urging them to be men, and finally succeeded in getting them quieted down, clinging to the ropes and chains that hung over the bow of the boat. The flames now began to lap around her with their fiery tongues. The men pleaded and urged her to jump into the water and thus save herself, but she refused, saying: "I might lose my presence of mind and be the means of the death of some of you." And so, rather than run the risk of becoming the cause of the death of a single person, she folded her arms quietly over her bosom and burned, a voluntary martyr to the men she had so lately quieted.

The wreck of the *Sultana* was drifting out of the channel into the shallows near the Arkansas shore. There were still people alive on board, but the fires were now burning down to the waterline and the boat had to be abandoned. Commodore Smith remembered this as the hardest moment of his life. The injured were begging to be thrown overboard, because they would rather drown than be burned alive. "While our hearts went out in sympathy for our suffering and dying comrades," Smith wrote, "we performed our sad but solemn duty."

The wreck by then was in a narrow channel between the bank and a chain of islets. The islets were submerged by the flood, but the tallest trees were still sticking up above the surface; some of the men were snatching at their branches and tying the lines to them. By then the last of the boat was aflame, and everyone still mobile had to jump into the water.

The fires reached the *Sultana's* waterline and began to gutter out. This made those in the water more frantic. As long as the boat had been burning, the glare cast across the water had faintly illuminated the forests along the shores and had given the swimmers a target to aim at, but once the flames vanished, they were lost in complete darkness. One survivor said mildly, "We could not tell which way to go and it was a very lonesome place to be in." Some of the survivors managed to thrash and lunge their way out of the current into the shallows and strike out toward what they thought was dry land—only to find when they arrived that the banks were overrun and the waters stretched on out of sight. Here and there were what looked like clumps of gnarled bushes poking above the river surface, and the swimmers grabbed on to them gratefully—but when they pushed their feet down into the water, feeling for solid ground, they found only more of the shapeless river murk: the bushes they were clinging to were treetops. Other swimmers managed to bump into the rooftops of farmhouses and drag themselves out of the water; some were able to break through the roofs into the attics, where they collapsed in exhaustion onto the sacks and barrels stored there. Still others did at last succeed in reaching firm land, only to be faced with a danger as bad as what they'd just escaped. The banks north of Memphis were being patrolled by Union troops who had no idea what had happened to the *Sultana;* when the men began straggling ashore, some of the patrols thought they were Confederate infiltrators and began firing at them.

The majority of those still alive, together with the corpses and the countless clusters of debris, were being carried downriver. Among the living a strange new terror was spreading. Some of them couldn't put a name to it. Chester Berry, who'd caught hold of a snag in the river, recalled: "I was out of my head and imagined that some terrible danger threatened me"—some danger, that is, worse than what he was currently going through. But several of the survivors were able to be more specific: they were tormented by the fear that, as they were thrashing through the water, they would be attacked by the *Sultana's* pet alligator. "I guess everyone that was on the 'Sultana' knew something about the monstrous alligator that was on the boat," remembered one soldier, Ben G. Davis. "It was nine and one-half feet long. While the boat was burning the alligator troubled me almost as much as the fire." Another, Ira B. Horner, wrote: "Although I felt that I would not drown at the same time I did not feel comfortable from the fact that there was an alligator seven and one-half feet long keeping me company." Some soldiers became convinced that they had actually gotten a glimpse of the alligator, and they were driven into a suicidal panic. One survivor recalled how a horse swimming downstream rested his nose on a log that several men were clinging to; the men mistook this dim, snorting silhouette for the alligator and all dived away into the water.

As it happened, the fear of the alligator was misplaced. During the worst of the fire, a soldier named William Lugenbeal had been searching belowdecks for something he could throw overboard; when he'd found that the rooms had all been stripped already—"every loose board, door, window and shutter was taken to swim on"—he'd thought of the crate the alligator was kept in. It was exactly the right size and shape for a lifeboat. The only problem was the alligator itself—but Lugenbeal made quick work of that: "I got [the crate] out of the closet and took him out and ran the bayonet through him three times." Then he lugged the crate to the bow, threw it overboard, and jumped in after it. He grabbed hold of it once it bobbed back to the surface, and he began kicking his way out of the mêlée around the wreck. He remembered: "When a man would get close enough I would kick him off, then turn quick as I could and kick someone else to keep them from getting hold of me. They would call out 'don't kick, for I am drowning,' but if they had got hold of me we would both have drowned."

By then hundreds of people were drowning. Of those who were alive when they'd gone into the water, many were unconscious or in shock or had been scalded by the blast and were too disoriented to understand what was happening; some were so badly injured they were helpless; some simply couldn't swim. But most were succumbing to hypothermia. The river had been flooded by meltwater from its northern tributaries and it was deadly cold. Some were surviving only by clinging desperately to the bodies of drowned horses and mules, because they still had some lingering warmth. Others were bunching themselves together into tight clusters, which gradually fell apart as their strength weakened and some of them helplessly let go. The current was irresistibly pulling everyone away from each other. Their voices grew weaker and more remote, and gradually fell silent.

The river swept them onward into pitch darkness. The sky was starless, and rain was falling in thin, hissing cascades. Then in the distance ahead a hazy glow appeared. It was Memphis, looming on its high bluff through the drizzle and the river mist. As the current carried them closer, the men began shouting and screaming for help. They wailed and banged their shards of driftwood and flotsam together, and they shrieked at the top of their lungs. They were terrified that they'd be whisked past the city and back out into the night again. Many of them sobbed with relief when they heard the city answer.

Boat whistles and church bells were ringing out from the riverfront. The boat city off the levee was breaking up and putting out into the water: steamboats, packet boats, flatboats, rafts, and canoes. Elsewhere up and down the river were voyageurs and raftsmen who had seen the pillar of fire and smoke rising above the hills, and as the first gray of the dawn light spread along the river, they, too, set out to look for survivors.

Over the course of the next several hours, the rescuers took seven hundred people alive out of the river. They were found everywhere, clinging to flotsam, perched on drowned treetops, and waving from half-submerged farmhouse roofs—wounded, injured, scalded, exhausted, corpse-blue with hypothermia. One man was rescued ten miles downriver from Memphis. A rescuer remembered, "We found men almost dead, hanging to the trees about two miles out into the river, and among those that I rescued was one man so badly scalded that when I took hold of his arms to help him into the boat the skin and flesh came off his arms like a cooked beet." One survivor, Perry S. Summerville, remembered that when he was taken out of the water, he couldn't stand up; he was wounded, he was scalded, and he was spitting up blood. "Was rescued at Memphis," he wrote, "by a colored man who picked me up in a canoe and took me to a boat to get warm. After I had been there a few minutes a young man was brought in who was so badly scalded that his skin slipped off from the shoulders to the hands." The scalded man paced around the room, unable to sit still or lie down, before he finally collapsed and died.

About two hundred of the rescued died over the next few days—of their injuries, of exposure, or of the medical care they received after they'd been brought ashore. (The only treatment available then for severe burns, for example, was to cover them in oil and flour and wrap them in gauze.) The rest of the survivors, some five hundred of them, left Memphis just as soon as they were able to travel. They got aboard other steamboats—it was still the quickest way out of the South. Many of them, once they reached Cairo, stepped onto the docks and declared that they would never set foot on a boat again.

From Cairo they caught trains bound north and east. The farther away from the river they got, the less anyone cared about the *Sultana*. Its loss was barely mentioned in the Eastern newspapers. This was the worst naval disaster in American history (more people died on the *Sultana* than would die on the *Titanic*), but there was a general sense back east that it was, after all, just another sunken frontier steamboat. And besides, everyone was still in mourning for Lincoln. In town after town, the returning veterans arrived expecting to find cheering crowds and celebratory storms of red, white, and blue bunting but instead discovered nothing but somber-faced citizens and silent streets hung with long, listless streamers of black crêpe.

No final count was ever established of the lives lost. Only a few of the dead were recovered; the rest were carried off by the river. A couple of days after the explosion, a gunboat coming upriver was met by a drifting mass of what the crew assumed to be fallen trees: as they got closer, they saw that it was a flotilla of hundreds of bodies. The gunboat had to be deliberately beached on a sandbar to avoid running them over. No attempt was made to collect them; they were permitted to glide past untouched, and soon vanished around a river bend. They ended up the way the river's dead always did—buried in the river mud or devoured by the alligators and the other carrion eaters of the lower valley.

The wreck of the *Sultana* was sunk about twenty feet down in a channel along the Arkansas shore, around seven miles north of Memphis. Over the next few years, the river shifted course, and the channel was emptied of its current. The great banks caved in, and the bottom was covered over by wash after wash of mud and silt deposited from upstream. Eventually the last traces of the channel and its islets were swallowed up. The soil grew rooted with meadow grasses and wildflowers and trees; then the land was cleared and cultivated, and the *Sultana* rested deep beneath the soybean fields of Arkansas.

PART FIVE

THE GOOD AND THE THOUGHTLESS

16

The Last of the Floating Life

IN 1882, MARK TWAIN TOOK A steamboat ride on the Mississippi. There would have been nothing unusual about such a trip in the old days—Twain had once been a steamboat pilot and had made countless runs up and down the river. But that had been before the war; now he was middle-aged and the celebrated author of *The Adventures of Tom Sawyer,* and this was the first time he'd been on the river in more than twenty years.

He began at St Louis. The first sight of the famous levee came as a shock. The warehouses were all shuttered; the docks were deserted; where there had been a hundred packed steamboats arriving and departing each day there were now only a lingering handful. "This was melancholy, this was woful," he wrote. "Half a dozen lifeless steamboats, a mile of empty wharves. . . . Here was desolation, indeed."

When he asked the few remaining crews what had happened, they all looked straight up. They weren't gazing at the heavens; they were glaring at the new bridge. "The mighty bridge, stretching along over our heads," Twain wrote, "had done its share in the slaughter and spoliation." It was the first bridge across the lower river: its construction had begun after the war and had taken seven years to complete. It was being hailed all over the world as one of the wonders of the modern age—and it had ruined the steamboat business. With the lower river successfully spanned, the railroad networks on opposite sides were finally connected, and rail had become a safe, quick, and reliable alternative to the steamboats. There was really no reason any longer for the river to be used for transport at all. Within a few years, essentially everybody and everything that moved in the river valley went by rail. By the time of Twain's visit, the big steamboat lines had all gone bankrupt and the few remaining boats were running mostly empty.

"Mississippi steamboating," Twain wrote, "was born about 1812; at the end of thirty years, it had grown to mighty proportions; and in less than thirty more, it was dead! A strangely short life for so majestic a creature."

Twain took one of the still-running steamboats downriver to New Orleans. The Mississippi wasn't the river he remembered, either—but at least that was something he'd been expecting. He'd never lost his old river man's habit of perpetually redrawing the map of the river in his mind. Twenty years meant a lot of shifting and twisting and writhing; almost all the old familiar landmarks had been altered or obliterated. Everywhere Twain went, he ticked off the places he remembered and noted how they'd been remade: "Beaver Dam Rock was out in the middle of the river now, and throwing a prodigious 'break;' it used to be close to the shore, and boats went down outside of it. A big island that used to be away out in mid-river, has retired to the Missouri shore, and boats do not go near it any more. The island called Jacket Pattern is whittled down to a wedge now, and is booked for early destruction. Goose Island is all gone but a little dab the size of a steamboat."

And so on, and on, down every bend and twist: new cutoffs, new oxbow lakes, channels that had filled in, islets that had sprouted up or had melted away. The "great and once much-frequented" Walnut Bend was now "set . . . away back in a solitude far from the accustomed track of passing steamers." The famous Graveyard south of the confluence of the Mississippi and the Missouri, "among whose numberless wrecks we used to pick our way so slowly and gingerly," was, he found, "far away from the channel now, and a terror to nobody." He was most surprised by his first sight of Vicksburg. The town was standing on its bluff the way it always had, and around it on the hills, the "signs and scars still remain, as reminders of Vicksburg's tremendous war-experiences." But the river had shifted, and Vicksburg no longer had a riverfront. A cutoff had formed near the spot where the Yankees had tried to dig their canal, and the bend before Vicksburg Landing had emptied out. The cutoff, Twain observed, had made Vicksburg into "a country town."

All this was the normal routine of river life. Other changes were more dismaying. Twain's original plan had been to stop off at all the towns he remembered from his youth to see how they'd altered over time. But he quickly dropped that idea: there was no point. Even from the steamboat rail, he could see enough. Town after town, the scene was the same as he'd found in St. Louis. The rowdy riverfront districts were silent and the levees were empty. Behind them, the decorous towns on the bluffs were themselves growing dismal and shabby—all of them, Twain noted, could have used a fix-up and a good coat of whitewash. Several of the towns he best remembered were simply gone—burned down and not rebuilt, flooded out and left abandoned.

And there was another reason to stay in the boat: the riverbanks were dangerous. There were armed camps of squatters in the derelict riverfronts. Many of them were farmers who'd lost their homesteads after the war ended (peace had brought a catastrophic collapse in agricultural prices); others were veterans, many suffering severe psychic trauma from battle, who'd found themselves unable to fit in back at home or anywhere else. Some of the squatters were organizing into hunting parties that were terrorizing the river towns like the land pirates of the old days. It was as though the river valley were reverting back to the worst times of the Crow's Nest.

But the greatest shock for Twain was the solitude. Not just the steamboats but all the old river traffic was gone: the flatboats and the keelboats, the pirogues and shanty boats and arks. "All day we swung along down the river," he wrote, "and had the stream almost wholly to ourselves. Formerly, at such a stage of the water, we should have passed acres of lumber rafts, and dozens of big coal barges; also occasional little trading-scows, peddling along from farm to farm, with the pedler's family on board; possibly, a random scow, bearing a humble Hamlet and Co. on an itinerant dramatic trip. But these were all absent." Just once did he come across a scene that reminded him of the great days. His steamboat encountered an enormous convoy of lumber rafts heading downriver from the northern valley. But as he looked more closely, the disillusionment set in. The rafts were not "floating leisurely along, in the old-fashioned way, manned with joyous and reckless crews of fiddling, song-singing, whiskey-drinking, breakdown-dancing rapscallions; no, the whole thing was shoved swiftly along by a powerful stern-wheeler, modern fashion, and the small crews were quiet, orderly men, of a sedate business aspect, with not a suggestion of romance about them anywhere."

The rest of the voyage glided by in eerie silence. There were no longer any glittering boat cities gathered in the evenings before the levees, no lashed boats making their way down the channels by first light, no steamboats furiously racing each other upriver and casting lesser boats aside like kindling—just more of the empty river down each bend.

> We met two steamboats at New Madrid. Two steamboats in sight at once! an infrequent spectacle now in the lonesome Mississippi. The loneliness of this solemn, stupendous flood is impressive—and depressing. League after league, and still league after league, it pours its chocolate tide along, between its solid forest walls, its almost un-tenanted shores, with seldom a sail or a moving object of any kind to disturb the surface and break the monotony of the blank, watery solitude; and so the day goes, the night comes, and again the day—and still the same, night after night and day after day,—majestic, unchanging sameness of serenity, repose, tranquillity, lethargy, vacancy,—symbol of eternity, realization of the heaven pictured by priest and prophet, and longed for by the good and thoughtless!

Twain wasn't alone on his river journey. There were other passengers on board: "river men, planters, journalists, and officers of the River Commission"—a thinned-out, modern version of the great riotous throngs of the prewar days. Twain spent a lot of idle time chatting with them. He was continually surprised to discover that they didn't share his despondency about what had happened to the river. In fact, they were bubbling over with optimism. As the half-empty boat made its way down past the deserted shores, on the deck and in the common rooms there was nothing but upbeat talk about the grand future of the river valley. "Mississippi Improvement is a mighty topic, down yonder," Twain wrote. "Every man on the river banks, south of Cairo, talks about it every day, during such moments as he is able to spare from talking about the war."

The most outlandish proposals for remaking the river were being soberly discussed. There were plans to regulate the river current as though with a giant faucet; to build artificial lakes and rivers in order to drain off the floodwaters; to use the Great Lakes as reservoirs for replenishing the current whenever it ran low. The possibilities were dizzying and endlessly contradictory. "Wherever you find a man down there who believes in one of these theories," Twain wrote, "you may turn to the next man and frame your talk upon the hypothesis that he does *not* believe in that theory." Twain began to think that "Mississippi Improvement" was an incurable epidemic of competing and irreconcilable proposals. "You will have come to know, with a deep and restful certainty, that you are not going to meet two people sick of the same theory, one right after the other," he wrote. "You may vaccinate yourself with deterrent facts as much as you please— it will do no good; it will seem to 'take,' but it doesn't; the moment you rub against any one of those theorists, make up your mind that it is time to hang out your yellow flag."

In all this welter of talk Twain heard, there was one name that kept recurring—James Eads, the man who was currently the biggest celebrity associated with the Mississippi, other than Twain himself.

Eads, the designer of the diving-bell salvage boats, had gone on to several new ventures in the last few decades. Some of them had washed out—a factory to make fancy window glass, for instance. Others had been triumphs—like a series of armored gunboats for the Union navy, which were later said to have revolutionized naval warfare. And one project had made him world-famous: he had designed and built the bridge at St. Louis.

Eads had had no formal training in engineering or architecture. He hadn't even had a high-school education. All he'd had was an unshakable certainty that he could build the bridge. The professionals had scoffed at its radically original cantilevered design, and they claimed that its innovative new construction material, structural steel, wouldn't hold up. But Eads persisted despite their opposition; he persisted in the face of chronic underfunding, a maze of political chicanery, and a blizzard of lawsuits from the steamboat companies; he persisted even when the unfinished bridge took a direct hit from a tornado. But when the bridge triumphantly opened to railroad traffic in 1874, he immediately gave up bridge building and moved on to something else.

His new project was the remaking of the Mississippi itself. He wanted to install a system of jetties along the entire length of the river to control its course and reduce its flooding. By the time of Twain's river journey, Eads had already completed a pilot project—a jetty at the river mouth. It was intended to shape and focus the immense outflow of the current spewing into the Gulf of Mexico, in order to dredge a deeper channel and punch through the centuries of accumulated sandbars. If it worked, it would enable oceangoing ships to enter the river delta safely for the first time, without immediately going aground. It turned out to work perfectly.

Eads was one of those people whose brains are perpetually, almost involuntarily, brimming over with new ideas. Even as he was pressing the government for backing for his full-scale jetty system, he was dreaming up other projects for the Mississippi. He had already worked out a plan for revitalizing the river traffic. He wanted to build a fleet of gigantic cast-iron industrial barges to replace the steamboats. His friend and partner Richard Smith Elliott later recalled Eads's boundless enthusiasm for the barges, and his ultimate disappointment: "Though the air was for a year or more as full of iron barges as ever the atmosphere of Utah was of grasshoppers, yet the barges did not actually get on the water." (Decades after Eads's death, they were the dominant form of traffic on the Mississippi.)

Eads wasn't fazed by this or by any other setback. In the midst of his long and finally futile campaign for the jetties, he was devising a grander and stranger proposal. He wanted to construct a new transport system across the Central American isthmus at Panama. An idea had been mooted to build a canal there, inspired by the recent opening of the canal at Suez, but he'd opposed it—he considered the whole apparatus of locks and dams to be obsolete technology. He had something else in mind. He was going to load all the ships onto gargantuan flatbed railway cars, which he would design and build, and shuttle them by train between the Atlantic and the Pacific.

Could this have worked? Twain observed that any sane man would have dismissed Eads's river-mouth jetty project as "clearly impossible," and yet it had worked: "We do not feel full confidence now to prophesy against like impossibilities."

While Eads was the biggest name involved in remaking the Mississippi, he wasn't ultimately the one with the most clout. That was the federal government. After the Civil War, it had created a new authority, the Mississippi River Commission, to take over the management of the river. It reflected a new attitude toward federalism in the wake of the Union victory. Before the war, the idea of the national government engaging in large-scale infrastructure improvements had been fiercely resisted; now such projects were expected, even demanded.

By the time of Twain's trip, the commission and the U.S. Army Corps of Engineers had already launched a series of radical new projects. They had begun by clearing the Mississippi of snags. This was something that had been undertaken earlier by independent entrepreneurs (including, inevitably, Eads), but only along small stretches of the river, on commission by individual communities. The corps sent out a fleet to sweep the entire river. It had taken them years, but gradually they'd rid the river of the thousands of pockets of sawyers and sleepers and preachers and planters that had been rotting in place for generations. "They have rooted out all the old clusters which made many localities so formidable; and they allow no new ones to collect," Twain wrote in amazement. "The government's snag-boats go patrolling up and down, in these matter-of-fact days, pulling the river's teeth."

The corps had gone on to an even more dramatic project. They had installed more than seven hundred beacons along the length of the river. A few of these were full-scale lighthouses built of brick; the rest were simple oil lamps set on tall poles planted securely in the riverbanks. (Local residents were hired to keep the oil tanks filled and to turn the lamps on and off.) Now, each day at sunset, the beacons flared to life, and the entire course of the river was illuminated. The river's murkiest reaches—its shadowy islets, its dangerous shallows and shoals, its foaming and turbulent junctions—were for the first time visible all night, every night. "The national government has turned the Mississippi into a sort of two-thousand-mile torch-light procession," Twain wrote. "There is always a beacon in sight, either before you, or behind you, or abreast. You are never entirely in the dark now."

Yet more projects were getting under way. Twain could see the evidence of them everywhere. "They are building wing-dams here and there, to deflect the current," he wrote, "and dikes to confine it in narrower bounds; and other dikes to make it stay there; and for unnumbered miles along the Mississippi, they are felling the timber-front for fifty yards back, with the purpose of shaving the bank down to low-water mark with the slant of a house-roof, and ballasting it with stones; and in many places they have protected the wasting shores with rows of piles."

What was it all for? The corps was setting out on a successor project to the snag clearing: they were going to dredge the river of its sandbars and establish a minimum depth in the channels. Then they were going to construct an immense new maze of levees and spillways to regulate the river current and reduce its annual flooding. (They had rejected Eads's large-scale jetty proposal—too hastily, as it turned out. Eventually they would incorporate elements of it in their designs.) And they were beginning to consider an even more ambitious proposal: permanently stabilizing the river's course. Twain wrote:

> One who knows the Mississippi will promptly aver—not aloud, but to himself—that ten thousand River Commissions, with the mines of the world at their back, cannot tame that lawless stream, cannot curb it or confine it, cannot say to it, Go here, or Go there, and make it obey; cannot save a shore which it has sentenced; cannot bar its path with an obstruction which it will not tear down, dance over, and laugh at. But a discreet man will not put these things into spoken words; for the West Point engineers have not their superiors anywhere; they know all that can be known of their abstruse science; and so, since they conceive that they can fetter and handcuff that river and boss him, it is but wisdom for the unscientific man to keep still, lie low, and wait till they do it.

It did not escape Twain's notice that all these projects were being carried out at a time when the Mississippi was almost entirely devoid of traffic. So what was the point? In *Life on the Mississippi,* he vented his doubts by way of a surrogate—a cranky, eccentric steamboat pilot of the old school named Uncle Mumford, who denounced the remaking of the river in a long monologue:

> When there used to be four thousand steamboats and ten thousand acres of coal-barges, and rafts and trading scows, there wasn't a lantern from St. Paul to New Orleans, and the snags were thicker than bristles on a hog's back; and now when there's three dozen steamboats and nary a barge or raft, Government has snatched out all the snags, and lit up the shores like Broadway, and a boat's as safe on the river as she'd be in heaven. And I reckon that by the time there ain't any boats left at all, the Commission will have the old thing all reorganized, and dredged out, and fenced in, and tidied up, to a degree that will make navigation just simply perfect, and absolutely safe and profitable; and all the days will be Sundays.

But Twain knew that he and Uncle Mumford were on the losing side. The river was bound to be transformed—even if generations would pass before anybody made any use of it. "The military engineers," Twain concluded, "have taken upon their shoulders the job of making the Mississippi over again,—a job transcended in size by only the original job of creating it."

Or, as Richard Smith Elliott, the friend and partner of Eads, put it, in words that are virtually a death warrant for the old, wild river:

> The United States will have a population of about sixty-three millions in 1890, and eighty millions in 1900. The majority will be west of the Alleghenies. To say that we shall allow the great river to remain in its present imperfect and destructive condition, is to say that we do not understand the interests of the nation, or our own power.

Here and there on his journey downriver, Twain could glimpse, among the ruins of the old river economy, the first stirrings of new life. A few of the towns that he had expected to find abandoned turned out to be flourishing. There was never any mystery about why: "We found a railway intruding at Chester, Illinois; Chester has also a penitentiary now, and is otherwise marching on. At Grand Tower, too, there was a railway; and another at Cape Girardeau."

The riverfronts may have been derelict, but the areas around the railway depots were alive with fresh growth. The shanties had been replaced by squat fortresses of brick: brick warehouses were rising alongside the rail yards, and there were brick smokestacks poking up from factories on the bluffs. Twain was particularly impressed by a tour of a cotton mill in Natchez. It was a hulking three-story factory that could turn out millions of yards of fabrics a year—the South was at last milling its own cotton for export.

Around New Orleans, the run-down old mansions and plantation houses of the sugarcane country were being rehabbed into factories and manufacturing plants. Twain visited one of them. It was, he said, "a spacious house, with some innocent steam machinery in one end of it and some big porcelain pipes running here and there." But as he looked closer, he found that he was wrong: "No, not porcelain—they merely seemed to be; they were iron, but the ammonia which was being breathed through them had coated them to the thickness of your hand with solid milk-white ice."

The house had been turned into an ice factory. The floors of the great rooms were lined with rows of countless tin boxes, each filled with filtered water and packed around with bags of salt. The ammonia chilled the water, and workers stirred it to keep it from clouding up. When the blocks of ice were ready—"hard, solid, and crystal-clear"—they were cut out of the tin boxes and lifted onto carts. The carts were then wheeled from the big hall out the back door, where a row of flatcars waited on a newly constructed spur line of the local railroad. Then the train trundled off to the street markets of New Orleans.

The ice blocks were being sold as decorative centerpieces for dinner tables. Lovely and curious objects had been frozen within them: coins and toys, bouquets of tropical flowers, French dolls dressed in silk. The blocks were set out in shallow bowls, and during the sultriness of the delta afternoons, they would slowly melt, cooling the diners gathered around the table. By twilight, as the last of the ice dissolved, the toys and trinkets in their depths would be left floating in the brimming bowls: dolls and flowers and gifts and party favors, like flotsam from a modern kind of flood. It made Twain marvel at how the world was changing. "In my time," he observed, "ice was jewelry; none but the rich could wear it. But anybody and everybody can have it now."

Epilogue

JOHN BANVARD TOOK HIS Mississippi River panorama on a tour of England in the early 1850s. It was a tremendous success. The "Three-Mile Painting" awed Queen Victoria and got a rave review from Charles Dickens—in fact, Dickens greatly preferred Banvard's panorama to his actual experience of the Mississippi. Banvard himself became a celebrity. He served as his own narrator at the showings; after years of practice he had become a superb and polished entertainer. One reviewer in London praised his "Jonathanisms and jokes, poetry and patter, which delight his audience mightily." (A Jonathanism was a wild hyperbole, which was regarded then as the hallmark of American speech.) The way Banvard told it, his creation of the panorama had been as exciting as anything shown on the canvas itself. His journeys up and down the river, to paint each scene from life (or so he claimed), had been one long epic of frontier adventure. He made it sound as though he had been sketching with one hand while fighting off wild animals, savage Indians, and menacing desperadoes with the other. He clearly gloried in the role of the heroic frontiersman. He liked to claim that he was entirely self-taught as an artist and had only taken up his paintbrush because he had been so inspired by the great river itself. ("No—he had a teacher," his promotional pamphlet clarified. "He studied the omnipresent works of the One Great Living Master! Nature was his teacher.")

Banvard had competition on his English tour: John Rowson Smith and his *Leviathan Panorama of the Mississippi River*. But Smith was nowhere near as theatrical a personality as Banvard. He hired other people to be his narrators while he supervised from offstage. His great pitch for his panorama wasn't its romance, but its documentary veracity. It was, he claimed, a wholly exact rendering of the river, painted with scrupulous on-the-spot accuracy. He was particularly careful about his steamboats—there were steamboat buffs in the audiences then, ready to debate the most hairsplitting details of their design. He specifically guaranteed in his advertisements that every steamboat in his panorama was a faithful rendering of a real steamboat currently afloat somewhere on the Mississippi. His panorama even took an intermission from the vistas of the river for a detailed tour of basic steamboat design, including a cutaway schematic of a typical interior.

Smith was irked by Banvard and considered his panorama a sham. During their English tours they got into a fierce feud in the London newspapers over the truthfulness of their respective creations. This may have been a publicity stunt—and if it was, then it was a clever one: it kept the attention of the English public for months, and drove up attendance at both panoramas. But the artists themselves seem to have been entirely serious about it. Or at any rate Smith was. He was exultant when his attacks on Banvard received crushing, even conclusive support from a world-renowned authority. This was the artist and writer George Catlin, famous for his books on the Missouri Territory and the Plains Indians. (His *Manners, Customs and Condition of the North American Indians,* first published in 1841, is still highly regarded today.) Catlin went to a showing of the Banvard panorama in London and declared that in his opinion its scenes of the Missouri River were faked. He found so many important landmarks missing, and so many inaccuracies in the ones that were shown, that he doubted Banvard had ever been on the Missouri at all. Smith immediately trumpeted Catlin's charges in his ads; Banvard never refuted them.

But while Smith won the fight over accuracy, he lost with the public. His realistic panorama was never as popular as Banvard's grand extravaganza. In the end he seems to have surrendered: he finished his tour and came back to America in 1853, long before Banvard did, and he immediately retired from the panorama business. There's no evidence that after he returned from England he ever showed *Leviathan Panorama* again. He resumed his old career as a theatrical scene painter, and he died in obscurity in 1864.

It was around this time that the other Mississippi panoramas began to drop out of sight. Their original owners wearied of the touring life and sold them, their new owners were unable to get enough bookings for them, and they eventually were lost or destroyed. One of the panoramas was abandoned in Havana when a Caribbean tour went bust. Another was sold to a potential exhibitor in Asia, and the last recorded trace of it was when it was transshipped through Calcutta on its way to Java—there's no evidence whether it ever reached its destination. One disappeared in a more spectacular fashion: Leon Pomarede had unwisely added special effects to his *Original Panorama of the Mississippi*, big billows of smoke and steam that came writhing out of the wings to enhance the illusion that the audience was on a steamboat with its boilers at full power; something went wrong before a showing in New Jersey and the canvas roll caught fire. The panorama went up like a torch and was irretrievably damaged within a few minutes.

By the middle 1850s, Banvard's panorama was the only one still on tour. Banvard cashed in on the absence of competition: after England he continued on for the next several years through Europe and the Middle East. He was wildly popular wherever he went. By the time he finally returned to America, he was a wealthy man. He bought a mansion outside of New York City. He wrote travel books and poetry. He opened Banvard's Museum in New York, a hall of curiosities and theatrical exhibitions in imitation of Barnum's American Museum; the Mississippi panorama was the opening attraction. In his travels he'd collected material for several new panoramas as well, including one of the Holy Land and another of the Nile, and he debuted them in New York to great acclaim. By 1860 he had become the most famous artist in America.

The Mississippi panorama retained its popularity for several years. Banvard was careful to keep it fresh. During the Civil War he repainted large sections of it to include the latest news from the Mississippi River campaigns; when he exhibited it in 1863, he drew big crowds all over again—people were eager to get a look at the grand events they'd been reading about, the ironclad battles and the surrender of New Orleans and the siege of Vicksburg. But after the war was over, Banvard put the panorama in storage. He didn't show it again for more than a decade.

Its next recorded display was in 1881. By then Banvard's fortunes had taken a steep dive. The museum and an assortment of other big-budget ventures had failed, and he was going broke. If he'd hoped to make back some money with a revival of the panorama, he was disappointed. The vogue for panoramas had faded, and the Mississippi itself wasn't of much interest to people then. The frontier had moved on west, and the river was no longer the edge of the world; it was just an immense obstacle the railroads had to cross. Banvard's panorama was viewed as no more than an interesting historical curiosity. Soon afterward, Banvard's luck ran out. His museum was closed down for good and his mansion repossessed. Banvard fled New York to escape his creditors.

He went west—first back to the Mississippi valley. But he, too, found it to be of little interest any longer. It was much the same as Twain described: empty, shabby, overregulated, tamed. So he kept on going, up the Missouri into the freshly settled territories beyond. He followed the outer tendrils of the new railroads until he reached the Glacial Lakes region of South Dakota. There he came to rest in Watertown, a railroad stop on the Big Sioux River, about a hundred miles north of Sioux Falls. Banvard was in his late sixties then, but he soon started a new career as a construction contractor.

He didn't wholly give up on his theatrical art. A couple of years after he arrived in Watertown, he presented to the locals his new work. It wasn't a panorama this time: it was a moving diorama that re-created the burning of Columbia, South Carolina, at the end of the Civil War. The premiere was a big event. Everyone in town showed up at the local hall to see it. It proved to be a wonderfully elaborate and cunning piece of work—but the real highlight of the show was Banvard himself. He narrated, pulled curtains back and forth, raised and lowered flats with windlasses, rang bells, blew whistles, and set off firecrackers. The people of Watertown were amused no end. He briefly toured with it around the Glacial Lakes until everyone in the region had seen it. Then he put the diorama away and retired from the entertainment business for good.

He lived with his wife and his children and grandchildren in a big house on the outskirts of town. Down in the basement was the one possession he'd managed to salvage from the wreck of his fortunes back east— the Mississippi panorama. But he never put it on display in Watertown. Later one of his grandsons remembered playing on it as a child: it was a titanic roll twenty feet long and six feet thick, perpetually hidden under a tarpaulin, as silent and ominous as a sleeping dragon.

Banvard died in 1891. Shortly after the funeral, the family got rid of the panorama. They said that nobody cared about it anymore and it was just taking up space. Besides, it could no longer be shown: after so many years of storage in that dank basement, the canvas had rotted and the images were unrecognizable. So it was carted off to the town dump.

But that may not have been the end of it. Decades later, after the Second World War, a historian named John Francis McDermott wrote a book about the panoramas, and he solicited the people of Watertown for their memories of Banvard. The editor of the local newspaper, Richard Albrook, wrote to McDermott with a story he had heard when he was young. According to Albrook, somebody had found the panorama in the dump and had rescued it; the salvageable vistas all along its length had been cut out and had been used to decorate the walls of a local building. But that was all that Albrook remembered. He couldn't say what building it was: he'd forgotten, or maybe he'd never learned in the first place, and he'd never seen the building himself. McDermott wasn't able to find out anything more, either; nobody else he contacted remembered hearing anything like Albrook's story. He ended his book with the question of the panorama's fate still open.

The question remains open to this day. No trace of the Banvard panorama has ever been found. Watertown today is a city of twenty thousand people, and there has been a century's worth of new construction downtown. But many of its original buildings are still standing. It's at least possible that the panorama survives in one of them, unsuspected by the current occupants, hidden under layers of lath and plaster and paint and wallpaper. It might even turn up again someday. An ancient wall might be knocked down, and a scrap of painted canvas might come to light: a glimpse of wide water, a burning steamboat, a lone human figure posed on a distant bluff—an authentic souvenir of the wicked river, the way it had been in the old times.

A Note on Sources

My first and largest debts are to three anthologies: *A Treasury of Mississippi River Folklore: Ballads, Traditions and Folkways of the Mid-American River Country,* edited by B. A. Botkin (Crown, 1955); *The Mississippi River Reader,* edited by Wright Morris (Anchor Books, 1962); and *Before Mark Twain: A Sampler of Old, Old Times on the Mississippi,* edited by John Francis McDermott (Southern Illinois University Press, 1968). Without these any further exploration of the river culture would have been impossible.

PART I: THE RIVER RISING

Chapter One: Gone on the River

For the geography, topography, and natural history of the river, I've primarily used *The Navigator; Containing Directions for Navigating the Monongahela, Allegheny, Ohio, and Mississippi Rivers, with an Ample Account of These Much Admired Waters,* by Zadok Cramer (eighth edition; Cramer, Spear, and Eichbaum, 1814); and *The History and Geography of the Mississippi Valley,* by Timothy Flint (third edition; E. H. Flint, 1833). I've also made heavy use of the volumes of the Works Progress Administration's American Guide Series devoted to the Mississippi river valley states. Descriptions of the "floating life" of the river derive from *Recollections of the Last Ten Years, Passed in Occasional Residences and Journeyings in the Valley of the Mississippi,* by Timothy Flint (Cummings, Hilliard, 1826); *Letters from the West, Containing Sketches of Scenery, Manners, and Customs,* by James Hall (Henry Colburn, 1828); *Delineations of American Scenery and Manners,* by John James Audubon (E. L. Carey and A. Hart, 1832); *Fifty Years on the Mississippi, or Gould's History of River Navigation,* by Emerson Gould (Nixon-Jones, 1889); *Old Times on the Upper Mississippi: The Recollections of a Steamboat Pilot from 1854 to 1863,* by George Byron Merrick (Arthur H. Clark, 1909); and *A Traffic History of the Mississippi River System,* by Frank Haigh Dixon (National Waterways Commission Document No. 11; U.S. Government Printing Office, 1909).

Chapter Two: Old Devil River

For river meanders and helicoidal flow, see *River Mechanics,* by Pierre Y. Julien (Cambridge University Press, 2002). The flooding of the river is described in countless sources, perhaps most vividly in John Audubon's *Mississippi River Journal* (reprinted in

Writings and Drawings, Library of America, 1999). The 1805 tornado is described in *The Pioneer History of Illinois,* by John Reynolds (Fergus, 1887). Thomas Bangs Thorpe's "A Storm Scene on the Mississippi" is collected in his book *The Hive of "The Bee-Hunter": A Repository of Sketches* (Appleton, 1854).

Chapter Three: The Comet's Tail

The story of the Crow's Nest and the New Madrid earthquakes is based on the accounts in Timothy Flint's *Recollections* and Emerson Gould's *Fifty Years* (see above, chapter 1), as well as *Natural and Statistical View, with an Appendix Containing Observations on the Late Earthquakes,* by Daniel Drake (Looker and Wallace, 1815); *Travels in the Interior of America, in the Years 1809, 1810, and 1811,* by John Bradbury (Smith and Galway, 1817); *View of the Valley of the Mississippi, or The Emigrant's and Traveller's Guide to the West,* by Robert Baird (H. S. Tanner, 1834); *The Rambler in North America,* by Charles Joseph Latrobe (Seeley and Burnside, 1835); *The New Madrid Earthquake,* by Myron L. Fuller (U.S. Geological Survey Bulletin 494; U.S. Government Printing Office, 1912); and *The New Madrid Earthquakes,* by James Lal Penick Jr. (revised edition; University of Missouri Press, 1981).

Chapter Four: Like Bubbles on a Sea

For Timothy Flint's life, I've used *Timothy Flint: Pioneer, Missionary, Author, Editor, 1780–1840,* by John Ervin Kirkpatrick (Arthur H. Clark, 1911); and *Timothy Flint,* by James K. Folsom (Twayne, 1965). The account of the Natchez tornado is based on the newspaper reports reprinted in *Early American Tornadoes, 1586–1870 (History of American Weather),* edited by David M. Ludlum (American Meteorological Society, 1970).

PART II: "DO YOU LIVE ON THE RIVER?"

Chapter Five: The Desire of an Ignorant Westerner

For the general account of the westward migration, I've used *Notes on a Journey in America, from the Coast of Virginia to the Territory of Illinois,* by Morris Birkbeck (Ridgway, 1818); *A Woman's Story of Pioneer Illinois,* by Christiana Holmes Tillson (Lakeside Press, 1919); and the memoirs and travel books excerpted in *The Opening of the West (Documentary History of the United States),* edited by Jack M. Sosin (Harper and Row, 1969). The actions of the committees and the courts of Judge Lynch are described in detail in *Frontier Law and Order: Ten Essays,* by Philip D. Jordan (University of Nebraska Press, 1970). The story of James Ford derives from *Chronicles of a Kentucky Settlement,* by William Courtney Watts (Putnam, 1897); and *The Outlaws of Cave-in-Rock,* by Otto A. Rothert (A. H. Clark, 1924).

Chapter Six: Bloody Island

William Johnson's diary has been published as *William Johnson's Natchez: The Antebellum Diary of a Free Negro,* edited by William Ransom Hogan and Edwin Adams Davis (Louisiana State University Press, 1951). I've also consulted the biographical sketch by the diary's editors, *The Barber of Natchez* (Louisiana State University Press, 1954); as well as *The Unhurried Years: Memories of the Old Natchez Region,* by Pierce Butler (Louisiana State University Press, 1948). For dueling in the lower valley, I've used *The Field of Honor: Being a Complete and Comprehensive History of Duelling,* by Ben C. Truman (Fords, Howard, and Hulbert, 1884). The Biddle-Pettis duel is described in many books and has accumulated a number of curious details in the retelling (according to Truman, for instance, the guns used were the actual ones from the duel between Aaron Burr and Alexander Hamilton). The version offered here is based mostly on the account in *Personal Recollections of Many Prominent People Whom I Have Known, Especially of Those Relating to the History of St. Louis,* by John F. Darby (G. I. Jones, 1880); *A Centennial History of Missouri: The Center State, 1820–1921,* by Walter B. Stevens (S. J. Clarke, 1921); and the detailed modern summary in *Duels and the Roots of Violence in Missouri,* by Dick Steward (University of Missouri Press, 2000). The stories of Alonzo Phelps and the Foote-Prentiss duels are in Henry Stuart Foote's memoir, *The Bench and Bar of the South and Southwest* (Soule, Thomas, and Wentworth, 1876).

Chapter Seven: The Roar of Niagara

The Mike Fink stories are collected in *Half Horse, Half Alligator: The Growth of the Mike Fink Legend,* edited by Walter Blair and Franklin J. Meine (University of Chicago Press, 1956). For the Davy Crockett almanacs, I've used the facsimile reprints in *The Tall Tales of Davy Crockett: The Second Nashville Series of Crockett Almanacs, 1839–1841,* edited by Michael A. Lofaro (University of Tennessee Press, 1987); and *Davy Crockett's Riproarious Shemales and Sentimental Sisters: Women's Tall Tales from the Crockett Almanacs, 1835–1856,* edited by Michael A. Lofaro (Stackpole Books, 2001). Many of the Annie Christmas stories are summarized in *The French Quarter: An Informal History of the New Orleans Underworld,* by Herbert Asbury (Knopf, 1936), though it isn't clear whether Asbury realizes, or cares, that Annie Christmas is a modern construct. (The story of the invention of Annie Christmas is told in Botkin's *Treasury;* see headnote above.) The oddity of Lincoln's conversation is noted in many memoirs; these examples are from David Porter (see below, chapter 14). Stories of prodigious drinking were universal on the frontier; the picnic is from William Johnson's diary (see above, chapter 6). The description of the camp meetings derives from *An Excursion Through the United States and Canada During the Years 1822–23,* by William Newnham Blane (Baldwin, Cradock, and Joy, 1824); *Autobiography of Peter Cartwright, the Backwoods Preacher* (Philips and Hunt, 1856); *Autobiography of Rev. James B. Finley, or Pioneer Life in the West* (Methodist Book Concern, 1858); *History of Cosmopolite, or The Writings of Rev. Lorenzo Dow, Containing His Experience and Travels in Europe and America, Up to Near His Fiftieth Year* (Anderson, Gates, and Wright, 1859); *A Short History of the Life of Barton W. Stone, Written by Himself, Designed Principally for His Children and Christian Friends,* reprinted in *The Cane Ridge Meeting-House,* by James R. Rogers (Standard, 1910); and two modern histories, *And They All Sang Hallelujah: Plain-Folk Camp-Meeting Religion, 1800–1845,* by Dickson D. Bruce Jr. (University of Tennessee Press, 1974), and *The Frontier Camp Meeting: Religion's Harvest Time,* by Charles A. Johnson (Southern Methodist University Press, 1955).

Chapter Eight: The Cosmopolitan Tide

The description of the steamboats is based primarily on Emerson Gould (see above, chapter 1) and Robert Baird (see above, chapter 3), as well as *Domestic Manners of the Americans,* by Frances Trollope (Whittaker, 1832); *Narrative of a Tour in North America,* by Henry Tudor (Duncan, 1834); *Men and Manners in America,* by Thomas Hamilton (Blackwood, 1843); *Excursion Through the Slave States, from Washington on the Potomac to the Frontier of Mexico,* by George Featherstonhaugh (Harper and Brothers, 1844); and *The New World,* by Marie de Grandfort, translated by Edward C. Wharton (Sherman, Wharton, 1855). The life of the sharpers (and their question, "Do you live on the river?") is from *Forty Years a Gambler on the Mississippi,* by George H. Devol (Devol and Haines, 1887). For information about Thompsonian medicine and on other assorted quackeries and frauds, I'm indebted to *American Medicine in Transition, 1840– 1910,* by John S. Haller (University of Illinois Press, 1981). The maneuverings with paper money and counterfeit detectors described here can be found in William Johnson's diary (see above, chapter 6) and in E. F. Ware's memoir and regimental history, *The Lyon Campaign in Missouri, Being a History of the First Iowa Infantry* (Crane, 1907), and in Philip D. Jordan's *Frontier Law and Order* (see above, chapter 5—and for green thumbs and black thumbs as well).

Chapter Nine: A Pile of Shavings

The description of conditions of urban life along the Mississippi derives from Frances Trollope (see above, chapter 8); *A Diary in America, with Remarks on Its Institutions,* by Frederick Marryat (Baudry's European Library, 1839); the excerpted texts and the topographical plates collected in *Cities of the Mississippi: Nineteenth-Century Images of Urban Development,* by John W. Reps (University of Missouri, 1994); and the modern history *The Urban Frontier: The Rise of Western Cities, 1790–1830,* by Richard C. Wade (Harvard University Press, 1959). The account of the St. Louis fire is from *The Makers of St. Louis: A Brief Sketch of the Growth of a Great City,* edited by William Marion Reedy (Mirror, 1906). The epidemics of the river valley are described in *Autobiographical Sketches and Recollections During a Thirty-five Years' Residence in New Orleans,* by Theodore Clapp (Tompkins, 1863). There is more on the cholera outbreak during the Black Hawk War in *Memoirs of Lieut.-General Scott, LL.D., Written by Himself* (Sheldon, 1864).

Chapter Ten: The Coasts of Dark Destruction

The description of New Orleans is based on *The Journal of Latrobe,* by Benjamin Latrobe (Appleton, 1905); *The Homes of the New World: Impressions of America,* by Fredrika Bremer (Harper, 1858); *A Journey Through the United States and Part of Canada,* by Robert Everest (Woodfall and Kinder, 1855); *Rambles and Scrambles in North and South America,* by Edward Sullivan (Bentley, 1852); *Scenes in the South and Other Miscellaneous Pieces,* by James Creecy (Lippincott, 1860); *Life and Liberty in America, or Sketches of a Tour in the United States and Canada in 1857–8,* by Charles Mackay (Harper, 1859); and *America Revisited, from the Bay of New York to the Gulf of*

Mexico, by George Augustus Sala (Vizetelly, 1886). Stories of the voodoo ceremonies are from *New Orleans as It Was: Episodes of Louisiana Life,* by Henry C. Castellanos (L. Graham, 1905); and *New Orleans: The Place and the People,* by Grace Elizabeth King (Macmillan, 1917). I've also relied on a series of modern books on New Orleans reprinted by Pelican Press in Baton Rouge, particularly *Fabulous New Orleans,* by Lyle Saxon; *Voodoo in New Orleans, The Voodoo Queen,* and *Mardi Gras as It Was,* by Robert Tallant; and *End of an Era: New Orleans, 1850–1860,* by Robert C. Reinders. The remark about the Jabberwock is in the Works Progress Administration's guide to New Orleans.

PART III: THE COURSE OF EMPIRE

Chapter Eleven: The Mound Builders

The best survey of nineteenth-century theories and fantasies about the Mound Builder civilization is *Mound Builders of Ancient America: The Archaeology of a Myth,* by Robert Silverberg (New York Graphic Society, 1968). I've also used *Behemoth: A Legend of the Mound-Builders,* by Cornelius Mathews (Langley, 1839); *Traditions of De-Coo-Dah and Antiquarian Researches: Comprising Extensive Explorations, Surveys, and Excavations of the Wonderful and Mysterious Earthen Remains of the Mound-Builders in America,* by William Pidgeon (Horace Thayer, 1858); *The Prehistoric World, or Vanished Races,* by E. A. Allen (Ferguson, Allen, and Rader, 1885); and *The Ancient Earthworks and Temples of the American Indians,* by Lindesey Brine (Farmer and Sons, 1894). For Cole's *Course of Empire,* I've used *The Life and Works of Thomas Cole,* by Louis L. Noble (Sheldon, Blakeman, 1856).

Chapter Twelve: A Young Man of Splendid Abilities

The story of John Murrell was told and retold throughout the nineteenth century, never the same way twice. This version is based mostly on *A History of the Detection, Conviction, Life and Designs of John A. Murel, the Great Western Land Pirate* (undated pamphlet); *The History of Virgil A. Stewart, and His Adventure in Capturing and Exposing the Great "Western Land Pirate" and His Gang* (Harper and Brothers, 1836); *Proceedings of the Citizens of Madison County, in the State of Mississippi at Livingston, in July 1835, in Relation to the Trial and Punishment of Several Individuals Implicated in a Contemplated Insurrection of the Slaves in That State* (undated pamphlet); *A Casket of Reminiscences,* by Henry Stuart Foote (Chronicle, 1874); *A Stray Yankee in Texas,* by Philip Paxton (Redfield, 1853); and *The Great Western Land Pirate: John A. Murrell in Legend and History,* by James Lal Penick Jr. (University of Missouri Press, 1981). The fullest account of the later outbreaks of the Murrell excitement is in *American Negro Slave Revolts,* by Herbert Aptheker (International Publishers, 1983). I've also used *American Slavery as It Is: Testimony of a Thousand Witnesses* (American Anti-Slavery Society, 1839); *Slavery in the South: First-Hand Accounts of the Antebellum American Southland from Northern and Southern Whites, Negroes, and Foreign Observers,* edited by Harvey Wish (Farrar, Straus, 1964); and *Slave Testimony: Two Centuries of Letters, Speeches, Interviews, and Autobiographies,* edited by John W. Blassingame (Louisiana State University Press, 1977).

Chapter Thirteen: The Oracles

The visions troubling Calvin Stowe are recorded in *Life of Harriet Beecher Stowe, Compiled from Her Letters and Journals,* by Charles Edward Stowe (Houghton, Mifflin, 1891). The story of Herschel's telescope and the moon creatures is told in detail in *The Moon Hoax, or A Discovery That the Moon Has a Vast Population of Human Beings,* by Richard Adams Locke (William Gowans, 1859). The hysteria about Millerism on the Mississippi is described in *Streaks of Squatter Life, and Far-West Scenes,* by John S. Robb (Carey and Hart, 1847); for general information on Miller, I've used *God's Strange Work: William Miller and the End of the World,* by David L. Rowe (Eerdmans, 2008). For showboats and theatrical boats, I've used *Struggles and Triumphs, or Forty Years' Recollections of P. T. Barnum, Written by Himself* (Warren, Johnson, 1873); *Dramatic Life as I Found It: A Record of Personal Experience, with an Account of the Rise and Progress of the Drama in the West and South,* by Noah Miller Ludlow (G. I. Jones, 1880); *Children of Ol' Man River: The Life and Times of a Show-Boat Trouper,* by Billy Bryant (Furman, 1936); and *Showboats: The History of an American Institution,* by Philip Graham (University of Texas Press, 1951). For minstrel shows, I've relied on "Three Years as a Negro Minstrel," by Ralph Keeler (*Atlantic Monthly,* July 1869); *Talks, by George Thatcher, the Celebrated Minstrel* (Penn Publishing, 1898); *Negro Minstrels: A Complete Guide to Negro Minstrelsy, Containing Recitations, Jokes, Crossfires, Conundrums, Riddles, Stump Speeches, Ragtime and Sentimental Songs,* by Jack Haverly (Frederick J. Drake, 1902); and the modern history *Blacking Up: The Minstrel Show in Nineteenth-Century America,* by Robert C. Toll (Oxford University Press, 1974). James Eads's salvage operations are described in *Road to the Sea: The Story of James B. Eads and the Mississippi River,* by Florence Dorsey (Rinehart, 1947). The wreck of the St. Louis levee is described by George Byron Merrick (see above, chapter 1).

PART IV: BEHEMOTH

Chapter Fourteen: The Sky Parlor

The siege of Vicksburg, like every other event in the Civil War, has been exhaustively documented and analyzed. For the general course of the military campaign, I've used *Personal Memoirs of U. S. Grant* and *Memoirs of William Tecumseh Sherman* (both in the recent Library of America editions) and, in particular, *Incidents and Anecdotes of the Civil War,* by David Porter (Appleton, 1886). For modern tactical and strategic analysis, I've used *Triumph and Defeat: The Vicksburg Campaign,* by Terrence J. Winschel (Savas, 1999); and *Vicksburg Is the Key: The Struggle for the Mississippi River,* by William L. Shea and Terrence J. Winschel (University of Nebraska Press, 2003). The account of the town during the siege is based on *My Cave Life in Vicksburg,* by Mary Ann Webster Loughborough (Appleton, 1864); *A Southern Record: The History of the Third Regiment, Louisiana Infantry,* by W. H. Tunnard (privately printed, 1866); "A Child at the Siege of Vicksburg," by William W. Lord Jr. (*Harper's* magazine, 1909); *Brokenburn: The Journal of Kate Stone, 1861–1868,* edited by John Q. Anderson (Louisiana State University

Press, 1955); *Vicksburg, Southern City Under Siege: William Lovelace Foster's Letter Describing the Defense and Surrender of the Confederate Fortress on the Mississippi,* edited by Kenneth Trist Urquhart (Historic New Orleans Collection, 1980); the memoirs and other testimony collected in the modern anthologies *Vicksburg: 47 Days of Siege,* edited by A. A. Hoehling (Prentice Hall, 1969), and *The Siege of Vicksburg,* edited by Richard Wheeler (Crowell, 1978); and the modern history *Vicksburg: A People at War, 1860– 1865,* by Peter F. Walker (University of North Carolina Press, 1960).

Chapter Fifteen: The Alligator

The account of the *Sultana* disaster derives primarily from *Loss of the* Sultana *and Reminiscences of Survivors,* by Chester D. Berry (D. D. Thorp, 1892). I've also made very heavy use of *Disaster on the Mississippi: The* Sultana *Explosion, April 27, 1865,* by Gene Eric Salecker (Naval Institute Press, 1996). I also consulted *Cahaba Prison and the* Sultana *Disaster,* by William O. Bryant (University of Alabama Press, 1990); and *Andersonville: The Last Depot,* by William Marvel (University of North Carolina Press, 1994).

PART V: THE GOOD AND THE THOUGHTLESS

Chapter Sixteen: The Last of the Floating Life

For Twain, I've used the Penguin American Library edition of *Life on the Mississippi,* edited by James M. Cox, which has substantial passages from the manuscript omitted in earlier editions. For James Eads, I've used *Addresses and Papers of James B. Eads* (Slawson, 1884); and *Notes Taken in Sixty Years,* by Richard Smith Elliott (Studley, 1883). The work of the U.S. Army Corps of Engineers is described in *The River We Have Wrought: A History of the Upper Mississippi,* by John O. Anfinson (University of Minnesota Press, 2003); and *Structures in the Stream: Water, Science, and the Rise of the U.S. Army Corps of Engineers,* by Todd Shallat (University of Texas Press, 1994).

INTRODUCTION, PROLOGUE, AND EPILOGUE

The description and history of the panoramas derive from *The Lost Panoramas of the Mississippi,* by John Francis McDermott (University of Chicago Press, 1958). John Banvard's descriptive pamphlet for his panorama is reprinted in *Before Mark Twain* (see headnote above). Some details of Banvard's later career are drawn from *Pioneer Photographers from the Mississippi to the Continental Divide: A Biographical Dictionary, 1839– 1865,* by Peter E. Palmquist and Thomas R. Kailbourn (Stanford University Press, 2005).

The manhole is north of the intersection of Lincoln and Belmont avenues in Chicago.

Index

About the Author

Lee Sandlin is an award-winning essayist and jounalist. His essay "Losing the War" was included in the anthology *The New Kings of Nonfiction*. He lives in Chicago.

www.leesandlin.com

A Note About the Type

This book was set in Adobe Garamond. Designed for the Adobe Corporation by Robert Slimbach, the fonts are based on types first cut by Claude Garamond (c. 1480–1561). Garamond was a pupil of Geoffroy Tory and is believed to have followed the Venetian models, although he introduced a number of important differences, and it is to him that we owe the letter we now know as "old style."

Composed by North Market Street Graphics
Lancaster, Pennsylvania

Printed and bound by Berryville Graphics
Berryville, Virginia

Designed by M. Kristen Bearse